To Betty,
Happy Christmas

WORKING IN CORK

Everyday Life in Irish Steel, Sunbeam Wolsey
and the Ford Marina Plant

1917–2001

WORKING IN CORK

Everyday Life in Irish Steel, Sunbeam Wolsey
and the Ford Marina Plant

1917–2001

LIAM CULLINANE

CORK UNIVERSITY PRESS

First published in 2020 by
Cork University Press
Boole Library
University College Cork
Cork
T12 ND89
Ireland

© the author 2020

Library of Congress Control Number: 2020934772
Distribution in the USA: Longleaf Services, Chapel Hill, NC, USA

All rights reserved. No part of this book may be reprinted or reproduced or utilised in any electronic, mechanical or other means, now known or hereafter invented, including photocopying and recording or otherwise, without either the prior written permission of the publishers or a licence permitting restricted copying in Ireland issued by the Irish Copyright Licensing Agency Ltd., 25 Denzille Lane, Dublin 2.

British Library Cataloguing in Publication Data
A CIP record for this book is available from the British Library.

ISBN: 978-1-78205-413-9

Printed in Poland by BZ Graf
Print origination & design by Carrigboy Typesetting Services
www.carrigboy.com

COVER IMAGES – Front: Silk hose spinner at Work, 1944, by permission of Cork City and County Archives – B505 Sunbeam Photos Temp 75; Front flap: Ford Marina plant workers leaving the facility, 1929. Photo reproduced with the kind permission of the *Irish Examiner*; Back flap: top – Irish Steel plant in 1958. Photo reproduced with the kind permission of the *Irish Examiner*; bottom – workers in the half-hose knitting department, Sunbeam Wolsey, *c.*1944. Photo reproduced with the kind permission of Cork City and County Archives – B505 Sunbeam Photos Temp 75.

www.corkuniversitypress.com

For my parents

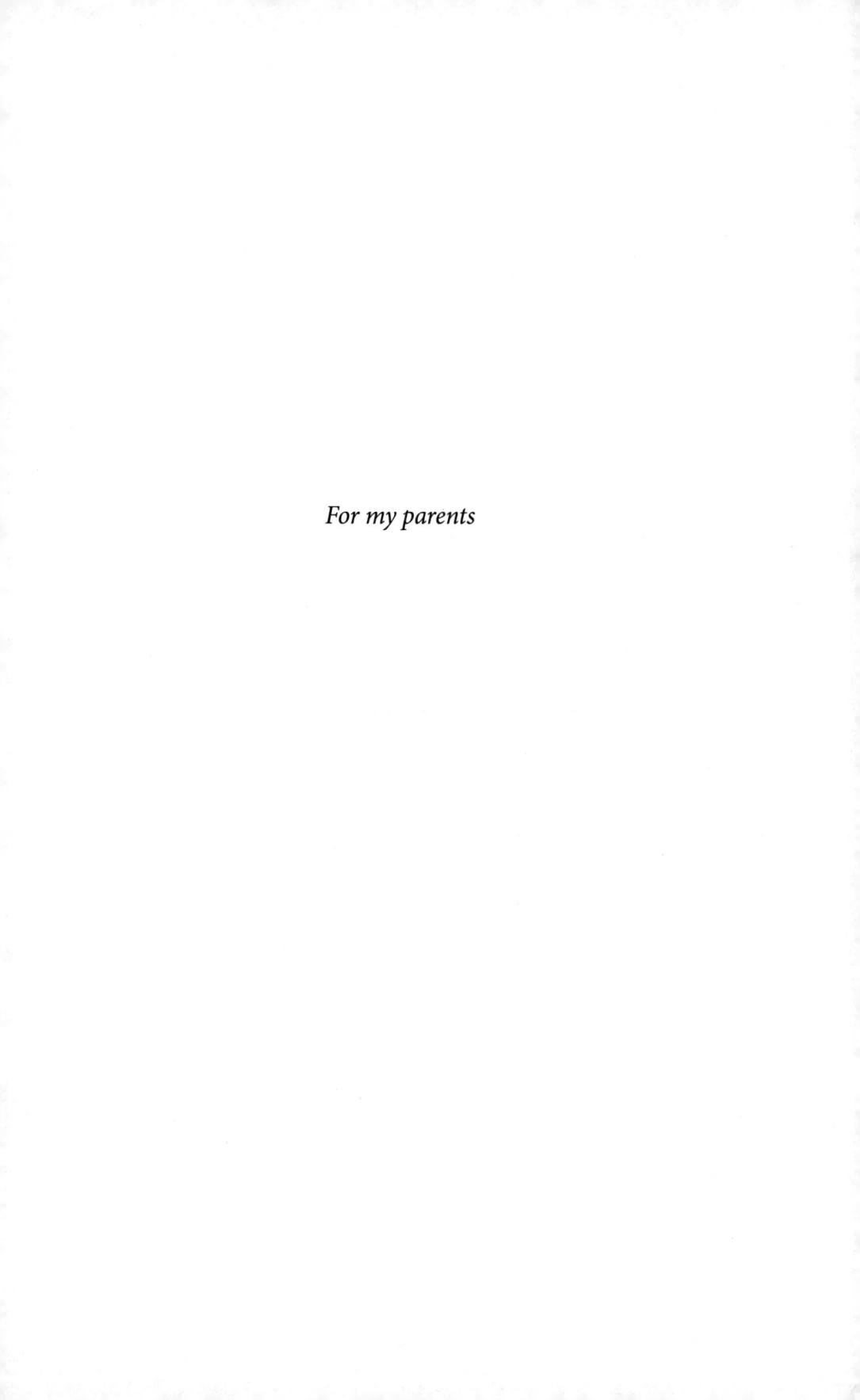

Contents

MAPS, FIGURES AND TABLES	viii
ACKNOWLEDGEMENTS	ix
ABBREVIATIONS	xi
NARRATORS	xiii
INTRODUCTION	1
1. 'The towering giant of the Irish automotive industry': The Ford Marina plant, 1917–84	16
2. 'Giving the nation socks': Sunbeam Wolsey, 1927–90	33
3. 'Endeavour, struggle and survival': Irish Steel, 1939–2001	51
4. Working for Fords, 1917–84	72
5. Working for Sunbeam Wolsey, 1927–90	112
6. Working for Irish Steel, 1939–2001	140
7. Employment, Inequality and Emigration	173
8. Gender, Status and Resistance	196
CONCLUSION	235
ENDNOTES	243
BIBLIOGRAPHY	272
INDEX	293

Maps, Figures and Tables

Map 1	Cork harbour area in relation to the rest of Ireland	12
Map 2	Cork harbour area	13
Figure 2.1	William Dwyer admiring a scale model of the Sunbeam complex at Millfield, 1949	37
Figure 2.2	Sunbeam Wolsey complex at Millfield, date unknown	38
Figure 3.1	Irish Steel plant in 1958	61
Figure 4.1	Ford Marina plant workers leaving the facility, 1929	83
Figure 4.2	Michael Lenihan installing a window at the Ford Marina plant, 1984	104
Figure 4.3	Workers at the Ford Marina plant, 1984	110
Figure 5.1	Workers in the half-hose knitting department, Sunbeam Wolsey, c.1944	116
Figure 6.1	Irish Steel tongsmen at work, 1951	145
Table 3.1	Irish Steel, profits and losses, 1976–92	69

Acknowledgements

The nature of a project which incorporates significant amounts of oral history is one of collective endeavour and collaboration. As such, I must begin by thanking all those who agreed to be interviewed by me and to share their experiences, in no particular order: Rita Sisk, Eleanor Ford, Mary Cronin, Patsy Corcoran, Marian Courtney, John O'Shea, Frank Wallace, Kevin Dwyer, Tom Scott, Billy McMurty, Christy Buckley, Donal Brady, Fionnán Kerrigan, Robert Walsh, Jim Shealy, Tony Cummins, James Cronin, John Phelan, Denis Forde, Gus McLoughlin, Michael Costelloe, Michael Lenihan, Tim Murphy and Pat Dunlea. Others who provided significant practical help and assistance in the completion of this project include: Henry and Ann Cunningham, Aisling and Sarah Kerrigan, Edna Leahy, Donal Varian, Marian O'Sullivan, Sinéad Gunning, Miriam Nyhan, Evelyn Roche, Maeve Amphlett, Máire Leane, Elizabeth Kiely and Diarmuid Ó Drisceoil. In addition I would like to thank the patient and helpful staff of the National Library of Ireland, Cork City and County Archives, SIPTU College Library, Irish Labour History Society Museum and Archives, the Benson Ford Research Centre, UCC Library, Cork City Library Local Studies Department, the National Archives of Ireland and the Cork Folklore Project, in particular Mary O'Driscoll.

The completion of this work was made a great deal easier by the existence of a supportive and welcoming staff and postgraduate community in the School of History, University College Cork. Among the many colleagues whose support, advice and constructive criticism was of great value I would like to thank Andy Bielenberg, David Toms, Peter Hession, David Convery, Sara Goek, Michael Dwyer, Shane Faherty, John Borgonovo and Sarah-Anne Buckley. I would particularly like to thank my supervisor Donal Ó Drisceoil. Terry Murphy and Patrick Walsh (Uncle Pa) warrant a mention also, for providing free and much-needed accommodation in Dublin during my many research trips to the capital. My friends outside of academia all provided much-needed encouragement and support. I would like to thank all of them, but particularly Tadhg Crowley, Leah Ring and Amy Ring. Finally, I would like to acknowledge the support and encouragement of my family, Lily, Richie and Niamh Cullinane.

Abbreviations

AGIBS	Ancient Guild of Incorporated Brick and Stonelayers
AIFTA	Anglo-Irish Free Trade Agreement
AUEW	Amalgamated Union of Engineering Workers
BFRC	Benson Ford Research Centre
CCCA	Cork City and County Archives
CFP	Cork Folklore Project
CIÉ	Córas Iompar Éireann
CIO	Committee on Industrial Organisation
CTF	Commercial Travellers Federation
EEC	European Economic Community
ESB	Electricity Supply Board
ESRI	Economic and Social Research Institute
ETU	Electrical Trade Union
FUE	Federated Union of Employers
GATT	General Agreement on Tariffs and Trade
ICTU	Irish Congress of Trade Unions
IFI	Irish Fertiliser Industries
ISH	Irish Steel Holdings
ISTC	Iron and Steel Trades Confederation (UK)
ITGWU	Irish Transport and General Workers Union
MNI	Miriam Nyhan Interviews
NAI	National Archives of Ireland
NEETU	National Electrical and Engineering Trade Union
NET	Nítrigin Éireann Teoranta
NUVB	National Union of Vehicle Builders
SIPTU	Services, Industrial, Professional and Technical Union

TD	Teachta Dála
UCATT	Union of Construction Allied Trades and Technicians
UCC	University College Cork
WOHP	UCC Women's Oral History Project

Narrators

SUNBEAM WOLSEY

Rita Sisk: Born 1949. Grew up in Shandon, Cork city. General operative at Sunbeam, 1965–72.

Eleanor Ford: Born c.1950. Grew up in Gurranabraher, Cork city. Worked as a general operative at Sunbeam during the mid-1960s before emigrating to London. Later returned to Ireland.

Mary Cronin: Born 1938. Grew up in Farranree. Worked as a 'runner' at Sunbeam, 1953–7 before emigrating to Britain. Later returned to Cork with her family.*

Patsy Corcoran: Born c.1940. Grew up in the Bandon Road area of Cork city. Half-hose operative at Sunbeam Wolsey, 1956–65.

Marian Hickey: Born c.1950. Grew up in Farranferris, Cork city. Worked at Sunbeam from the late 1960s until her marriage in the early 70s. Later returned to work at Sunbeam on a part-time basis in the 1980s.

John O'Shea: Born in Ballymacthomas area of Cork city in 1932. Moved to Gurranabraher with his family in the mid-1930s. General operative at Sunbeam Wolsey, 1951–5. He has written a memoir, *Cork's Red City* (Cork: Litho Press, 2005).

Frank Wallace: Born in Blackpool, Cork city, in 1933. Worked at Sunbeam from c.1950, first as a general operative, then as a full-time

---

* Asterisk indicates a narrator who has chosen to use a pseudonym. The biographical notes above pertain only to narrators who were interviewed directly by the author.

ITGWU shop steward. Later became a full-time organiser for the ITGWU.

KEVIN DWYER: Born 1944, grandson of William Dwyer, the founder of Sunbeam, and son of his successor, Declan Dwyer. Worked at Sunbeam from 1962 to '74 as an advertising executive and, later, manager of the design and development department.

TOM SCOTT: Born in Nottingham, UK. Worked in the textile industry in Britain before being taken on as a manager at Sunbeam c.1958 to set up their design and development department. Became managing director of Sunbeam Wolsey following Declan Dwyer's retirement in 1967. Remained in this position until he left the company in the early 1980s.

IRISH STEEL

BILLY MCMURTY: Born 1938 in south Armagh before moving to Cobh with his family. Worked at Irish Steel from the 1960s as a crane driver and, later, a security guard. Left the company in the early 1990s.

CHRISTY BUCKLEY: Born 1930 in Cobh, County Cork. Foundry operative at Irish Steel, 1950s–1990s.

DONAL BRADY: Born 1932 in Shanbally, County Cork. Electrician at Irish Steel, 1960–94.

FIONNÁN KERRIGAN: Born in the Lough area of Cork city in 1967. Worked at Irish Steel from 1987 until closure in 2001, first as a general operative and later as production manager for the plant.

ROBERT WALSH: Born in the Lower Harbour area of County Cork in 1950. Fitter's mate at Irish Steel from the 1960s until the late 1980s.*

NARRATORS

Jim Shealy: Born in Cobh, County Cork in 1950. Worked in Britain for a while before returning to Cobh. Tongsman in the Irish Steel rolling mills, c.1973–80.

Tony Cummins: Born 1944 in Cobh, County Cork. Rolling mill operative at Irish Steel, 1966–2001.

James Cronin: Born in Cobh, County Cork in 1945. Worked at Irish Steel from 1958 until 2001 in the payroll department.

John Phelan: Born in the 'Jewtown' area of Cork city in 1940. Started work in the costing office of Irish Steel in 1958. Later became production manager. Left the company in 2000.

FORDS

Denis Forde: Born in 1928 in the Greenmount area of Cork city. Worked at Fords from 1942 until closure in 1984, first as a general operative, later as projectionist for the Ford film unit. Spent periods of times working at Ford plants in Leamington Spa and Dagenham.

Gus McLoughlin: Born in Blackpool, Cork city, in 1924. Started work at the Dagenham Ford plant in 1942. Later returned to Cork and worked as a general operative at the Marina plant, excluding stints in Dagenham, from 1948 until closure in 1984.

Michael Costelloe: Born in Duagh, County Kerry, in 1940. Briefly lived in Britain and began work at the Marina plant in the late 1960s as a warehouse operative. Remained there until 1989 when the Ford stores were shut down, five years after the main plant ceased manufacturing.

Michael Lenihan: Born 1958. Grew up in the Blarney Street area of Cork. General operative at Fords from c.1979/80 until closure in 1984. He has written a number of local history books relating to Cork city.

TIM MURPHY: Born near Blarney c.1940. Worked at Fords from 1960 until closure in 1984, first as a general operative, later as a supervisor.

PAT DUNLEA: Born 1945. Grew up in Ballyphehane, Cork city. General operative at Fords, 1963–84.

Introduction

In *Locked Out*, David Convery complains of what he perceives as the subordinated place of the working class within Irish historical writing, claiming that

> the study of an independent working class [in twentieth-century Ireland] is neglected in favour of an all-embracing focus on nationalism in politics, culture and wider society … this neglect has stretched at times to an actual denial of the existence of an Irish working class. [The idea] that class, rather than ethnicity, religion, or […] national identity could have a role to play in politics and cultural production is an alien one to mainstream Irish debate. *The working class has been locked out of history.*[1]

He proceeds to argue that rescuing the Irish working class from this neglect would not only benefit Irish labour history but also have a positive effect on Irish historiography more generally: 'Exploring history from the position of the working class would further offer new perspectives on familiar events, and challenge our tendency to view Ireland in isolation from the rest of the world, allowing for a more complete understanding of society and the dynamics of change in history.'[2]

Convery is not alone in his criticisms. Fintan Lane also takes issue with the dominant narratives of modern Ireland. He complains that mainstream Irish history 'has yet to fully integrate the research and information made available by labour historians over the past few decades', while universities have failed to recognise that 'the experience of working people should be a fundamental element in any attempt to holistically apprehend the Irish past'.[3] Moreover, he remarks,

> misconceptions still exist with regard to the contours of labour history, which is defined narrowly by some as primarily the study of organised labour, with a special focus on industrial relations and political history. This is a hopelessly inadequate vision for labour history, which needs to embrace the entire history of the working class, from politics to leisure, from workplace behaviour to family relations, from socio-economic conditions to socio-cultural values.[4]

These points are echoed by Conor McCabe and Emmet O'Connor, who write that most Irish labour historians 'remain fixated with the so-called "bigger" picture, with high politics and the national question'.[5]

Peter Winn – writing in relation to Latin American labour history in 1979 – outlined a similar situation to that delineated by McCabe and O'Connor. He described workers, the 'presumed protagonists' of labour history, as being present only as abstractions.[6] Winn's suggested solution to this problem was to use the factory study approach, arguing that the scale of the local study could facilitate a holistic reconstruction of workers' lives.[7] To date, only a few such studies have appeared in Irish labour historiography but the factory study has a strong pedigree in American, British, Canadian and Latin American historiography.[8] Winn's other solution to the perceived limitations of labour history 'from above' was the employment of the techniques associated with oral history. Oral testimony, he argues, can provide a more total picture of working lives than would otherwise be possible. It is especially useful in capturing those subjective aspects of working-class life that would otherwise be obscured in traditional sources.[9]

This book differs from much previous research in Ireland in its emphasis on workers and the workplace. Eschewing a traditional focus on high politics and trade unions, it instead concentrates on just three workplaces: Irish Steel (1939–2001), Sunbeam Wolsey (1927–90) and the Ford Marina plant (1917–84) and the men and women who worked in these iconic factories. This is not the first study of a firm or workplace to be conducted in an Irish context. However, it is the first to compare several side by side.[10] By means of this comparative factory study approach (a variation on the method suggested by Peter Winn) combined with the use of extensive oral testimony, this book looks away from the 'bigger picture' of Irish labour history to instead focus on workers and their lived experiences.

The book begins with an examination of the business history of each factory, utilising extensive archival material to place the lives of narrators in their local economic context (Chapters One, Two and Three). It then proceeds to a comparative analysis of the lives of employees in each plant in terms of industrial relations and the experiences of work (Chapters Four, Five and Six). Finally, the study takes a step back from these more specific and comparative concerns to investigate the lives of narrators in terms of work–life patterns, gender, and trade unionism more broadly (Chapters Seven and Eight).

In those chapters that compare and contrast the industrial relations record of Sunbeam, Irish Steel and Ford, the book seeks to answer questions that arose naturally from the approach taken. Why, for example, did Sunbeam experience decades of industrial quietude before a significant increase in strike activity in the 1970s? What were the factors that won the workers of Irish Steel a (generally well-deserved) reputation for industrial militancy unequalled by either Sunbeam or Ford? Why was it that trade union recognition was won so early and easily at Sunbeam and

Irish Steel while taking several decades and a hard-fought strike to be achieved at the Ford Marina plant? Why did organised resistance in the form of strikes decline in all three firms from about 1980 onwards? The first six chapters, combining economic, labour and social history, answer these questions by looking at the underlying factors determining industrial relations and working lives in each firm.

The final two chapters step back from the particularities of each firm to look at the broader picture of working lives in Ireland over the course of this study. What, for example, were the factors that determined the overall pattern of working lives in Ireland as evidenced in the recollections of narrators and other available evidence? What were the meanings of work as reflected in the autobiographies of narrators? How did men and women experience work differently? In answering these questions, a combination of oral and documentary evidence is employed. The oral component of this evidence differs in several respects from the use of more traditional sources. As such, a note on interviews, methodology and ethics in the collection and storage of oral testimony follows.

A NOTE ON INTERVIEWS

In total, this project accessed sixty-six audio interviews with workers, managers and others associated with Irish Steel, Sunbeam Wolsey and the Ford Marina plant. Thirty-three of these interviews were conducted by Miriam Nyhan in her research on the Ford factory, which were provided to the present author in exchange for digitising these tape-recorded interviews. Two interviews with former Sunbeam workers were conducted as part of the University College Cork Women's Oral History Project (WOHP), seven were provided by the Cork Folklore Project (CFP) and the remaining twenty-four were conducted by the present author. As such, the oral testimony sample available was considerable.

My own interview sample was generated primarily by means of snowball sampling. Personal and community contacts were used to make initial contact with potential interviewees, who were then, after the interview itself, asked to provide names and contact details for other potential narrators. In addition, I placed newspaper advertisements and utilised noticeboards and other resources to generate an initial group of interviewees. In total, my own sample consisted of interviews with twenty-four narrators. Of these, twenty can be considered 'primary' narrators, in terms of fulfilling the requirements of being manufacturing workers (strictly defined to include only 'blue-collar' labourers) with the remainder described as 'ancillary' narrators, mainly consisting of management and others who did not meet the relatively strict criteria for being considered among the 'primary' sample.

While the initial aim of the project was to collect a broadly representative sample of narrators, representing a cross-section of manual workers of varying genders and age groups, the final sample did not conform exactly to this ideal. For example, there are few surviving Ford workers who were employed in the plant in the pre-1932 period and, as such, their testimony was unavailable. This lacuna was addressed both by examining the social memory of Ford workers in former decades and by reading against the grain of archival documents to seek out the hidden voices and experiences of long-deceased employees. Similarly, the fact that all three firms reached peak employment in the 1960s and '70s (and were employing declining numbers in subsequent decades) meant there was a bulge in the number of interviews conducted with narrators who began their working lives in the 1950s and '60s. While not ideal, this bulge was inevitable, given the available pool of potential narrators and the economic history of the firms themselves. Consequently, we are limited in our ability to examine generational change in terms of attitudes regarding work and class. Therefore the book mainly provides a representative snapshot of the post-war working class, defined as those who entered paid employment in the twenty years following the Second World War, though tentative conclusions could be drawn regarding the generations that preceded and succeeded this cohort. An additional lacuna might be the fact that only one tradesman was interviewed. While it was hoped that the final sample would include at least two craftworkers, the fact that such workers represented a small minority in the workforces of each plant militated against the inclusion of a larger number of tradesmen. This numerical disparity in the interviews reflects the actual numerical disparity in numbers of tradesmen employed when compared to general operatives.

Finally, a minor problem was identified regarding gender. Due to the length of male working lives in comparison to those of women (these differences are discussed in more detail in Chapter Eight), the period covered in the interviews with the male narrators tended to be longer than those of their female counterparts, often spanning many decades of employment in a single firm. While the sample, from the very beginning, was designed with the intention of having a broadly representative mix of male and female narrators, reflecting the male-dominated nature of Fords and Irish Steel and the majority female labour force at Sunbeam Wolsey, it proved necessary to interview two male Sunbeam workers in order to get a better picture of changes over time in the firm. The result was that, of the twenty primary respondents interviewed, only five were women. It was unfortunate that time constraints prevented the conducting of more interviews with female narrators (although the balance was actually reflective of the demographic mix of employees in each factory) but it proved possible to rectify this balance by accessing a large number of interviews with female Sunbeam workers available through the CFP and the WOHP. As such, while the interview sample is not ideal it is broadly representative, and (combined with other sources) more than satisfactory for the purposes of this book.

During the interviews themselves, I employed a modified life-story approach – a compromise between a highly open life-story method ('tell me about your life') and a more traditional questionnaire format. I devised a question sheet that included a list of open-ended questions that roughly corresponded with the overall life story of narrators. In general, the question sheet served as a guide, rather than a questionnaire, the question format serving as a backup in case I drew a blank during the interview. In general, every effort was made to ensure that the interviews resembled a normal, flowing conversation.

The nature of oral history means that ethical concerns were foremost in my mind during the collection of interviews. It was important that narrators possessed 'informed consent' when agreeing to be interviewed. The nature of the project, and of the interview, was explained when contact was first made with potential interviewees (usually over the phone). Following this initial contact, I met with each narrator to conduct the interview. Before interviewing began, I again explained the nature of the project and the purpose and subject matter of interviews and presented them with a consent form/contract. The consent form was a modified version of the template used by the CFP. It gave interviewees the option of using a pseudonym to protect their identity, though the overwhelming majority were willing to waive anonymity. It also gave them the choice of either having the interview available only to me for use in my own research (as well as conference presentations and publications resulting from this research) or else to be deposited in the CFP for use by future researchers. Furthermore, interviewees (as made clear in the consent form) maintained the right to withdraw their interviews either from myself or the CFP at any time. Most of these interviews are being made accessible from the CFP as part of the 'Liam Cullinane – Cork Working Lives' collection.[11]

Following the completion of the interviews, narrators received a copy of the interview on CD and, where requested, in the form of a transcript. At this point, narrators were asked if they wished to have any portion of the interview deleted (they were also informed of their right to do so immediately before and after the interview), if they did not want certain sections to be available to either myself or future researchers. Interviewees were contacted a third time (after the submission of the thesis on which this book is based) to ensure they were still content with their interviews being used, if they wished for any sections of the interviews to be deleted, if they were still happy to have their testimony deposited with the CFP (where relevant) or if they had any further questions or requests. Finally, the consent form contained a section which allowed narrators to stipulate any further conditions they wished to have placed on the use of their testimony.

Every effort was made to ensure the comfort and consent of respondents. Interviews were largely conducted in narrators' own homes to ensure they were relaxed. Only in one or two cases, at the request of narrators, did interviews take place elsewhere. Most interviews were one-on-one. Only in one case, again at the request of a narrator, was a group interview conducted, and even then, this only involved two interviewees. As in the two cases just mentioned, the duty of care to narrators on the part of the interviewer (myself) meant that changes to the overall approach were made in line with narrators' wishes. For example, one narrator was happy to discuss her working life at Sunbeam, but for personal reasons did not wish to answer questions pertaining to her life outside the factory. While this represented a departure from my preferred approach, the desires of the interviewee had to take precedence and the request was granted.

Finally, the importance of the relationship between popular and individual memory was considered. What of the lingering legacy of the three workplaces? How has popular memory been shaped in the decades since closure? What effect has this popular memory had on the oral testimony? Here we find a complicated legacy. Sunbeam and Fords are remembered primarily with positivity and nostalgia. The former has been the subject of two highly popular comedy-musicals, while the latter has been the subject of a play and a TG4 television documentary (the latter largely celebratory in tone). Irish Steel meanwhile does not feature nearly so prominently.[12] This divergence in popular memory (celebration on the one hand and silence on the other) reflects the subsequent economic experiences of Cobh and Cork city. While the latter eventually recovered from the devastating closures of the 1980s, Cobh was subject to continued de-industrialisation and loss of prosperity that continued through the period of the 'Celtic Tiger' (see Chapter Six). Moreover, the nature of Irish Steel's eventual closure, the subsequent struggle over redundancy, the cynical behaviour of the multinational company Ispat (who operated the plant between 1995 and 2001), as well as the history of injury, death and ill-health in the factory, all rendered the legacy of Irish Steel a bittersweet one for former employees and for the town of Cobh. Redundancies and the terms on which they occurred were also important in shaping the cultural legacy of the workplaces. Ford employees, in sharp contrast to Irish Steel, were granted generous redundancy packages. Narrators stressed their gratitude for the good terms on which their employment in the Marina was terminated. All these factors combined to shape public and popular memory in different ways.

Penny Summerfield notes that private recollections are invariably influenced by public discourses.[13] The effects of the diverging public memories of all three workplaces – celebration and silence – were clear as early as the interview phase of this project. Former Sunbeam and Ford employees were much more positive and forthcoming about consenting to interviews. In the case of Irish Steel, the trust of important contacts had to be won before former employees were comfortable in speaking about the plant.

Throughout the book I have taken every care to balance the need for objective, scholarly investigation with a respect for the significance of each workplace for both the narrators themselves and the communities to which they belong. This work does not seek to be uncritical or merely celebratory but rather to balance the historian's craft with a respect and affection for the experiences of those who so kindly agreed to contribute their stories to this volume. Every effort was made to ensure that the anonymity of those narrators who chose to adopt a pseudonym was maintained, that the interpretations and memories of narrators were never simply dismissed (even when there was a divergence between their recollections and the conclusions I reached in my capacity as historian) and that those who worked in each factory but were not interviewed for this project had their privacy and dignity protected.

Finally, it must be noted that oral history at its best is always a collaborative endeavour. Those I interviewed were not merely 'interviewees' but collaborators and co-authors, equal partners in a project larger than any single individual. I do not regard them simply as 'sources' but as storytellers employing the raw material of their own rich and complex lives. Hence, they are referred to as narrators throughout the work, their recollections each contributing to the telling of a broader story in which I am simply one collaborator among many.

THREE CORK FACTORIES

Before telling our story in earnest, we must examine the central geographical setting of this study (the Cork harbour area) to set the broader context for the chapters that follow. As two of the factories (Sunbeam Wolsey and the Ford Marina plant) were situated in Cork city, this section focuses on the city itself. Cobh is poorly served by historical research and (given its specific importance only in relation to Irish Steel) is examined in tandem with that firm in Chapters Three and Six.

The second largest city in Ireland with a population of 208,000, Cork's economic and commercial life has, for most of its existence, been based on its status as a port city with a strategic location in Cork harbour.[14] At the beginning of the twentieth century Cork was a city with little in the way of either industry or industrial workers. While the nineteenth century had been an era of industrial revolution for Britain and America, it had been one of industrial stagnation and decline for Ireland. Indeed, by 1900 Cork possessed a smaller and less varied industrial sector than it had in 1800.[15] The lack of local industry was not just due to economic degeneration.[16] Cork had never been a significant industrial centre. Even the establishment of the Ford Marina plant in 1917 (detailed in Chapter Four) was significant only as an exception to the overall industrial malaise of the city.

If Corkonians had expected the securing of limited Irish independence with the establishment of the Free State in 1922 to be a harbinger of economic expansion, they were quickly disappointed. The local and national economy remained largely stagnant (with industry actually declining) throughout the 1920s. Fianna Fáil's coming to power in 1932 saw a decisive shift in the economic policy of the Irish Free State, with the introduction of import substitution and protectionism.[17] While its achievements

Map 1. Cork harbour area in relation to the rest of Ireland. Map by Sarah Kandrot.

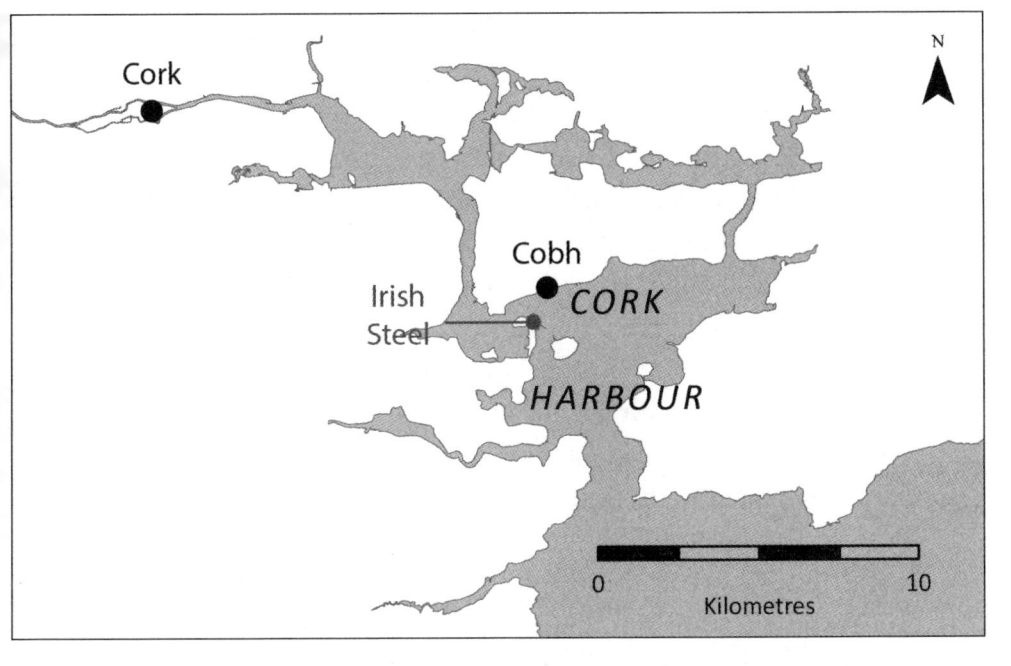

Map 2. Cork harbour area.
Map by Sarah Kandrot.

were limited, this new policy did provide some spur to industrial development, with industrial employment increasing from 110,000 to 166,000 between 1931 and 1938.[18] Cork too benefited from these new policies, with manufacturing employment (excluding construction) rising from 7,301 to 8,285 between 1926 and 1936, an increase of 13.5 per cent.[19] Sunbeam Wolsey in particular reaped the benefits of this new dispensation, expanding from a small concern into a virtual monopoly within its industry, a process examined in Chapter Two.[20]

By the 1950s, the limits of these protectionist policies had become clear. The industrial base of Cork actually shrank between 1951 and 1961, with the total number of manufacturing jobs in the region falling from 12,000 to 10,000.[21] Despite this decline, Cork had managed to develop a basic industrial base. It was now the country's second largest industrial centre, with over half of its 10,000 manufacturing jobs in traditional domestic trades like clothing, textiles, brewing and food processing.[22] By 1971 total manufacturing jobs had risen again to 13,000 and there was also some evidence of diversification, with US chemical multinational Pfizer establishing a base at Ringaskiddy.[23]

Significant changes in Irish economic policy began in the late 1950s, which would see a switch from protectionism to free trade. Important stages in this process included Ireland's signing of the General Agreement on Tariffs and Trade (GATT) in 1967 and its joining of the European Economic Community (EEC) in 1973.[24] Cork's reliance on its traditional industries was problematic as these sectors were highly vulnerable without the shield of tariff protection. It was in the 1980s that Cork truly felt the effects of this economic transition. Sunbeam Wolsey and the Ford Marina plant numbered among the casualties while Irish Steel struggled to limp through the decade that followed.

The 1980s were bleak years. Manufacturing employment fell by almost a fifth, with 5,400 job losses in the first half of the decade. New openings and expansions only provided 1,270 new jobs. Cork became an unemployment black spot with over a fifth of its workforce unemployed.[25] The devastation of the 1980s proved to be relatively short-lived, however. The city regained its prosperity in the following decade and became a major beneficiary of the 'Celtic Tiger' economic boom. But this recovery lies outside the scope of this study.

Having established the narrative of Cork's industrial development throughout the twentieth century, our attention now turns to the firms themselves. The following three chapters are narrative in nature, reconstructing the business histories of the Ford Marina plant, Sunbeam Wolsey and Irish Steel, respectively. These chapters consider the similarities and divergences of the business histories of each firm, examining their establishment, the extent to which their ownership (multinational, domestic or state-run) affected business decisions, how each was able to achieve success within its respective sector, how each responded to the removal of the tariff protections on which their survival depended, and why all three firms were eventually compelled to cease operations in Ireland.

1

'The towering giant of the Irish automotive industry': The Ford Marina plant, 1917–84

INTRODUCTION

The nineteenth century saw thousands of Irish men and women travel to Michigan in search of a better life. As early as 1850 Irish migrants accounted for 16 per cent of the population of Detroit and a quarter of all foreign-born residents in the state.[1] While emigrants from all areas of Ireland settled in the region, those from County Cork were particularly well represented. Among the many Corkonian emigrants who arrived in the Great Lakes region before 1850 were the ancestors of Henry Ford.[2]

In 1912, Henry Ford arrived secretly in Cork. He had just completed a European business trip and wanted to take advantage of a rare opportunity to visit the land of his forefathers. His vacation brought him to Cork city. While there he visited Fair Lane, an overcrowded street in one of the city's extensive slum districts, and the former home of his maternal grandfather.[3] Ford's experience of the poverty-stricken city affected him profoundly. Some years later he wrote how he had found 'a city of casual labour and extreme poverty' with 'no real industry'. The men and their families, he noted, 'did not really live. They had no homes – only hovels. No clothing but what they had on.'[4]

After experiencing these horrific conditions first-hand, Ford began to consider seriously the idea of establishing a factory in the city, entrusting Percival Perry, chairman of the Ford Motor Company (England), with the task of investigating the viability of such an undertaking. This process would result in the creation of a plant that was 'from the point of view of layout and equipment … way ahead of anything in Europe'.[5] This chapter examines the fortunes of Henry Ford's Cork plant from its establishment in 1917 to its closure in 1984.

FORD COMES TO CORK

Other historians have highlighted the significance of Ford's 1912 visit to Cork on his eventual decision to establish a plant in the city. Wilkins and Hill comment that Ford 'liked the idea of a great factory in the land of his ancestors rising like a creative monument to his accomplishments'.[6] Miriam Nyhan and Thomas Grimes both conclude that patriotism and sentiment influenced the magnate's decision to locate in Cork but disagree as to how much weight can be attributed to pragmatic and philanthropic factors respectively. Nyhan argues that, while Ford's family heritage influenced his decision, it was not the primary factor in his choice of a Cork location.[7] She instead highlights the more tangible advantages offered by the city, such as favourable transportation links and a large pool of low-paid labour. Thomas Grimes differs slightly in this regard. He echoes Wilkins and Hill in arguing that 'Ford's overriding motivation was philanthropic' but suggests that this philanthropic motivation overrode more pragmatic concerns about the viability of Cork as an industrial location, claiming that Ford was willing to take risks in establishing a factory in the city.[8]

Grimes' analysis is the more convincing. A 1913 report by Percival Perry suggests that the advantages of Cork were outweighed by the disadvantages. On one hand, the low price of land and favourable lease terms in Ireland were identified as being superior to those of Britain.⁹ The Marina site itself, with its access to Cork's excellent natural harbour and maritime transport links to Britain, was championed by Perry as the best conceivable site for an Irish factory: 'I cannot imagine any other location which would be more suitable.'¹⁰ Perry was also positive about the local labouring population: there was widespread unemployment, and the wages of unskilled labourers were lower than those of their counterparts in Britain, while there was also a weaker trade union influence among the local working class. But while cheap local labour was undoubtedly attractive to Ford, it was also the case that there was a severe shortage of skilled labour in the region, which Perry described as being 'very inadequate in all areas affecting our business'.¹¹ Additionally, Ireland's insignificance within the British market (accounting for only 10 per cent of total car sales in the United Kingdom) meant that the majority of products would have to be transported across the Irish Sea to buyers on the British mainland, with associated freight costs of an estimated £15 per car.¹² Also, the absence of locally available raw materials and other industrial necessities would require a Cork plant to import materials and equipment by sea.¹³

The report concluded with the frank warning that 'for some years at least you will never secure so large a profit from an Irish factory as would be obtained from a similar factory operating in England. The risk of loss is considerably greater; the difficulties in every Department ... are augmented.'¹⁴ However, Perry's letter suggests that Ford was willing to proceed despite these difficulties: 'It must be recognised that the move is fundamentally a philanthropic one.'¹⁵ From a strictly business point of view, locating a manufacturing facility in Cork was illogical. Investment in a plant on the British mainland would have carried less risk, provided greater profits and presented fewer problems than were likely to occur in Ireland. As such, the defining basis for the decision to locate in Cork, aside from the handful of advantages presented by the Marina location, was sentimental, patriotic and philanthropic, rather than economic or pragmatic. This conclusion is supported by a 1918 letter to a senior Ford official (the uncompromising Dane Charlie 'Cast-Iron' Sorensen) in which Perry remarks that 'the principal reason why Mr. Ford started the institution at Cork was social and political rather than commercial and economic'.[16] Indeed, Henry Ford himself later stated that 'we chose Ireland for a plant because we wanted to start Ireland along the road to industry. There was, it was true, some personal sentiment in it.'[17] As such, when Ford branched out into tractor manufacturing (the 'Fordson' tractor was launched in 1917) it was Cork, rather than a more sensible location in mainland Britain, that was chosen as the centre of Fordson production for the United Kingdom.

In February 1917 Ford entered negotiations for the purchase of a site in Cork Marina. Initially, the identity of the purchaser was unclear, but on 1 March it was revealed that it was Henry Ford and that he would be establishing a factory there. The following month a new company, 'Henry Ford and Sons Limited', was incorporated.[18] The firm signed a lease with Cork Corporation that provided very generous terms – albeit requiring certain commitments on the part of the new company. Cork Corporation would lease land to the company for 999 years from 9 June 1917 for a one-off payment of £11,500 and a yearly rent of one penny while Ford would be obliged to spend £200,000 on industrial construction and maintain 2,000 employees at a minimum salary of one shilling per hour for five years.[19]

By mid-1919 the new plant on the banks of the Lee was completed. The first 'Fordson' tractor left the assembly line on 3 July.[20] Henry Ford and Sons was a truly international concern, with an Irish workforce, American management team (led by the strong-willed managing director Edward Grace, formerly a plant superintendent in Dearborn, Michigan) and markets spread throughout North Africa and Europe.

TRACTOR PRODUCTION AND MASS MANUFACTURE, 1919–32

The early years of the factory in Cork coincided with some of the most tumultuous times in the city's history: those of the War of Independence and subsequent Civil War. However, despite the turbulent situation that existed in the city generally, business at Fords was largely unaffected. Even during the burning of Cork in December 1920 the plant did not suffer directly, being located sufficiently far from the city centre to avoid the direct effects of the conflagration.[21] Writing to company headquarters in the United States, Edward Grace assured his superiors that

> as far as the works are concerned, we are in no danger: firstly, because it is owned by an American and they fear that it might involve multinational complications, and next because we have about 1,500 men employed, and while so employed they have no time to think of matters other than their work.[22]

A more serious threat to the plant's survival came not in the form of war but a quarrel with Cork Corporation in 1922. The dispute emerged due to the clause in the original lease agreed by Ford and the corporation which stipulated that the company maintain 2,000 men in employment, at a minimum of one shilling per hour.[23] In July 1921 the corporation attempted to press the issue of employment in the plant. Grace initially tried to resolve the question quietly through meetings with local councillors but by February 1922 the corporation had grown weary of waiting for a resolution and voted to force the company to comply with the lease.[24] Reacting strongly to the corporation's actions, the company stood its ground. Sorensen instructed Grace via telegram: 'MAKE NO CHANGES IN YOUR OPERATIONS. STOP ALL CONSTRUCTION AND INSTALLATION WORK. EMPLOY NO MORE HELP. CLOSE UP EMPLOYMENT DEPARTMENT.'[25] Henry Ford himself was infuriated by the corporation's decision and instructed Grace to shut down the Cork operation and transfer it elsewhere unless the corporation backed down. During the stand-off, local business interests, media and the Ford workers themselves sided with the company, fearing the economic repercussions of a closure. On 7 March Ford upped the ante by reducing its workforce by 500 men.[26] This action, allied to the fact that the tide of local public opinion was turning swiftly against the corporation, resulted in the latter backing down. The well-paid and stable jobs provided by Ford, in the economic context of high unemployment and poor job opportunities, led the workers themselves to side with the company against the forces of local government.

Despite the initial optimism surrounding the plant, Henry Ford and Son Ltd struggled to play the role required by its parent company. A letter from Sorensen to Grace in November 1920 painted a grim picture of the difficulties faced in Cork:

> I keep looking at your plant, from the point of view that you are not producing enough tractors and are spending an awful lot of money. Have you got it clearly in your mind that both ends are going to meet and are you going to keep up the present gait? Are your incoming funds and those at hand such that you are going to keep your head above water for an indefinite period, with no more prospects for future business than you have at the present time?[27]

Sorensen was clearly unimpressed with the plant's performance and concluded with a stark warning to Cork management: 'I am afraid with your very limited output and the way expenditures are being made at the present moment that you will soon be yelling for funds, and I assure you there will be none available.'[28]

By January 1921 it was clear that the initial undertaking had failed. Grace complained that sales had 'almost fallen off to nothing'.[29] John O'Neill, later to become managing director himself, attributed the collapse in sales to 'the world-wide depression, the collapse in prices' and 'the lack of demand for tractors in sufficient quantity to keep the plant in economical operation'.[30] Later that month all tractor production at the factory ceased, resulting in the dismissal of 600 men.[31] The foundry (where liquid metal was cast into parts for the vehicles) operations at the plant were re-directed towards the production of Model T parts to supply Ford's Manchester factory, as well as the construction of complete Model T cars for the Irish market. Such an arrangement was only possible due to the lack of a foundry in the Manchester assembly plant. Had Ford possessed a foundry anywhere on the British mainland, it is likely that the Cork factory would have been closed or significantly downgraded.

The firm continued to struggle even as the facility faced less onerous production demands. Sales of the Model T were falling off in both Ireland and Britain.[32] A letter from manager E.L. Clarke[33] to Sorensen in late 1926 revealed that the Cork plant had been forced to introduce a five-day week and reduce the workforce by over a hundred in order to reduce costs.[34] Additionally, as with the struggling Manchester plant, the Ford company had serious concerns about the quality of production in Cork. One inspector complained of a 'significant number of cases of poor workmanship and sub-standard parts'.[35] As Wilkins and Hill remark, 'the making of Model T parts in Cork at a considerable distance from Manchester was not an efficient arrangement. Soon it would become an impossible one.'[36] More worrying was the

1924 purchase of a site at Dagenham in Essex, where the company was planning to construct a gargantuan new manufacturing and assembly centre which would make the Marina plant surplus to the requirements of Ford in Europe. The future of Henry Ford and Sons in Cork looked bleak.

However, despite these inauspicious circumstances, the Cork plant was about to undergo a metamorphosis. As part of a broader re-organisation of Ford's European operations, Cork was to return to its initial purpose: the production of Fordson tractors. The Ford company's so-called '1928 plan' was ambitious. The task given to Cork management was daunting: the factory was to be the global centre of Fordson tractor production, supplying the continental market and the rapidly industrialising Soviet Union. Percival Perry predicted in 1929 that 30,000 Fordson tractors would be sold on the European market, the overwhelming majority of which were to be supplied by Cork.[37] Unwilling to waste the expensive foundry and experienced technicians in their Irish plant, Ford and Perry were committed to the success of the Cork operation. Indeed, Wilkins and Hill note that Henry Ford was 'still hopeful of establishing an industrial centre in Ireland' even though 'the Irish factory could not have turned out tractors as cheaply as could Dearborn'.[38]

By 28 February 1930 the Cork plant's workforce had mushroomed to 6,924 and the factory had been significantly expanded in order to cope with its massively inflated production requirements.[39] As Chapter Four demonstrates, the concentration of so many workers in such a large modern establishment created unique difficulties for Irish Ford employees, who were unused to factory work on such a large scale and at such high levels of organisational and technological sophistication.[40] While at first glance the prospects for the Cork plant appeared bright, other factors were conspiring against the facility. At the onset of the

1930s Henry Ford and his company found themselves in crisis. The industrial patriarch had initially ignored the burgeoning Great Depression, pushing ahead with expansion plans in Dagenham and elsewhere, claiming 'the immediate cure for depression … and by depression I mean a period when men are out of work … is told in one word, "quantity" – quantities of goods pushed out into the world'.[41] Ford's own relentless positivity proved to be quixotic in the face of economic reality. Wilkins and Hill describe how by 1930 the economic crisis had inflicted severe damage on the Ford company and was now spreading to its European holdings, which imploded 'like a collapsing house of cards'.[42]

Operations in Cork were the first to suffer. By 1931 the facility was reporting an adverse trading balance of £129,316.[43] Falling demand saw the production of tractors fall from a high of 15,196 units in 1930 to just 3,088 in 1932.[44] The international depression and endemic problems relating to production in the Cork plant meant that the firm found 'the tractor operation at Cork hanging about its neck like the ancient mariner's albatross'.[45]

In 1932, the tractor-production experiment at Cork came to an ignominious end. The completion of the Dagenham foundry had lessened the importance of its Cork equivalent, which was now reduced to making castings until the Dagenham foundry was fully operational. The inexperience of management, the rapid transfer of machine tools, constant changes in tractor design, the rawness of the Cork labour force, and over-optimistic production demands issued from Michigan that were 'far in excess of anything we could live up to' led to 'not only a hold-up in production but considerable expense in redistribution'.[46] Such problems were not unknown among inter-war Ford establishments in Europe where the abilities of management and labour frequently fell short of the ambitious plans of the engineers.[47] Consequently, Perry proposed that tractor production be moved to Dagenham as soon as possible.[48] With low demand for tractors, there was little justification for an entire plant dedicated to tractor production. Manufacturing assembly in Cork was to cease completely, with the Marina factory reduced to 'a distributing centre for Irish Free State [sic] for our motor car and tractor products'.[49]

Less than a month after this exchange, plans for Cork had to be altered quickly as the newly elected Fianna Fáil minority government began to implement protectionist policies. On 6 May 1932 the new government imposed an overnight tariff of '75% ad valorem or £60 ($300) whichever was the less, on automobile bodies'.[50] The suddenness of the legislation's introduction was such that the Ford company 'had 35 trucks fitted with cabs and commercial bodies in transit from Dagenham to Cork when this duty was put on and to clear the consignment ... had to pay £1,200 ($6,000) of unexpected duty'.[51] The company was taken aback by the new tax, which, Perry remarked, 'is so prohibitive that it would practically put us out of business unless we either buy or assemble our own bodies'.[52] Dearborn was also acutely aware that other car-assembly firms would take advantage of the new opportunities provided by the protections offered to the industry in Ireland, with Perry noting that 'our competitors already have made arrangements with body builders'.[53] To that end he sought, and received, permission to convert the Cork plant into an assembly operation, the estimated cost of which (£3,400) paled in comparison to the losses the company would face from paying import duties or losing the small but lucrative Irish market.[54] As Chapter Four demonstrates, this change from mass production for a world market to limited production for a small, domestic market fundamentally altered the nature of work in the Ford Marina plant.

CAR ASSEMBLY AND TARIFFS, 1932–69

The revamped assembly plant would be a much less impressive operation than it had been during the 1929–30 period. The new equipment recommended by Perry, which did not even include a conveyor, would 'give an output of 24 bodies per 8 hours, which at the present time is ample to satisfy the demand in the Free State'.[55]

The 1933 directors' meeting at Henry Ford and Sons announced that

> from January 1st 1933 [sic] your Company's trading activities shall be mainly directed to the assembly of chassis and production of bodies for the Irish Free State market and the sale therein of automobile, tractor and service parts. Arrangements for the equipment of parts of your factory as an Automobile Assembly Plant have accordingly been made and production has already commenced. The demand for our products appears to be favourable.[56]

The implementation of duties on the importation of car bodies ensured the survival of the Marina plant as an assembly centre for another half a century.

Even though the plant had survived the threat of closure, the new assembly operation was a dwarf in comparison to the industrial behemoth that had ballooned into being during the second period of tractor construction. Protectionism also precipitated the diversification of the Irish automobile market. As Perry had foreseen, other automobile manufacturers either set up their own operations in Ireland or formed partnerships with domestic body builders to circumvent import duties. By the end of the decade there were 1,500 Irish men and women employed in twenty-one car assembly firms.[57] Most of these operations were tiny. Unlike the large and egalitarian car market of the United

States, car ownership in Ireland remained a luxury, though there was a slightly larger market for commercial vehicles. The small and slow-growing nature of the Irish automobile market in the 1930s was demonstrated by the fact that there were only between 36,000 and 37,000 cars in use in the Free State at the start of 1936.[58] Legislation designed to promote domestic motor assembly also resulted in cars in Ireland becoming one-third more expensive than their British or Northern Irish counterparts which, combined with the effects of the great depression, actually saw a fall in the number of cars in use in the Free State between 1933 and '34 and an overall increase of only 300 between 1931 and '34.[59]

By the outbreak of the Second World War 'practically the entire car requirements of the country were being supplied from home sources', with the Irish motor assembly industry 'in a prosperous state and ... giving substantial employment'.[60] Despite market penetration by other forces, Ford remained the dominant player within the Irish industry, constituting more than half of all car sales in the state.[61] However, given Ireland's isolation and the necessity of importing all materials required for car production, the factory was ill-prepared for the effects of the war, which saw 'operations coming to a complete standstill from 1941 to the end of 1945' due to a lack of supplies.[62] The introduction of petrol rationing also inflicted a heavy burden on the vehicle assembly industry. *The Cork Examiner* reported in 1940 that garages across Cork were 'bone dry of petrol' and that one firm of undertakers had been forced to let go its entire driving staff due to the scarcity of fuel.[63] The subsequent ban on private motoring was merely the final nail in the coffin for Irish vehicle production. The effects of this closure were mitigated, however, by the expansion of Ford plants in Britain, which willingly took on experienced workers from the Cork operation. In 1947 the Cork plant re-commenced production at pre-war levels. The experience of the hundreds of Ford employees who were transferred to British facilities is examined in more detail in Chapter Four, while working-class emigration more generally is discussed in Chapter Seven.[64]

The post-war motor assembly industry in Ireland was characterised largely by small manufacturers with low production volumes, often employing fewer than a hundred workers. A 1962 Committee on Industrial Organisation (CIO)[65] report noted that most firms employed between 800 and just a few dozen, while output varied from 14,000 vehicles to fewer than 10.[66] These firms were all subject to considerable variations in demand, with rapid fluctuations in numbers employed. Between June and October 1960, the number of manual workers employed in the industry dropped from 2,500 to 1,722.[67] Smaller firms with limited market share were particularly vulnerable to these variations in demand. During a brief industry-wide recession in the mid-1950s, for example, Buckley Motors saw its workforce contract from 163 to just 18 in the space of one year while another firm was forced to lay off two-thirds of its workforce.[68] Ford, due to its superior resources in terms of plant and its consistent domination of the Irish market, was able to respond to such shifts in demand far better than smaller concerns. Regardless, the firm's primacy within the Irish market was far from reassuring given the weak state of the industry more generally.

None of these Irish vehicle assembly operations were competitive by international standards, and did not need to be. Ford's Cork operation, the most extensive and modern vehicle assembly plant in the country, was considered 'uncompetitive in the extreme, costs being higher there than in any other Ford plant in Europe'.[69] Regardless, these companies remained highly profitable.[70] Profitability did not, however, mean value for money. Prices of Irish cars were higher than they would have been had they been imported fully assembled.[71]

In 1962 Seán Lemass attended a banquet to celebrate the forty-fifth anniversary of Henry Ford and Sons' presence in Cork. During his speech he allayed fears for the future of the motor assembly industry, claiming that 'it will not be too difficult [for the car assembly industry] to adapt … to operations which will be viable under free trade conditions'.[72] These remarks were inaccurate and disingenuous. A 1968 *Business and Finance* article laid out the reality in stark terms, declaring that the future of the Irish motor assembly industry under free trade conditions was 'both limited and grim'.[73] A 1962 CIO report had reached much the same conclusions, declaring that 'the motor vehicle assembly industry would have no economic prospects of survival under free trade conditions' and predicted job losses of 2,000 people directly employed by the industry and a further 450 to 600 jobs lost in supplying industries.[74]

END OF AN ERA, 1970–84

In 1969 Ford remained the single most important brand within the Irish car market, accounting for 27 per cent of new car registrations.[75] Moreover, as the economy improved after the nadir of the 1950s, car ownership ceased to be a luxury. In 1968, some 49,500 cars were assembled in the Republic, which was more than the total number of private cars in the country in 1935.[76] However, even this large market share did not necessitate huge production requirements, with *The Irish Times* reporting that the Cork plant was producing eighty cars per day in 1969.[77] While this was a 400 per cent increase on the number produced by the factory in the early 1930s, it paled in comparison to other European Ford facilities. Dagenham, for example, in 1963 had an output of almost 1,200 units per day.[78] Regardless, Ford focused on maintaining its enviable position within the Irish market, completing a £1.5 million modernisation project at its Marina facility in 1967.

Given the weaknesses of the domestic assembly industry in general, Ireland's accession negotiations with the EEC were watched closely by those associated with car assembly. Surprisingly, the signing of the Anglo-Irish Free Trade Agreement (AIFTA)[79] in 1965 did not have an immediate negative impact on the industry. A Dáil question from TD David Thornley in 1971 revealed that the numbers employed in car assembly had actually increased slightly following the signing of the agreement, up from 3,600 in 1964 to 3,800 at the end of 1970.[80] The industry was given a stay of execution when, during the negotiations that led Ireland to join the EEC, the Irish government was able to ensure that industry protections would be extended until the end of 1984 as part of a transitional period for manufacturers in 'sensitive' economic areas. The government claimed that prospects for the industry were bright. Indeed, even a broadly pessimistic article in *The Irish Times* in March 1979 expressed the belief that, while most assembly firms would be unable to survive, it was 'virtually certain that Ford will stay assembling in Cork'.[81] Managing Director Paddy Hayes confirmed that same year that the Cork facility was viable and could match the far larger and more modern Genk plant in Belgium in terms of price and quality.[82] However, just four years later he was admitting that the Cork plant was unlikely to survive.[83] One newspaper noted frankly that the Irish plant was 'in grave danger and easily expendable'.[84] At this stage (October 1983), most of the other car assembly plants in the country had already ceased production. The Fiat plant in Dublin had closed its doors in 1981 while Toyota and Nissan maintained token assembly operations with fewer than thirty people employed in each plant.[85] Even before the crucial year of 1984 dawned, Ford was the country's last major automobile assembler.

On 17 January 1984, Paddy Hayes called a meeting of the Fords workforce and its various trade union representatives. Explaining in stark terms the dire economic situation that the Irish company faced, Hayes confirmed that the plant would close later that year, resulting in the total Ford workforce in the country being reduced from 1,000 to 200.[86] Following the eventual acceptance of a satisfactory redundancy agreement by the Ford trade unions, the plant closed its doors in July 1984. The short-term effects of the closure were devastating. The high wages in the plant meant an estimated annual loss of £34 million to the Cork economy, a particularly grievous blow in the wake of almost one thousand redundancies in other industries between September 1983 and January 1984.[87] When Henry Ford II (grandson of the original Henry Ford and his successor as head of the company) was informed of the decision to finally end manufacturing and assembly operations at Cork he was reported to have been 'upset', while also acknowledging the economic necessity of the closure.[88] His grandfather's ambitious vision, of a great industry that would bring employment and prosperity to the working men of Cork, had finally come to an end.

CONCLUSION

For the final five decades of its existence Ford's Cork operation was 'a relatively straightforward business, a virtual haven of stability and calm as it fulfilled the role of assembling vehicles to meet the needs of the local Irish market'.[89] As John O'Neill (managing director of the Cork plant from 1932 to 1959) put it in 1960, 'the postwar history of the Irish firm has been humdrum. There have been no scandals or explosions, no front page stories. We keep on selling and keep on making money.'[90] This quiet prosperity was predicated on the continuation of tariff protection. Indeed, the

Department of Industry and Commerce had recognised this fact since the early 1960s, with other sources such as *The Irish Press* in agreement.[91]

The extension of the motor industry quota (one of the guarantees given to Ireland for entry into the Common Market) represented a stay of execution for Ford and the broader motor vehicle industry. However, by the time the quota was finally removed in 1984, the Ford Motor Company had accepted that it was no longer economical to continue motor production at Cork. Unlike some other protected industries, which desperately attempted to survive in a free-trade environment, the company was able to abandon its Irish operations with little fanfare and at little cost. Indigenous firms such as Sunbeam Wolsey faced a far more dramatic and uphill struggle under changing economic conditions.

2

'Giving the nation socks': Sunbeam Wolsey, 1927–90

INTRODUCTION

As you drive into Cork city by the Mallow Road – just as you reach the suburbs, it's nestling in a hollow on the right-hand side of the road – Sunbeam Wolsey Ltd, Millfield. A big, many-windowed, red-brick, five-storey building, with single-storey buildings, squat and solid and new, sprouting from it … The whirr of machinery, the purring of dynamos, the deft movements of hundreds of trained workers, all the sound and fury of a modern factory in full, healthy production.[1]

In the early decades of the twentieth century Cork was a city in economic decline, but also an area that had long been an active centre of the textile and clothing trade. In 1919 D.J. Coakley identified the city and county as representing the 'chief seat of the woollen industry in Ireland', which was giving employment to about two thousand people in the region.[2] In 1890, for example, the suburb of Douglas possessed two woollen mills employing 750 people between them.[3] In 1911 linen manufacturing was employing over a thousand people in the city and environs.[4] Among the largest of these concerns was the Millfield Flax Spinning and Weaving Company, established in 1867, which employed around 630 people.[5] The plant was closed during the depression of the 1880s before being reopened by businessman James Ogilvie as the

Cork Spinning and Weaving Company in 1889, which, by 1897, was employing over 600 workers.[6] By 1919 the company had become one of the largest industries in the city with upwards of a thousand employees.[7] The firm survived until 1927 when the impressive factory on the Commons Road was again left vacant.[8]

The Dwyer family were among the most established of Cork's clothing manufacturers, having been significant employers there since the early nineteenth century. In the 1920s, they could still be counted among the most important families of the city's economic elite, operating several significant textile and clothing concerns such as the Lee Hosiery and Lee Boot Company. At a company meeting on 24 March 1927, the ambitious scion William Dwyer announced he would be leaving the company.[9] William's intent was to strike out on his own by establishing a knitwear firm in the city.

In the decades that followed, William Dwyer's gamble paid off spectacularly as his new venture grew into what was (by Irish standards) an industrial giant. In a city blighted by unemployment and which had relatively little in the way of modern manufacturing industry, the Sunbeam factory was one of the most important employers of labour in the region. At its height it employed close to two thousand people, over half of whom were women.[10] At a time when the average post-war manufacturing establishment employed fewer than twenty people, Sunbeam was a behemoth, one of the top 1 per cent of Irish manufacturing establishments when measured by numbers employed.[11] In spite of the importance of the firm, however, there has been little substantial research on its history. This chapter rectifies this lacuna in Irish economic history and provides the industrial and economic context for the discussion of work and industrial relations in later chapters.

PROTECTIONISM AND EXPANSION, 1928-65

The company William Dwyer established in 1928 (Sunbeam Knitwear Ltd) initially operated out of the small Shandon butter market and had a workforce numbering in the dozens. One woman who was hired by Sunbeam in 1929 estimated that there were no more than fifty people working there at the time.[12] The small factory was typical of the broader textile and clothing industry in Ireland. The Irish woollen industry was characterised by small firms, with most employing fewer than fifty people.[13] The tiny cotton industry consisted of only five mills.[14] Moreover, the textile industry was in decline, with the number of workers in the Irish woollen trade alone falling by a third between 1917 and 1925.[15] A factory inspection conducted in four western counties in 1927 found that the hosiery industry was also in a dire state, with the three hosiery plants inspected employing just twenty-eight people.[16] Ready-made clothing was in a better situation due to the recent imposition of a tax on imported clothes.[17] The gradual decline of the industry led to the otherwise laissez-faire Cumann na nGaedheal government introducing a number of tariffs, which were developed further under the Fianna Fáil government that succeeded it in the 1930s. Fianna Fáil expanded the existing tariff on ready-made clothing to also include woollen and linen imports, and in 1935 introduced a quota system for all sectors of the textile and clothing industries.[18]

Sunbeam benefited from these protections. However, for the company to expand it required an injection of capital for investment in machinery and to increase its workforce. This injection was provided by Charles Orr (C.O.) Stanley, a Waterford-born capitalist who had made his fortune in the UK electronics industry, having turned the Pye radio company into a major player there. Still true to his Irish roots, Stanley had begun making investments in the Free State.[19] The first of these investments saw the opening of a Dublin branch of his advertising agency, Arks Publicity, in 1930. William Dwyer initially contacted Stanley with the intention of securing his company's advertising services. Stanley's biographer claims that the radio magnate then discovered that the managing director had barely managed to cover the previous week's payroll.[20] This convinced Stanley to make a major investment in the fledgling operation in exchange for a directorship. The company became 'Sunbeam Wolsey' in 1933 as a result of an arrangement made with Wolsey Knitwear, one of Stanley's advertising clients.[21] However, even before the merger with Wolsey, William Dwyer's firm had already outgrown its small premises in the butter market, leading him to announce in 1932 that the company was planning to relocate to the much larger Millfield mill, former site of James Ogilvie's Cork Spinning and Weaving Company.

Sunbeam's move to the new site was greeted with enthusiasm. The Cork Workers' Council noted that it was 'very glad to see that a local firm was about to open the Blackpool factory',[22] while *The Irish Times* predicted that the new industry would 'raise the city to a position of commercial pre-eminence'.[23] At the opening of the premises, at the time employing about 250 people, William Dwyer announced that 'my son, who is nineteen, and myself … signed a contract recently that on his twenty-first birthday we will employ two thousand hands here and on my fiftieth birthday, we are going to have five thousand'.[24]

Ambitious as these predictions were, they were not far off the mark. Benefiting massively from the protectionist economic policies introduced by Fianna Fáil in the 1930s, native clothing and textiles manufacturers flourished, with companies such as Sunbeam able to dominate their market.[25] Indeed, the firm was ruthless and monopolistic, soon accounting for nearly a third

2.1 William Dwyer admiring a scale model of the Sunbeam complex at Millfield, 1949. Photo reproduced with the kind permission of Cork City and County Archives. CCCA: B505/BND29/1 Temp 79 Sunbeam Wolsey Limited – Twenty-First Annual Report.

of employment in the domestic textile and clothing trade (the remaining two-thirds were spread across sixty-four separate manufacturers).[26] By 1936 it had already more than doubled its workforce and could afford to pay significantly higher wages than other companies in the hosiery industry. Sunbeam's 1936 annual report noted that,

> because of the number of factories which have now started, the competition which we are up against is practically altogether internal. That we can meet this competition and still pay 50 per cent higher wages to our workers is clear proof that our organisation is on the soundest possible basis.[27]

The broader Sunbeam Group (which included Sunbeam Wolsey and a number of other companies owned by the Dwyers) continued

2.2 Sunbeam Wolsey complex at Millfield, date unknown. Photo reproduced with the kind permission of Cork City and County Archives. CCCA: B612/BH.

to grow with the opening of the Cork Spinning Company, located adjacent to the original Millfield complex, in 1939.[28]

In this period, Sunbeam sought to implement Fianna Fáil's economic nationalism in practice and succeeded remarkably in doing so. In 1944, a promotional booklet issued by the company boasted that the factory had become 'as near as any industry can be, self-contained', and in 1940, with the setting up of Woolcombers Ireland, Sunbeam could function almost completely independently of imported materials.[29] Wool was bought from Irish farmers, combed through the subsidiary company and then processed at the Millfield factory. In just a few years, Sunbeam had achieved almost total autarky and continued to grow even in the face of economic difficulties posed by the 'Emergency' (as the years of the Second World War were known in Ireland). These problems were overcome largely due to the work undertaken by Dwyer for the United Kingdom Ministry of Supplies during the war, which allowed him to secure contracts from the British military.[30] Indeed, by 1945 the firm had actually expanded and was employing over a thousand workers.[31] Moreover, the expansion of the Sunbeam Group continued with the purchase of the Tullamore-based Industrial Yarns Ltd and the setting up of Midleton Worsted Mills and Seafield Fabrics in the years following the war.[32] It was this near-total domination of their industry, combined with protection against external market forces, that allowed Dwyer and his company to maintain a paternalist form of management (see Chapter Five).

While Sunbeam's success was based primarily on its domination of the Irish market, the company began to prepare for the onset of free trade from an early stage. In a 1951 editorial, *The Irish Times* was impressed by Sunbeam's successful attempts at expanding its export business.[33] The article noted that Sunbeam's products were being bought all over the world, and that the fame of Midleton Worsted wool (a Sunbeam subsidiary) had spread as far as Morocco and New York.[34] However, the company remained reliant on domestic sales and the maintenance of protectionism.[35]

Such concerns were likely to have been at the forefront of chairman C.O. Stanley's mind at Sunbeam's 1957 annual general meeting, where the company's prospects under free trade were discussed at some length:

> Your management … recognise that all the pundits have said that the textile industry must suffer in a Free Trade area. They are therefore moving out into new fields which are less likely to be affected by free trade and concentrating on developing, particularly in the export market, those sides of the business which are unlikely to prove to be the strength of any of the larger European textile industries. Your Directors appreciate

that to be an isolated industry in a small country would be a great handicap if a free trade area were established. They are therefore ready to take every advantage of a working understanding with their many friends and associates abroad.[36]

Unfortunately, the extent of the difficulties created by the introduction of free trade with the UK in 1965,[37] and Ireland's 1973 accession to the EEC, would prove to be considerably more challenging than Stanley and others had envisaged.

FREE TRADE, 1965–80

In the aftermath of the 1965 Anglo-Irish Free Trade Agreement, Sunbeam's strong economic position and expansion of its export markets initially allowed the company to perform reasonably well. In 1968, for example, its annual report noted a rise in sales from £183,000 in 1965 to £743,000 and commented that the order books for 1969 appeared 'very favourable'.[38] However, while the company appeared to be on relatively sound footing, the new dispensation was presenting serious difficulties, which would soon be exacerbated by Ireland's accession to the EEC. Indeed, Stanley was complaining as early as 1963 that

> during the year we have ... had to face ruthless competition, often coupled with political support and hidden subsidies, and frequently intensified by the uncertainty of the policy of our own country in continuing to reduce tariffs without any quid pro quo from Great Britain and the EEC countries.[39]

Tom Scott (born in Nottingham; emigrated to Ireland in 1958; manager and later chief executive of Sunbeam Wolsey, 1958 to early 1980s) recalls the state of play when he became chief executive officer in 1967:

The company ... when I took over things were very difficult in terms of free trade. It was difficult for people to adjust. You know it was a major shock. And a lot of people just couldn't adjust. They just couldn't recognise that things had changed.[40]

The medium-term impact of free trade and EEC accession on the textile and clothing industry was dramatic. Between 1968 and 1978, twenty woollen and worsted producers closed with the loss of 3,445 jobs, nearly half of all employment in the sector.[41] Among those to close were Murrough Brothers, Douglas; Irish Worsted Mills, Portlaoise; and Mulcahy-Redmond, Ardfinnan, which had been employing 120, 130 and 110 people respectively.[42] In 1970, C.O. Stanley complained of import dumping by British, American, Dutch and Belgian firms, declaring that he 'could not estimate how seriously this dumping ... would affect the overall performance of the group'.[43] He emphasised: 'It is now, and will increasingly, affect employment in our factories.'[44]

At a meeting of the raw materials section of the Sunbeam Group in 1971, one participant outlined how this broader decline in textiles was affecting the company. At the group's subsidiary Salts, the 'proportion of good business was getting less and less'; Midleton Worsted Mills and Woolcombers Ltd were 'lucky to break even' and there was 'no sign of improvement' at the struggling Tullamore Yarns Ltd.[45] The following years saw the closing of both the Cork Spinning Company and Salts Ltd, as loss-making operations had to be shed in order to for the group as a whole to survive. Kevin Dwyer (born 1944, grandson of William Dwyer; worked at Sunbeam from 1962 to 1974 as an advertising executive and later manager of the design and development department) decided there was no long-term future for the industry: 'I was thirty years of age in 1974 and I had two small kids and I said, "There's no way that I'm going to be retiring from a job in the textile industry.'"[46] These economic developments also had a major effect on the previously pacific industrial relations in Sunbeam which began to deteriorate from the late 1960s onwards, as we will see in Chapter Five.[47]

In addition to the more general problems generated by increased foreign competition, the broader European textile industry was itself in a process of structural decline. An EEC commission brochure issued in 1982 described a 'structural crisis' and market collapse that had seen production contractions of 5.9 per cent and 6.3 per cent in textiles and clothing respectively since 1973.[48] The decline was attributed to a number of factors. Foremost among these was increased competition from producers in the developing world. These emerging producers could sell similar products at much lower prices, with the result that 'between 1973 and 1980, the share of European consumption taken by non-Community imports rose from 21% to 44%'.[49] The effect of these changes on employment levels within the continental industry was considerable. Between 1973 and 1980 the numbers employed fell from 3.1 to 2.3 million, with 'an average loss of 115,000 jobs a year'.[50]

Ireland was in a particularly weak position to compete in a continental market that was struggling for survival. In 1976, Senator Fintan Kennedy, the general president of the Irish Transport and General Workers Union (ITGWU), addressed the problems of the industry:

> Clothing and textiles in Ireland were more than twice the size of the industry in West Germany, where less than 5% were employed in the manufacturing sector ... to suggest that the European textile industry was suffering a structural decline meant one thing for West Germany for its 5% and another thing for Ireland with its 11%.[51]

The significant percentage of Irish manufacturing industry accounted for by textiles and clothing meant that the effects of European structural decline, grim elsewhere, were nothing short of devastating in Ireland, with closures and redundancies occurring on a massive scale across the sector.

In the face of these new challenges Sunbeam engaged in a process of significant expansion. The company's 1965 annual report revealed that it was in the process of negotiating the purchase of two of its competitors, Allied Textiles Ltd and Salts (Ireland).[52] Later, the company looked abroad and began to purchase British companies. Scottish knitwear manufacturer Kilspindie Ltd was acquired in 1975 and London-based firm Wilcrest Ltd was purchased in 1977.[53] Indeed, by 1978 the Sunbeam Group was a genuine multinational consisting of twenty-two subsidiary companies, six of which were based abroad, and was in the process of negotiating the purchase of more British firms.[54]

While such rapid expansion would seem to suggest an improving economic position for the company, the slew of acquisitions made by Sunbeam post-1965 was, in fact, a response to deteriorating circumstances for the textile and clothing industry in Ireland. Tom Scott explains:

> There were a lot of companies in Ireland who were realising that, under free trade, it was going to be difficult for them to survive and so a lot of people, a lot of companies in the same types of business in Ireland, were looking to Sunbeam for both leadership to rationalise industry ... and financial support because the banks were recognising that, in free trade, it was going to be very difficult for many of these companies to survive ... There was a Dublin company called Mulcahys ... Sunbeam took over the whole business and Mulcahys ... this was all in an effort to rationalise industry. Mulcahys were

> making very similar products to Sunbeam ... you see it was only a matter of time. There was no point having a plant in Cork making a product and a plant in Dublin making the same product and then competing with each other ... [it was better to] put them together ... but it didn't mean that Mulcahys had to close down and that was the way that rationalisation took place.[55]

This rationalisation project was supported by the government, which heeded the conclusions of a 1963 CIO report that only the largest hosiery and knitwear firms could adapt to the new economic circumstances. The report was, however, optimistic about the future of the industry under free trade conditions, believing that it could weather the storm on the basis of consolidation and amalgamation under the larger, more export-orientated firms.[56] Indeed, Sunbeam's acquisition of Tullamore Yarns, Commission Dyers, Smith Haywood and Company, Allied Textiles, and Mulcahy Brothers Ltd was carried out with 'full government support'.[57] The effect of the Sunbeam-led rationalisation of the domestic textile and clothing industry was mixed. According to one commentator, the expansion met 'one half of the Government's desired policy of creating a stronger textile industry at home' but 'failed to have much impact on the other half, namely to create a strong textile force, strong enough at home to cope with new pressures from outside'.[58]

The purchase of British firms reflected a more desperate state of affairs: an attempt to subsidise the struggling Irish industry through the operation of profitable British firms and the use of banking facilities in the United Kingdom. The strategy was spelt out clearly in 1971 by Sunbeam Group director William Kiley:

> With the arrival of Free Trade conditions, it was felt that in future we must think of the U.K. as our market, with the

Home Market as a 'wind fall'. To enable us to sell profitably in the U.K. it was necessary to effect saving in every item of expenditure and at the same time increase profitability.[59]

Tom Scott elaborated further:

> The sudden shock [of free trade] was difficult to adjust to and so what in fact we did as a policy was we went out and bought UK companies. And, interestingly enough, you see we could go into the UK, buy companies in the UK, to be supported by the banks in the UK and our companies in the UK were doing alright when the Irish companies – which was ... which was the birth, was the nucleus of the operations – were struggling ... We bought a number of other companies which carried the company along for a while ... putting it another *way, we could support the losses in Ireland with the operations in the UK.*[60]

While a rational, immediate response to the difficulties of free trade, this strategy was problematic in the long term:

> That only went on for so long because ... it was very difficult for the board to operate a policy like that ... we did alright except it was still an Irish company, it wasn't a UK company and therefore that could only go on for so long.[61]

Despite adverse commercial conditions, the Sunbeam Group's strategy appeared to be paying off as the company performed remarkably well in a deteriorating economic situation. After having posted pre-tax losses of £206,836 and £850,000 in 1974 and 1975 respectively,[62] in 1977 the firm recorded a trading profit of £458,000.[63] This modest recovery, made possible in significant degree by the closure of loss-making subsidiaries, continued to the end of the decade with annual profits growing to

£604,000 by 1979.[64] Even acknowledging that this figure includes a government-provided employment maintenance subsidy of £114,000, Sunbeam appeared to have weathered the storm of EEC accession. However, the company remained cautious about the prospects for the Common Market, predicting, at best, a 'less rapid rate of deterioration in trading conditions within the EEC'.[65]

CRISIS AND CLOSURE, 1980–90

The company's cautious view of its future was shared by others. A 1983 report compiled by the Sectoral Consultative Committee of the Irish Textiles and Clothing Industries was sanguine about the prospects for clothing manufacture in Ireland. While the report noted that the textile sector was relatively stable, the clothing sector was in a far more precarious position. The committee complained that 'the level of technological development in the Irish clothing industry lags significantly behind that of other European countries and contributes to the comparative lack of competitiveness in the industry', and described the sector as one of low productivity, under-investment and 'a general lack of competitiveness'. It warned that 'unless urgent short-term measures are taken to assist firms in difficulty, a significant increase in closures and redundancies will occur in the coming months'.[66]

The report also revealed the extent to which imports had penetrated the domestic market: 70 per cent in the case of clothing.[67] If the prospects for Irish textiles were poor, the European perspective was little better. A meeting of the Irish Textiles Federation noted that short- and medium-term prospects in 'all EEC countries' were 'grim'.[68] Ireland was also proving itself unable to compete in these conditions, 'caught in a squeeze between the low prices available in the market place and rapidly rising prices'.[69]

The poor state of the Irish industry was reflected in the Sunbeam Group, whose 1980 report noted that 'the UK companies performed more satisfactorily than our Irish companies and were responsible for some 50% of the operating profit'.[70] The group only managed to survive through shedding loss-making subsidiaries and cutting employment in poorly performing units. Tullamore Yarns was closed in 1982 with the loss of 120 jobs (in a plant which had once employed over a thousand).[71] Midleton Mills had also been abandoned by Sunbeam.[72] The scale of redundancies was massive, with 200 jobs lost across the Sunbeam Group in 1981 alone.[73] These harsh measures allowed the company to double its pre-tax profits from £325,959 in 1980 to £676,130 in 1981.[74] However, even these modest profits were only possible due to continued government employment subsidies, which included grants of £213,035 in 1981 and £302,950 in 1980.[75] The company's apparent turnaround in 1981 also included a significant operating loss of £1.4 million.[76] Moreover, the firm was deeply worried about costs, with Chairman John O'Connell complaining that 'Irish costs are so out of line with other nations, even a world recovery will pose problems'.[77]

Nevertheless, Sunbeam fared relatively well in a difficult environment, much of which was accounted for by its exploitation of American export markets which proved receptive to Irish knitwear products. Domestic demand, however, remained sluggish and limited the company's ability to overcome its many problems; indeed, export sales by 1984 accounted for 70 per cent of the group's output.[78] In 1983 sales rose by 20 per cent in value, and as 1984 dawned, Sunbeam was able to report cash balances of £1.7 million despite the withdrawal of employment subsidies upon which the company had been heavily reliant since the advent of recession.[79]

However, this success proved to be fleeting. In 1986 the entire Sunbeam Group was taken over by the John Crowther Group of

Huddersfield. While the new parent company remained profitable, the Millfield factory was generating significant losses. Trevor Barker, the chairman of Crowther, reassured the workforce that he 'did not think there would be any need for significant job losses to get the company back to profit'.[80] Barker's intentions soon proved irrelevant. A few weeks later, the British Monopolies and Mergers Commission approved the acquisition of the Crowther Group by another British textiles giant (Coloroll Plc), resulting in Sunbeam changing hands for the second time in eighteen months.[81] In the face of further turmoil within the textile industry due to the 'Black Monday' stock market crash, Coloroll decided to sell its Irish holdings.[82] Reacting to the sale, a number of managers from the textile division of Sunbeam formed the 'Response Group', which purchased the few remaining Sunbeam plants.[83] However, the new consortium's attempt to rescue the once-great Sunbeam empire proved to be doomed from the outset. On 30 January 1990 the Response Group collapsed, and receivers were appointed to its four remaining subsidiaries: Sunbeam Ltd, Sunbeam Wolsey Ltd, Richard Ingham and Company, and Kerry Fashions Ltd.[84]

The news that Sunbeam was now on the verge of closure sent shockwaves through the city. The shutting down of Ford, the Verolme dockyard and Dunlop in the early to mid-1980s and the continuing poor performance of the Irish economy throughout the decade had turned Cork into an unemployment black spot. *The Irish Times* reported in 1985 that joblessness in some parts of the city had reached 21 per cent.[85] Four years later the situation had not improved, with nearly one-fifth of the city's workforce unable to find employment and many more having emigrated.[86] This widespread unemployment, combined with the precarious position of the plant, resulted in a rapid deterioration in the bargaining power of Sunbeam's workforce (see Chapter Five). While still a significant employer, Sunbeam had declined in tandem with the city. From having a workforce of thousands, by the late 1980s the number employed by the group and its subsidiaries was less than 950.[87] Though the Millfield factory was now employing only around 450 workers, it was still one of the largest workplaces in Cork and was particularly important on the northside, where most of its employees were based.[88] There was a significant campaign to save the factory from closure, but efforts by politicians and trade unions failed, and in 1990 Sunbeam Wolsey closed after sixty-three years as a cornerstone of Cork's industrial landscape.[89] Clothing production continued under different companies operating out of the Millfield site throughout the 1990s. These smaller ventures themselves came to an end in 2003 when the Millfield complex burned down, destroying the last physical evidence of a company that had been central to Cork's economy for more than half a century.

CONCLUSION

The actions of both the state and the Sunbeam company itself must be considered when explaining the early success of Sunbeam Wolsey and its later survival under rapidly deteriorating domestic and international conditions. The state initially provided protectionist legislation and, later, support for rationalisation, alongside grants and subsidies that helped the company survive the initial challenges posed by free trade and EEC accession. William Dwyer and his directors ensured that Sunbeam emerged as the leading operator within the domestically protected industry through aggressive expansion, marketing and consolidation. In the more difficult post-1965 period, Dwyer's successors (like most Irish and European textile and clothing operations) eventually proved themselves unable to respond to the enormous challenges of free trade. Sunbeam's fluctuating fortunes can, therefore, be best analysed through the matrix of objective economic conditions, government policy and the actions of the firm itself.

In the case of the last of the three firms under consideration (Irish Steel), the state played a far greater role given that it was a nationalised industry. As the next chapter demonstrates, while there are many similarities in the economic history of Irish Steel and Sunbeam Wolsey, state control of Irish Steel meant that the way in which that company responded to changing economic conditions over time contrasted sharply with the experiences of Sunbeam and other private sector firms.

3

'Endeavour, struggle and survival': Irish Steel, 1939–2001

INTRODUCTION

The story of Irish Steel is 'not one of triumphant success or spectacular achievements but rather a record not indeed of defeat, but of persistent endeavour, struggle and survival, interspersed with sunnier days as well as periods of acute crisis'.[1] These are the words of Sarsfield Hogan, the civil servant who unexpectedly became director and later chairman of Irish Steel. They were written in 1980, before more than a decade of crisis that led to the privatisation of the firm in 1995 and which saw the company sold for just a single punt to Indian company Ispat.[2] Irish Steel was a unique enterprise in many regards. Opened in 1939, it was the state's only steel mill, one of the largest factories in the country and, for most of its existence, a semi-state concern. Fine Gael TD Garret FitzGerald commented in 1961 that the number of activities 'undertaken indirectly by the State in Ireland through the medium of state-sponsored bodies is surprisingly wide for a small country in which there has never been any ideological pressure in favour of the nationalisation of sectors of private enterprise'.[3] Semi-state companies were a response to the historical weakness of Irish capitalism, specifically the lack of a sufficiently powerful industrial bourgeoisie to develop certain industries and services seen as necessary to the development of a strong national economy. Most state-sponsored bodies in Ireland, such as the transport company Córas Iompar Éireann (CIÉ), were service-based, with the government only rarely throwing its weight behind manufacturing concerns. Even when it did so, for example in the case of Irish Sugar, Nítrigin Éireann Teoranta and the Dairy Disposal Company, it was mainly to assist the agricultural sector. Thus, Irish Steel was unique among Ireland's state-sponsored companies.

FROM PRIVATE TO PUBLIC, 1938–47

The decision to set up a steel mill in Ireland originated with Scotsman David Frame, chairman of the Hammond Lane iron foundry in Dublin. Frame's decision to expand into steel production necessitated the formation of a new company in 1938 (Irish Steel Ltd) and the acquisition of a site that could contain the large-scale activities required by a modern steel mill. To facilitate Frame and his partners, the government implemented a duty of 37.5 per cent on raw steel imports from the continent and introduced legislation that prevented the export of scrap iron unless Irish Steel Ltd did not require it.[4] The government also granted Frame and his partners a loan of £450,000 to assist the new enterprise.

Frame decided to locate the new concern on Haulbowline, a tiny island in Cork harbour opposite the town of Cobh. This unusual choice of location would have serious ramifications for decades to come. Haulbowline is an island of about eighty-four acres that became significant as the location of a British naval base. There were some advantages to the site. These included access to deep-water berths for the transport of supplies and completed product,[5] as well as the nearby town of Cobh which could provide a 'pool of labour hungry for work'.[6] However, the tiny island, which had to be shared with a significant Irish naval base and an oil refinery, would inhibit future expansion. As early as 1949, the directors of the plant were complaining that 'there is no further room for factory expansion, dock facilities are limited and tipping ground for slag is almost exhausted'.[7] When the mills were initially being established, it was also discovered that the site 'was not suitable for a steelworks' due to 'serious defects in the sub-soil'.[8] Additionally, the fact that the island could only be accessed by ferry created logistical problems for labour and materials, a recurrent issue until the construction of a bridge to the mainland in 1966.[9]

Frame had originally intended the new steel plant to be established in the Arklow estuary which would have made sense due to its easy access to the sea and plentiful room for expansion.[10] However, it was pressure from senior figures in the government that convinced Frame to choose the Haulbowline site. Minister for Industry and Commerce Seán Lemass revealed in 1940 that 'it was I who urged the selection of the Haulbowline site'.[11] All of these discussions appear to have taken place in private between Frame and Lemass. The archival evidence suggests that there was no official debate regarding the location of the plant, and by the time the development of a steel mill was made known to the media, the Haulbowline location had already been selected. The nature of site selection in the case of Irish Steel was unusual but still within the powers of the minister for industry and commerce.[12]

The selection of Haulbowline was primarily a political move taken in response to the unemployment that was blighting Great Island (the small island containing the urban centre of Cobh). When Cobh was known as Queenstown, it was a strategically important port in the British Empire with a local economy almost entirely dependent on the presence of the British naval base. At its height in the late nineteenth century the port had easily supported a population of over ten thousand.[13] The period after the First World War was one of precipitous decline for the small coastal town. In 1911 the census recorded a population of just over eight thousand;[14] by 1936 the port had lost a quarter of its inhabitants.[15] That same year the urban district council complained that the town 'could no longer support its population'.[16] Local unemployment 'became a constant social problem. The once busy sea-port could be observed as a gaunt depressing place of vacant and run-down buildings, the shell of its former glory'.[17] However, the unemployment situation does not sufficiently explain the choice of Haulbowline, given that Cobh was far from the only town in the country that was suffering in this way. Contemporary attempts to acquire a new industry for a town usually saw intense lobbying efforts by local communities.[18] However, in the case of the steel venture, negotiations were conducted informally and secretly between Frame and Lemass. Had the process been more open, there would have been lobbying from other parts of the country, as was the norm in the period.

The most likely explanation for Fianna Fáil's support for a Cobh location is that much of the unemployment in the Cobh area was the direct result of a key Fianna Fáil policy: the return of the treaty ports (strategic seaports which remained in British control after the Anglo-Irish war). Indeed, *The Irish Times* explicitly noted that Irish Steel 'should go far to *compensate* Cobh and Haulbowline for the losses sustained by the departure of naval and military services from Queenstown harbour' following the handover of the treaty ports to the Irish state in 1938.[19] The compensation promised was generous. Reporters were taken on a tour of the island and told that the industry would soon be employing between 900 and 1,200 men.[20]

These hopes were quickly dashed. Seán Lemass was attending a dinner to celebrate the opening of the factory when news broke that Germany had invaded Poland.[21] Great Britain declared war on Germany a few days later. At the company's 1940 annual meeting the chairman outlined how the conflict had 'the gravest effects on our Undertaking', particularly the acquisition of raw materials.[22] Similarly, the sourcing of coal was a major problem, with local alternatives like turf being unsuitable for the furnaces.[23] Irish Steel went into liquidation in February 1941.

Demands for state intervention emerged from diverse sources. Local businesses that were reliant on steel supplies suffered from the sudden closure of the firm, with the chairman of one such concern complaining that it was 'very short-sighted of the government to permit the liquidation of Irish Steel Limited' and advised keeping the company 'intact so it could carry on immediately after the war as heretofore'.[24] Local politicians also viewed the company's liquidation with concern. A special meeting of Cobh Urban District Council passed a resolution demanding that 'action should be taken by public bodies, so that State assistance could be obtained for the purpose of maintaining these works in such a condition as would permit their restarting on the termination of the present emergency'.[25] Attempts to secure government assistance for the mill were thwarted, however. Frame and his syndicate approached the Department of Industry and Commerce with a loan request of £550,000 and were twice rebuffed by Seán MacEntee, who had taken over Lemass' portfolio in 1940.[26]

This refusal of government assistance is casually glossed over in most accounts of the steelworks, leaving one to assume that aid for the factory was withheld due to the war. In reality, the government's refusal was primarily a result of MacEntee's 'unfavourable opinion of the efficiency and creditworthiness of the Board of the Company and its advisers', a view which was shared by the minister for finance, Seán T. O'Kelly.[27] A memorandum drawn up by MacEntee's department in 1940 issued a damning condemnation of the company. Investigation by department officials found that Irish Steel Ltd had 'greatly underestimated' the amount of capital expenditure required when applying for the initial government loan of £450,000.[28] This sum had proven insufficient to purchase the necessary plant and equipment, leading to the application for a further £550,000. MacEntee, following interviews with the company and examination of the relevant documentation, concluded that 'the promoters of the Company had every reason to believe that the £450,000 to be raised on that document [the company prospectus] would have been quite insufficient for the purpose stated'.[29] Indeed, when shares in the company were floated publicly, '67,000 ordinary shares out of the total of 73,995 under-written were left in the hands of the Munster and Leinster Bank' due to scepticism on the part of potential investors.[30] The memorandum concluded that the company had not lived up to the claims in its prospectus. That document had envisaged a self-contained steel plant with a tinplate mill, sheet mill and fully mechanised merchant mill to be completed by 1939. Instead, the company abandoned the tinplate mill and had failed to mechanise the merchant mill which, at the time of the factory's opening, had 'not even been erected' but was 'lying idle at Haulbowline'.[31] The memorandum concluded that the money loaned had been 'squandered' and that the second loan was only necessary on the basis of the company having falsely estimated the initial cost of the undertaking.[32]

Additionally, the business practices of Frame and his associates were regarded with extreme suspicion by the government. The origins of the steel undertaking lay in Frame's 1937 decision to purchase plant from Belgium. A new company (Haulbowline Steel Syndicate) was then formed by Frame and some associates, which purchased the plant from Frame's own Hammond Lane Foundry, the majority in the form of shares which, though valued at £1, were issued at a premium of £1,000 per share, resulting in an 'admitted profit of £10,000'.[33] Further profits were garnered when the plant and shares were then sold to Irish Steel Ltd, which had significant overlap with the Haulbowline Steel Syndicate in terms of directors and shareholders. 'Grave exception' was taken to the way in which the operators of Irish Steel appeared to have benefited financially from each of these transactions.[34]

Eyebrows were again raised when it emerged that Frame had set up yet another entity (the Hammond Lane Steel Company) with the objective of handling 'practically all available scrap in Ireland'.[35] Irish Steel Ltd would thus be totally dependent on Frame's other company for all of its scrap needs, and would be the only steelworks in the world to rely entirely on scrap for its operation. In addition, the department was surprised to discover that Frame had been appointed 'sole buying and selling agent' for the British steel cartel and that, while Irish Steel was struggling to acquire steel billets from Britain, 'Mr. Frame has been doing a very lucrative business in supplying scrap metal to the English steel cartel', benefiting from the monopoly the government had given him over Irish scrap.[36] Frame and his partners were defended by the newly appointed minister for supplies, Seán Lemass. However, others in the cabinet did not concur:

> The Minister for Finance strongly endorses the opinion held by the Minister for Industry and Commerce, that the Government would be open to severe criticism in using Public funds for the purpose of salvaging an industry to which, according to the documents submitted, such suspicion and discredit attaches ... In view of the statements contained in the documents submitted by the Minister for Industry and Commerce it would appear proper, in the public interest, that the papers should be referred to the Attorney-General to consider whether any of the promoters of Irish Steel have laid themselves open to criminal proceedings.[37]

The official documents reveal, therefore, that the plant was nowhere near viable when it formally went into operation in August 1939, and still required hundreds of thousands more capital to produce economically. They also show how the government was opposed to giving further assistance to directors and promoters that they deemed untrustworthy. Despite their reservations, the cabinet was still open to the idea of providing state aid to Irish Steel. However, it was stipulated that a 'complete change of control should be made an essential condition of any assistance'.[38]

What is perhaps most striking about the cabinet investigation into Irish Steel is that senior figures in the government and civil service were unaware of significant issues regarding the company until the inquiries prompted by Irish Steel's wartime application for a loan. This lack of transparency was typical of Fianna Fáil's implementation of protectionism and the almost dictatorial role Seán Lemass played as minister for industry and commerce. Lemass had such wide-ranging discretion that neither the Dáil nor the cabinet were able to seriously examine deals drawn up between Lemass and investors like Frame.[39] Given the findings of the department's investigation, it seems likely that, had Frame's application for a steel mill been subject to proper cabinet and Dáil scrutiny at the outset, the proposal would have been rejected.

However, a lack of steel imports due to the war led to the factory being re-opened in 1942 on a limited basis to produce steel in small quantities for activities considered vital to the state. Employment in the factory at this time 'varied with the scope of production, construction activities and maintenance. At its peak, the maximum number employed would have been 250 (including contractors' gangs) and then only for short periods.'[40] The steelworks remained in operation until 1946 when, its cash resources exhausted, it went into receivership.[41] In February 1947 the receiver placed the company's assets on the market 'as a going concern'.[42] While offers were made 'by interests who wished to obtain the plant for export and reerection elsewhere', none was received 'from parties who proposed to carry on the concern [in Ireland]'.[43] The government came under pressure as local TDs lobbied for action to be taken to solve the unemployment problem in Cobh.[44] Cobh Urban District Council demanded that the industry be 'taken over by the state and run along similar lines to CIÉ'.[45] Lemass (returned to the Industry and Commerce portfolio since 1941) continued his previous patronage of Irish Steel and pushed for government intervention, arguing that it was necessary for Ireland to conserve a steel industry to maintain steel supplies in case of a national emergency.[46] Fine Gael TD Eamonn Coogan was one of the few to voice opposition to state involvement, arguing that, since the private firm was a failure, a state-backed version would be little better.[47]

Lemass' support for the project led to the formal announcement on 20 June 1947 that the state would intervene. A private company called Irish Steel Holdings (ISH) was formed and provided with a loan from the Department of Finance to purchase the assets held by the receiver. Three civil servants, Sarsfield Hogan, John Williams and Tom O'Shea, were entrusted with the directorship of the new company.[48] It was a rushed and haphazard rescue operation: none of the directors had any experience of steel manufacture, and the new enterprise was organised as a holding company 'to indicate what was hoped to be a temporary stage pending further arrangements, possibly in association with commercial interests if the new venture should prosper'.[49] Indeed, this cautious approach was likely due to the reservations of the Minister for Finance, Frank Aiken, who was 'worried about financing this uneconomic high-cost industry which, even though it enjoys the protection of a 25% duty, has been able to produce only at a very substantial loss', believing it 'highly undesirable … that the State should commit itself to the maintenance on a permanent basis of the Haulbowline undertaking'.[50] The firm retained the title Irish Steel Holdings until the late 1970s and was, until 1960, technically a private company operating 'under ministerial authority and direction'.[51] Despite the cabinet's hope that a private firm would take over the running of Irish Steel, it remained a semi-state company for the next forty-eight years of its existence.

'A NEW ERA OF PROSPERITY', 1947–70

The new company was formally incorporated on 23 June 1947. Sarsfield Hogan and Tom O'Shea inspected the idle plant, now under state control, 'which provided a depressing aspect, matched by the dejected demeanour of the key personnel. These were about a hundred in all, administrative, supervisory and labouring … so as to maintain the equipment and present the appearance of a going concern.'[52] The new directors got to work quickly and commercial production of ingots began in late 1947. Two years later, the company reported to the new inter-party government that it had recorded a net profit of £3,000 for the last six months of 1948 and had doubled production levels.[53] By June 1952 the company was employing 447 workers and was having a significant impact on the economy of Cobh with a 'new era of prosperity … promised for the town'.[54]

These achievements should not be overstated. Much of the firm's early success was due to the existence of extensive protection measures that were considerable even by the standards of post-war Ireland. These measures included the scrap monopoly that had been introduced for the initial private undertaking, alongside tariff protection of 37.5 per cent on all steel imports. Additionally, the early years of Irish Steel Holdings Ltd coincided with a significant boom in the global steel industry. Favourable international

3.1 Irish Steel plant in 1958.
Photo reproduced with the kind permission of the *Irish Examiner*.

market conditions concealed the weaknesses of the firm, although informed observers were not blind to the company's problems. In 1956, Minister for Finance Gerard Sweetman predicted a decline in demand for steel and pointed out that the company's highest annual profit prior to 1953 would still be insufficient to cover the depreciation of the plant's replacement value.[55] Regardless, Irish Steel Holdings had established itself as a going concern.

Many now thought it desirable that the plant be remade as a modern steel manufacturer of international significance. For example, the treasurer of Dublin Council of Trade Unions sent Tánaiste (Deputy Prime Minister) Seán Lemass a report from a member of the Amalgamated Engineering Union, who commented that the plant had

> fulfilled the role of a useful experemental [sic] station and training room for some years, but we cannot regard it as anything else but such. We consider the time is due for

development of this enterprise for the real production of Iron and Steel.[56]

These sentiments were shared by the directors of Irish Steel, who sought advice on expanding the steelworks. Several foreign experts were invited to advise the company on its future. One of these experts, a Canadian named Timmerman, was positive about the future of the factory, expressing favourable opinions on the efficiency of the plant and commenting that he had 'no doubt that the industry could be developed'. However, he expressed concerns about the Haulbowline site, being of the opinion that an expanded facility 'would have to be located on the mainland as there would not be sufficient space for development at Haulbowline'.[57] Others, such as Sir Ernest Lever, former chairman of the Steel Company of Wales, were more circumspect:

> Any steel industry in Ireland seemed to be under the handicap that its basic raw materials – ore, coal and oil – would have to be brought from afar and that it would not have within its perimeter … a multiplicity of large secondary industries disposing of finished steel products for export.[58]

He also expressed concerns about the Haulbowline site, commenting that it would be 'foolish to take the risks involved in establishing a steel industry at a place which did not appear to command any advantages', suffering as it did from 'striking disadvantages in relation to the source of its basic raw materials'.[59] Despite these objections, the success of the factory in helping to curb Cobh's extremely high levels of unemployment at a time of mass emigration meant that the firm's economic weaknesses were ignored by policy-makers. Regardless, a redevelopment project was approved.

These expansion plans were as ambitious as they were expensive, involving 'the enlargement of the existing furnaces, the erection of a blooming or cogging mill and the modernization of the existing merchant mill'. These measures would allow the company to enhance the quality of its products, increase employment and render it more competitive in the context of the country moving towards free trade conditions.[60] The expansion plan was approved in principle in 1958 and began in 1960, by which time the cost of the improvements was estimated at £3.5 million.[61] Initially, the impact of this massive expenditure led to the company posting losses for the first time since 1947, a total of £500,000 during the first half of the 1960s. By the end of the decade, however, an upsurge in the building trade had returned the company to profit. Despite a few rough years, Sarsfield Hogan could boast, in June 1969, that 'output, sales and profit are in all cases the highest in the history of the company'. The company's long-time patron Seán Lemass proudly noted that the firm had been 'exporting about 25% of its production' and contributing about £1 million per year to the country's exports.[62]

CRISIS TO CLOSURE, 1970–2001

The 1970s proved to be a challenging decade for Irish Steel. The end of the 1960s' building boom saw profits begin to fall as the domestic market contracted. These falling profits were a cause for concern; however, they were a mere prelude to the massive losses the company endured in the post-1976 period. In 1971, the company informed the minister for industry and commerce that 'the orders on hands [sic] are only half those required to maintain the existing scale of output' and that the company had been forced to dismiss over one hundred workers.[63] As profits fell again the following year, the directors sought to reassure themselves and the public of the economic benefits that Irish Steel had provided the country, publishing cumulative figures for the company's performance in its twenty-five years as a state-run enterprise. These figures were far from reassuring. The company's own numbers demonstrated that, in its twenty-five years, it could boast less than £2.5 million in pre-tax profits in return for nearly £6 million investment by the state. More worrying for the directors was the fact that the firm's cumulative export sales accounted for less than 15 per cent of total sales at a time when it was preparing for entry to the Common Market and the dismantling of protectionism.[64]

The industry's benefits to the wider economy and the state coffers were far from significant. Due to the capital-intensive nature of steelmaking, the investment required to maintain the plant in effective working order was considerable, including, for example, a £3.5 million modernisation programme completed in 1960.[65] That sum was the equivalent of the company's total turnover in 1967. The large amounts of capital invested in the plant yielded relatively small returns and could have been spent more effectively elsewhere. Furthermore, despite the argument repeatedly made by Irish Steel that the domestic construction industry could not survive without it, the industry was not especially important to the wider economy, given that there had never been major problems for Irish companies in the procuring of steel either before or after the existence of the Haulbowline plant. Moreover, the protectionist measures defending Irish Steel inflated steel prices and forced its suppliers to sell for less than they could have done otherwise due to the company's monopoly over Irish scrap. Thus, Irish Steel had limited importance in the wider economy.[66]

A fundamental flaw in the company's business model was its reliance on a limited and slow-growing domestic market – a typical feature of Irish protected industries more generally.[67] By 1970, the limitations of the domestic market had been reached, and the company's profits began to fall accordingly, from

£321,000 (pre-tax) in 1967 to a low of £59,000 in 1973.[68] Irish Steel's orientation towards the domestic market was particularly problematic as EEC entry loomed. The ban on exports of domestic ferrous scrap (vital to Irish Steel's ability to maintain low prices) was scheduled to be lifted in December 1977.[69] By then, all tariffs protecting the industry against British and European competition were to be removed.[70] As early as 1950, the Department of Industry and Commerce had accepted Irish Steel's inability to compete with larger and more productive plants in Europe:

> The immediate danger to the Irish industry is the ability of the large steel-producing countries to undersell the home product no matter what the Directors may do in the matter of prices. The cartel countries have no use for small steel plants and, with an output per week of more than a year's Irish production, many foreign (including British) mills are in a position to undertake the crushing of the Irish industry.[71]

Two decades later, these weaknesses had not been resolved. In fact, exports fell from 29.5 per cent of total sales in 1965 to just 14.3 per cent in 1969.[72] By 1976, exports as a percentage of total turnover were just over 14 per cent.[73]

A major disadvantage for Irish Steel was the small scale of the industry. Ireland was, in 1977, except for Uruguay and Central America, the smallest steel producer in the world.[74] Kenneth Warren notes that modern steel plants are generally enormous because steel producers can only remain competitive based on enormous economies of scale.[75] However, some exceptions to this rule did exist. During the 1970s and 1980s there emerged successful so-called 'mini-mills', which fulfilled highly specific niches within the global steel market and remained competitive with large producers by utilising the most modern technology available to manufacture a limited set of products. Although Irish

Steel later attempted to replicate this model, the company as it existed before the 1980s was not a mini-mill but a steel industry in miniature, which produced all steel products required in the domestic economy and exported surplus production. In 1974 Cockerill and Silberston estimated the minimum efficient scale of a modern steel plant producing (like Irish Steel) a broad range of products to be some 8 million tonnes per annum.[76] Warren, writing a decade later, estimated 6 million tonnes per annum to be the minimum scale necessary for a successful integrated steelworks.[77] In 1974, Irish Steel produced just 110,000 tonnes, a mere fraction of what either of those two studies considered the minimum necessary for viability.[78]

Irish Steel was unable to benefit from the economies of scale associated with the steel industry behemoths of Europe and remained entirely reliant on the purchase of scrap, given the absence of easily attainable raw materials. These weaknesses rendered the company uncompetitive by international standards. Only Luxembourg eclipsed Irish Steel in terms of prices.[79] Worse still, the company's ability to sell even at this high price was largely due to the cost savings arising from Irish Steel's scrap monopoly. Once the scrap monopoly was rescinded in December 1977, the cost of high-grade scrap supplies for the company was predicted to rise from £26 per tonne to £45 per tonne, which would immediately and dramatically inflate the already high cost of the finished product.[80]

In addition to the challenges faced by all domestic industries entering post-EEC membership economic conditions, Irish Steel was also facing entry into a global steel market that was experiencing its most disastrous years since the Second World War. Sparked by the 1973 oil crisis, global demand for steel began to decline, before plummeting in 1975, forcing the member states of the EEC to drastically cut output.[81] By 1976, redundancies in the European industry were running at over 1,500 a month, and plant utilisation was down 40 per cent.[82] British steel production fell from 24.3 million tonnes in 1967 to just 13.7 million in 1982.[83] Other traditional steel-manufacturing nations suffered just as badly. In the years 1974–8 alone, the number employed in the EEC steel industry fell from 792,191 to 698,483, with a further 100,000 redundancies expected under continent-wide rationalisation plans.[84]

By the late 1970s, the Irish government and the directors of Irish Steel had both concluded that the firm was no longer viable based on its existing buildings, fittings and equipment. Chairman Kevin McCourt[85] explained that, 'much of the plant is obsolete and in poor condition' and that the company was 'beset during the year [1979] by plant failures, resulting in interruption of production … We cannot produce economically in our present plant.'[86] Minister for Industry and Commerce Justin Keating sought approval from the government for a major redevelopment programme for the Haulbowline plant, noting that

> it is considered that at its present size and with its present plant ISH could not be viable after 1977 and, if it is to remain in operation, capacity must be increased and the plant made more efficient by modernisation and rationalisation.[87]

This modernisation and rationalisation required curtailing the considerable power of trade unions within the plant to reduce labour costs, which precipitated a sea change in industrial relations within the firm, including a devastating strike in 1977 (see Chapter Six).[88]

The proposed redevelopment plan for the factory was ambitious. The plant was to be re-invented as a mini-mill, with a 90-tonne electric arc furnace, new melting shops, a new modern rolling mill and other large capital investment in equipment and machinery at a total cost of £40 million.[89] The alternative to the development proposal was the loss of the industry, as it was widely recognised that the firm could not survive without substantial investment. Despite the objections of the Department of Finance, the plan was approved, and the modernisation programme began in early 1980. The expansion proved to be disastrous. The location of the enterprise presented massive difficulties in the installation of the new plant. Limitations of space meant that the new facilities and machinery had to be built as the old plant was demolished step by step, resulting in the cessation of production from June 1980 until July 1981.[90] There were further problems when a national steel strike in Britain delayed the arrival of essential new plant. The total cost of the development was £78.8 million, nearly double the 1977 estimate of £40 million.[91]

However, a few years after the completion of the programme, it appeared that many of the problems affecting Irish Steel's ability to compete had been remedied. By 1986, the plant was one of the most technically advanced in Europe.[92] Impressed correspondents for the respected industry periodical *Steel Times* were gushing in their praise of the redeveloped industry.[93] Production capacity had been greatly increased, and output per man was one of the highest in Europe: 400 metric tonnes compared with averages of 250 in Germany, 308 in Luxembourg and 351 in Denmark.[94] Finally, the company was now completely export-orientated, to the point that, by 1987, exports accounted for 82 per cent of total sales.[95] However, despite the newfound efficiency of the plant, the 1980s were the most disastrous decade in the firm's history (Table 3.1).

The losses recorded above do not fully represent the scale of Irish Steel's misfortunes in the 1980s, as these figures do not incorporate the additional state investment the company received. First was the massive over-cost of the modernisation programme.[96]

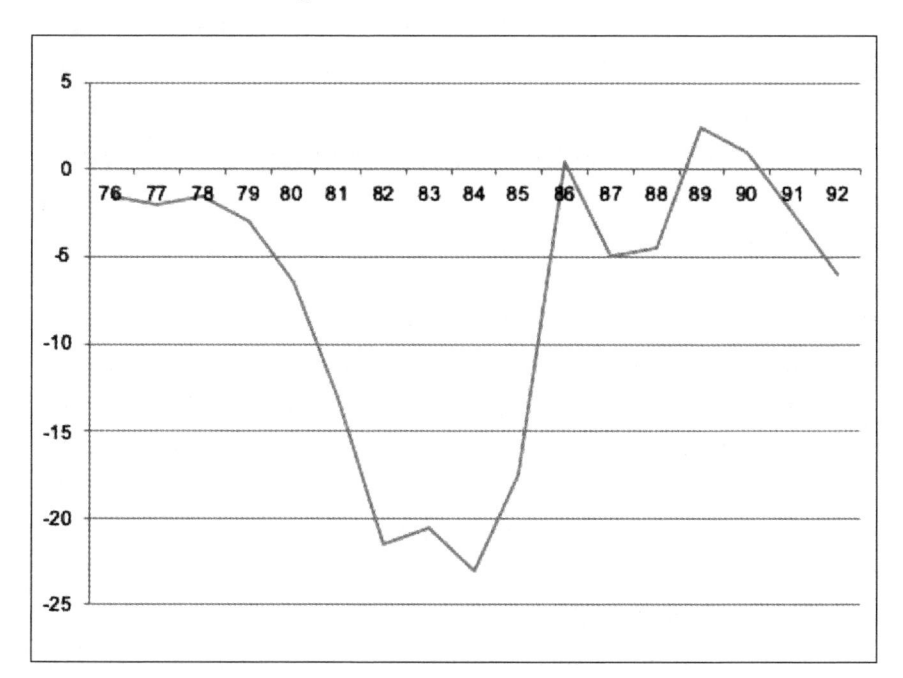

Table 3.1 Irish Steel profits and losses, 1976–92 (£ million)[97]

Second were two emergency cash injections of £89 million and £19 million in 1984 and 1985, respectively.[98] These injections were merely meant to cover the company's losses and did not represent investment in plant. Despite massive investment and overhauling, the firm had become, in the words of one commentator, 'the most anaemic white elephant in the country'.[99]

The spectacular failure of Irish Steel during the 1980s can be explained by the fact that, while the company's problems on the supply side had been resolved by the mid-1980s, newer and more dramatic difficulties had emerged on the demand side. From 1973 onwards, there was a series of damaging recessions within the steel industry, beginning with the international crisis of the mid-1970s. This series of recessions and crises was not a temporary downturn in the market but one stage in the broader decline of the Western steel industry. This period saw a great shift in steel production from Europe and America to emerging producers in Japan, Eastern Europe and the Third World. European steel production as a percentage of the world total declined from nearly 30 per cent in 1960 to just 17 per cent in 1984.[100] As a result, those European and American steel producers who remained in business were faced with low prices and weak demand, leaving them vulnerable to new competitors.

It was in this context that Irish Steel altered its business model to abandon its role as a domestic supplier, looking instead towards international markets for its survival. Even with a highly modern and efficient plant, the company simply could not survive in that climate, particularly as maximum production quotas enacted by the EEC under the Davignon plan prevented the revitalised factory from raising its output to the level of which the factory was capable.[101] Irish Steel had been initially reliant on a slow-growing and limited domestic market, but it had re-orientated itself towards a collapsing European export market and suffered accordingly. As discussed in Chapter Six, these years had profound effects on industrial relations within the firm, with the government increasingly important as an actor in relations between workers, trade unions and management. Moreover, the constant spectre of closure, though tempered by the political consequences of such an action, undermined the power of trade union organisation within the company.

By the late 1980s, Irish Steel was once again generating profits. However, this recovery was short-lived. By the time recession returned to the steel industry in 1992, there was little government appetite to maintain the Haulbowline mills. Indian multinational Ispat's purchase of the plant in 1995 came as a relief to the Irish government, which was happy to have the responsibility for the company taken off its hands.[102] Minister for Enterprise and Employment Richard Bruton explained in the Dáil that he was 'particularly pleased' to sign the contract for sale, given that the alternative was yet another state aid package, this time for £50 million.[103] The sale of Irish Steel saw the removal of what the government had long seen as an increasingly intolerable burden. It had freed itself from responsibility for the company's debts while simultaneously maintaining employment in the area – at least on a temporary basis. However, the firm, now in private hands, did not survive long. While many had hoped that Ispat would invest further in the plant to make it competitive, the company decided to close the operation as soon as it was able to do so, with steel production on Haulbowline finally ceasing in 2001.[104]

4

Working for Fords, 1917–84

INTRODUCTION

As discussed in the introduction, Cork in the early twentieth century was primarily a commercial rather than an industrial city. The region's economy was, in the main, agricultural, with 'no marked prevalence of any type of industry in the district'.[1] The 1917 establishment of a Ford factory in such a city had a major effect, not just on the locality and its economy, but also on a section of the region's urban and rural proletariat, who began to work in an industry utterly unlike anything else that existed in Ireland at the time.[2]

In theory, the Ford plant in Cork would be a mirror image of Ford production facilities in the United States. The pseudonymous 'J.C.P.' was optimistic:

> I have no hesitation in saying that the Cork factory is a complete replica in efficiency, organisation, plant, and labour conditions, of the world-famed headquarters of what is recognised to be the biggest business in the world.[3]

The development of the Ford Marina plant saw the importation of welfare practices, managers, business principles and production methods that had been honed in the automobile factories of Michigan (collectively known as 'Fordism') into an economically underdeveloped city with high unemployment and a semi-industrial labour force.[4]

While the business history of the Ford Marina plant between 1917 and 1932 has been recounted elsewhere and is summarised in the earlier part of this book, the lives of the thousands of Cork workers who flocked to the factory in search of employment in these years have not been examined in the detail presented here.[5] The first part of this chapter explores the nature of the Fordist system in the Marina plant, and how employees of the firm experienced that system. The chapter then analyses working conditions and industrial relations as they existed in the plant during the inter-war period. The next section, entitled 'Emergency and Emigration, 1932–47', discusses the impact of the Second World War on the factory workforce. Finally, 'Work and Industrial Relations, 1949–1984' begins by examining the post-war unionisation of the plant before analysing the nature of work and industrial relations in the Cork plant in its final decades.

FORDISM IN CORK, 1917–32

In March 1917, rumours of the creation of a Ford manufacturing facility in Cork harbour were officially confirmed, with construction beginning a few weeks later.[6] The establishment of the Marina factory generated considerable excitement in Cork, not just because of the introduction of a badly needed industry for the city, but also because of the welfare policies associated with the company. Familiar, through the media, with the company's employee welfare policies, many in the city expected similar generosity to be shown to workers in the new factory at the Marina. The monthly bulletin of the Cork Industrial Development Association was hyperbolic, but far from atypical of local media coverage:

> That the labourer is worthy of his hire – AND SOMETHING MORE – Henry Ford has made the fixed rule of his relationship with

those employed under him. It is for his belief in, and practice of that 'something more' that Henry Ford has won the plaudits and devotion of the hundreds of thousands of contented workers associated with him in his different undertakings, and has merited for him the goodwill and esteem of those millions of wage-earners in all lands, who have come to know of the justice and solicitous care with which Henry Ford treats his numerous and devoted employees.[7]

This enthusiasm was related primarily to the welfare capitalist programmes that had been introduced in American Ford plants, the most famous of which was the 'five-dollar day' instituted in the firm's Highland Park facility in 1914.[8] In this period, according to one historian, 'forward-looking managerial traditions of scientific management and industrial betterment coalesced and became a new strategy for the control of workers'.[9] This strategy entailed many benefits for workers, including recreational, educational and medical programmes, as well as the provision of bonuses and other positive gains for the workforce. However, as Stephen Meyer notes, there was a dark side to Ford labour practices, which were highly intrusive, involving a 'a wide-ranging and tightly-knit web of controls over the Ford workforce' which extended as far as close observation of workers' personal and family life.[10]

Though possessing its own peculiarities, Ford's welfare policy was just one example of a trend known as 'welfare capitalism', whereby large firms rejected the notion of the employment relationship as an impersonal market transaction and sought to meet the needs of their workforce beyond the provision of wages.[11] Welfare capitalist firms provided a range of benefits and facilities to their employees that were intended to maintain strong control over their internal labour market and to ensure loyalty and co-operation on the part of their workforces. Industrial welfare was about business rather than philanthropy.[12] Moreover, the policy was very much a phenomenon of the early twentieth century and differed markedly from the more traditional forms of industrial paternalism we discuss in relation to the Sunbeam factory in the next chapter. Like traditional paternalists, Ford and other welfare capitalist enterprises provided facilities and fringe benefits to employees that went beyond the cash nexus. Unlike traditional paternalists, Ford did so through the medium of a sophisticated managerial bureaucracy.

There appears to have been plans for some form of welfare service for the Marina factory even before the final decision had been made to establish it. In 1913, Percival Perry, the head of the British branch of the Ford empire, wrote a report on the viability of a Cork plant. In this report, composed the year before the introduction of the five-dollar day, Perry recommended that improvement measures would have to be taken by the company:

> The standard of living in Ireland is lower than that of Great Britain and I am of the opinion that a successful Manufacturer would deliberately have to set himself to improve the standard of living in order to obtain a proper production from the workers ... My suggestion in this regard would be to pay only the wages which unskilled labour is and has been in the habit of receiving, and devote the difference between such wages and adequate wages to providing facilities for raising the standard of living.[13]

He felt this approach was necessary because, had the company simply paid the workers equivalent wages to those received in Detroit, the Cork workforce 'would, because of inexperience, spend the money badly'. He concluded that 'careful organisation and assumption of responsibilities in respect of housing and improving conditions of living of Employees' was a 'positive necessity' if a factory was to be established in Cork.[14] Indeed, as late as 1918, Perry wrote to Sorensen expressing the opinion that 'we should have a policy here which will take cognisance of the home conditions of our workers'.[15]

By 1917, Ford labour practices were again undergoing a profound change. Stephen Meyer describes how, 'in the course of the [first world] war, Ford labor policies underwent a transition from a variant of welfare capitalism ... to a version of the American plan, which typified the more recalcitrant employer attitudes of the twentieth century'.[16] By the time the Marina plant had been established, the high point of Fordist industrial welfare was over. In his 1922 autobiography, Henry Ford explained that

> we make no attempt to coddle the people who work with us. It is absolutely a give-and-take relation. During the period in which we largely increased wages we did have a considerable supervisory force ... But it would not do at all as a permanent affair and it has been abandoned ... It is too late in the day for that sort of thing.[17]

This shift – from the extensive and intrusive welfare capitalism of the five-dollar day epoch to the more laissez-faire approach that came to dominate the company in the post-war years – created confusion among Ford managers at Cork. Henry Ford's autocratic management style demanded that local branches of the international empire imitate policy in Michigan and follow his instructions unquestioningly. For example, a letter from Percival Perry to Charles Sorensen in 1918 requested precise instruction as to the degree of welfare initiatives to be taken in Cork, insisting that 'we want to reflect, as accurately as possible, here in Cork, what you are doing at Dearborn'.[18] However, communication between Dearborn and Cork was often difficult, being conducted mostly through telegrams and brief letters, most of which were focused on immediate issues regarding production. The transition occurring in Ford welfare and labour practices in the United States led to confusion over the policies to be introduced in the Cork plant.

Thomas Grimes cites a telling example of this confusion in relation to Edward Grace's attempts to embark on a housing project for the accommodation of Ford workers.[19] Grace's initiative was based on the severity of the housing crisis in Cork, which was so grave that a 1926 report calculated that 15,763 people in the city were living in dwellings 'at the borderline of being unfit for human habitation' and recommended 'dispossessing and re-housing upon probably new sites 16,000 people, one-fifth of the total population'.[20] It is also likely that the initiative was influenced by Percival Perry's earlier recommendations to 'take cognisance of the home conditions of workers' and the house-building programmes undertaken by the Ford company in Dearborn. Grace was in the process of finalising the purchase of land for the construction of thirty to forty cottages when the proposal was shot down by Ford management. Following a severe financial crisis in 1919, Charles Sorensen had returned to ascendancy and adopted an attitude of hostility towards welfare programmes within the organisation.[21] Replying to Sorensen's irate condemnation of the housing scheme, Grace defended himself by saying that the initiative had been 'worked out from what was thought to be your wish'.[22] In the end, however, the managing director was forced to sever all connections to the scheme.

However, while welfare policies in Cork were not nearly as extensive as those initiated in the United States during the five-dollar day era, those that were introduced still went far beyond the welfare policies of any company in Ireland, with the sole exception of the Guinness brewery in Dublin.[23] One example of these policies was the large number of social clubs and outlets that were provided through the firm, including an Irish-language club that held weekly classes in the factory, the Fordson dancing club and, of course, the football team. The last of these was perhaps the most successful leisure project initiated in the factory. The footballers, known as the 'Tractor Boys', went from strength to strength during the 1920s, culminating in their 1926 winning of the Free State League, after which manager Edward Grace was presented with the match ball, an indication of the close links between the team and the factory management.[24] The Fordson football team differed markedly from the examples of 'bottom-up' recreational culture we examine in Chapter Eight, with management playing a much more significant role.[25]

At least part of the reason for the provision of these activities was rooted in the Ford company's own stated aim to contribute 'towards the development of men who in turn will be factors in constructive citizenship'.[26] Support for these clubs was in line with Henry Ford's own philosophy of philanthropy. In his 1922 autobiography, he condemned charity as a 'drug', 'coddling' and a 'cold and clammy thing'.[27] Instead, he championed the civilising nature of labour combined with opportunities for self-improvement, writing that 'industry organised for service removes the need for philanthropy'.[28] A 1918 letter from the Cork plant emphasised that 'the best way to make an industrious man is to give him work to do, and watch over him in the factory and see that he does it'.[29] The good wages and steady work of the factory would create disciplined and respectable workers who would then be in a position to be active and responsible citizens. Wholesome activities such as the football club and dancing societies would provide workers with opportunities for voluntary self-improvement, as well as being a productive use of leisure time.[30]

In addition to sports and entertainment opportunities, Henry Ford and Sons also provided more tangible welfare measures for its workforce. The Fordson store was established to 'provide for the Fordson employee a first-class article at rockbottom prices' and to 'do our little bit in checking the hitherto unfettered career of the profiteer'.[31] The store provided boots, clothing, overalls and other items of necessity at reduced prices and appears to have been popular among the workers. Cork labour policies also sought to provide financial security to workers and their families. Grace revealed, in a 1920 letter to Charles Sorensen, that only twenty-seven of his employees had over £100 worth of life insurance, 70 per cent had no insurance at all and five workers had died in the previous year, all of whom left dependants with no means of support.[32]

It was to remedy this precarious situation that the factory's investment scheme was introduced. Under the scheme, a worker could invest small amounts of money every week following pay day. After sufficient money had been accumulated, workers would receive certificates of £20 and £100, while their investments would accumulate interest at 3 per cent per year. By November 1921, about a quarter of the workforce had availed themselves of the scheme.[33] While the programme was no doubt beneficial for some, the high turnover at the plant meant that only a minority of workers reaped significant rewards from their investments.

The Cork plant was also notable in its provision of factory-based healthcare, a feature later adopted by other large factories in Ireland. A visitor to the Marina plant in the late 1920s described a visit to the welfare department, where

> every want is catered for and every need provided. The Medical Health Department is [staffed by] a fully trained doctor and a staff of trained assistants, who deal promptly with all cases of accidents and keep a strict supervision over

the general health of the employees. It is at all times open for a free consultation. I was informed that the Ford Company attached great importance to keeping every member of the firm in the best of health, as it is only by doing so that the goal of all-round efficiency can be reached.[34]

Employment reports from 1922 include references to a chemist, medical department head and first-aid men.[35] By 1925, there were also 'safety men' and 'Employment and Factory Service' workers included in the employment reports, suggesting that the health and welfare services had been extended in the intervening years.[36] The factory also reflected Ford's personal obsession with cleanliness.[37] One visitor described the plant as a 'perfect industrial picture … From the 600 feet wharf the factory is seen surrounded with the greenest of lawns, and inside the appearance of order and cleanliness strikes the visitor as a peculiarly pleasant feature of the place.'[38] Ford management were so confident about the cleanliness of the plant that they imitated Ford factories in Michigan by inviting members of the public to tour the plant at any time during working hours.[39] Additionally, health and safety practices were accorded great importance, and there appears to have been few significant or fatal accidents in the factory, in sharp contrast to Irish Steel.[40]

The *Fordson Worker* (a company paper distributed within the factory) actively encouraged participation in the clubs and societies within the plant while advertising the many welfare measures afforded to employees. The newspaper was also a method for the dissemination of Fordist ideology. The only surviving edition includes a lengthy article devoted to the business philosophy of Henry Ford and a poem extolling the values of work. Such publications were typical of American paternalist firms in the period. Andrea Tone notes that company newspapers served to remind workers how lucky they were to be the recipients of employer largesse.[41] The newspaper was a propaganda tool that demonstrated the 'proof' of mutual interest between worker and employer and an ideological accompaniment to the broader goals of industrial welfare in the firm.

Welfare measures in Cork were therefore considerable and provided opportunities and a safety net unavailable to most working-class people of the time. Nevertheless, a rose-tinted view of Ford's welfare capitalism would be mistaken. Imported into Ireland, the origin of Ford's welfare capitalism had been the company's desire to combat its high labour turnover in Detroit without giving up managerial autonomy and power.[42] At their core, the welfare measures instituted in the factory were a means of social control and a compensation for workers' lack of autonomy.[43]

WORKING CONDITIONS AND 'GREEN LABOUR', 1917–32

While workers benefited from the high wages and fringe benefits in the factory, these represented only two facets of employment in the Marina plant. The testimony of former employees describes working conditions in the plant prior to unionisation in 1949 as being strict, irregular and punitive. Gus McLoughlin (born 1924 in Cork city; general operative at Ford Dagenham and Cork Plants, 1948–84) recalled, from conversations with his father, who was employed at Ford from 1919 until the late 1930s, that 'conditions were very strict and difficult' and were 'nearly as bad when I started there in 1948'.[44] Bob Elliott noted that the factory was 'a tough place to work' and compared the plant in the pre-union days to a 'reform school' in terms of strictness.[45] Michael V. O'Donoghue, who began work in the factory in 1919, commented that while he was initially attracted by the high wages, he 'very shortly regretted' his decision.[46] The consistently high levels of unemployment in

Cork and the surrounding areas, the high desirability of work in the plant and the nature of Ford production methods, in which almost anyone could be quickly trained to play a productive role on the assembly line, meant that dismissal could be applied without restraint by management.[47]

As the oral testimony suggests, one of the notable features about working at Fords, from its establishment until unionisation, was the insecure nature of work at the plant. Employment in the factory was based on production, and when demand was slow workers were simply dismissed until production returned to previous levels. Nyhan notes that, between 1917 and 1957, frequent lay-offs were the norm for Ford employees.[48] This tendency was particularly pronounced prior to protectionist legislation in 1932; rapid fluctuations in the nature of the plant meant that the number of workers required in the Marina changed often and rapidly in accordance with the needs of the business. Wages and employment reports from 1922 demonstrated high rates of labour turnover.[49] The most dramatic fluctuations occurred in the period 1929–30, when the plant became the company's sole supplier for the European tractor market. The numbers employed in the Marina plant skyrocketed in a relatively brief period, rising from 1,314 in January 1929 to 6,510 in February 1930.[50] The influx of workers was so considerable that it placed huge pressure on accommodation in the city, with *The Cork Examiner* reporting that, 'it was no unusual occurrence for a Fordson worker to return home to occupy a bed that had just been vacated by another employee whose shift was just commencing'.[51] Immediately after this rapid growth in employment, in July 1930, more than four-fifths of the total workforce were made redundant in less than a month. While irregularity of work and periods of slackage were common in Irish industry until the 1970s, these oscillations in numbers were particularly unstable but typical of the company's

4.1 Ford Marina plant workers leaving the facility, 1929.
Photo reproduced with the kind permission of the *Irish Examiner*.

practices in other areas.[52] As Huw Beynon writes, 'the motor industry at that time was a hire-and-fire industry. There were no seniority rights. Everyone was employed from day to day ... Labour turnover rates were extremely high.'[53] However, given the lack of other manufacturing jobs in the Cork area, and the importance of the factory's workforce to the local economy, the sudden loss of thousands of jobs was particularly devastating. E.L. Clarke, who replaced Grace as managing director in 1926, reported to an official in the Free State Department of Industry and Commerce in July 1930:

> We have had to lay off almost 6,000 men during the past three weeks, which is a very serious consequence in a city of this size, and where there are practically no other industries of any importance. Naturally, these men are all on the dole.[54]

The establishment of a modern manufacturing industry in a city otherwise characterised by commerce and agriculture had a significant impact on Cork. Stephen Meyer describes how the Highland Park Ford factory in Detroit attracted thousands of immigrant workers from agricultural and pre-industrial backgrounds and the difficulties this created: 'Not possessing the traditional skills and discipline that came from the traditional craft system, former peasants and former farmers created special problems for Ford factory managers.'[55] In Michigan, workers from as far afield as Eastern Europe were drawn to the expanding automobile industry by the availability of jobs. In Cork, however, this process occurred in reverse as the plant was established in a region with a semi-industrial labour market, where even urban dwellers were more likely to work on a farm than in a factory. A 1932 article in *The Irish Times* described how

> hundreds of agricultural workers a few years ago flocked into Cork to obtain work in Ford's factory, where they received sometimes three times as much as they had been earning on the land, although in many cases the work did not last long.[56]

Unsurprisingly, management in Cork experienced similar difficulties to those encountered in Michigan.

There were just 4,000 industrial workers in the entirety of Cork city at the turn of the twentieth century.[57] The Ford plant, when it was first established, was a giant by the standards of other manufacturing concerns in the metropolis, despite employing fewer than 2,000 workers. At its height, in late 1929 and early 1930, the factory was a behemoth, briefly becoming the largest Ford facility outside the United States. The expansion of the company's workforce meant that, by 1930, Ford was the biggest private employer in the Irish Free State, with nearly 7,000 men engaged in the Marina plant.[58] As stated previously, this figure was a five-fold increase in employment in the space of just thirteen months. As numbers increased, the proportion of the workforce with any industrial experience shrank as inexperienced craft and agricultural workers flooded into the factory. According to one report, in August 1929, 1,095 of the total labour force were considered 'green'. By March 1930, that number had increased to 2,131, about a third of the total workforce.[59]

The adjustment to the industrial discipline of the factory was a significant challenge for these employees. *The Cork Examiner* described the situation:

> The majority of the employees are Corkmen – city and county – but there are many others from other counties in the South. The work may not be quite as easy as they had hitherto been accustomed to; for men who have worked in the field, free from the annoyances of timetables and other regulations which are essential observances in a factory, must find the beginning of employment in any factory irksome, and even irritating. But the difference between the wages paid on the land, and what could be earned from work on the land, is more than ample recompense for whatever loss of liberty submission to discipline is supposed to involve.[60]

The article also noted that the lack of workers with high technical qualifications was proving to be a problem.[61] A 1929 report by plant superintendent Harry Scott described the scale of the difficulties:

> We have, approximately, 3300 men on the pay-roll. We know this is far too many for what we are doing, but as most of these men *know absolutely nothing about machines* we find it necessary to put someone on practically every machine until we have the new men trained in and then can commence

wedding [sic] out. They are rather slow to take hold of some of the jobs, particularly the grinding and similar operations.[62]

Similarly, Ford official William Squires complained that they did not have enough foremen and mechanics to train in the constant flood of new workers. He described the Cork labour force as 'very anxious to have employment' and 'good workmen' but 'hard to break in, afraid of grinders especially, and the multiple tooling of some of the machining operations seems too much for them to master'.[63]

Workers in the foundry were a particular cause for concern. Writing a few weeks after Squires, E.L. Clarke explained that,

> possibly the biggest of our troubles is the labour. We now have 2,300 men in the foundry and they are all more or less 'green'. The supervision also is inexperienced. This is a state of affairs which every day gets better, but I know you will appreciate how difficult is foundry labour anywhere when it has to work to your methods, but particularly in Cork where men have to be taught everything.[64]

The working conditions in the foundry were particularly harsh. In the massive River Rouge plant in Dearborn, for example, transfer to the foundry was used as punishment for workers who were thought to be courting trade unions.[65] One ballad describing the Ford Dagenham foundry (which was almost identical to the one that had existed in Cork) provides some indication of the conditions faced by workers in this horrific environment:

> At the fettlin' [fettling] wheel, you ground your steel with the smoke, the heat and the smell.
> I saw strong men drop in the knockout shop. It was only one step from hell.

Half hour on, half hour off was how they worked the shift,
Till your eyes were red and your poor feet bled and your lungs near came adrift.[66]

A Kerry-born narrator working the foundry in Dagenham put it more laconically: 'God help us: the heat and the sweat!'[67] It is no surprise then that foundry absenteeism constituted a major problem for the plant. Clarke complained that, on one day in March 1930, 223 men, over 10 per cent of the foundry workforce, were absent, 'unable to stand the pace'.[68]

Although there is almost no contemporary testimony from workers entering the factory in the 1920s, interviews with employees who came in later decades offer some indication of the culture shock of entering a modern, high-pressure industrial concern when coming from craft or agricultural backgrounds. Tim Murphy (born 1940s near Blarney, County Cork; general operative and floor supervisor in Ford, 1960–84), who came from a farming family, described the experience of entering the Marina plant: 'Even though I worked in Blarney Woollen Mills before I entered into Fords … it was quite a big step for me and, you know, working in a city factory was ah, almost traumatic at the start really, because it was very busy, there was a noise and a buzz all the time … fellows around you … It wasn't like an ordinary factory at that time.'[69] Given that the factory in 1960 was both smaller and less intense in terms of production than it had been in the 1920s, this later testimony indicates how drastic the entry into Fords was for agricultural and craft labourers in the earlier decade.

INDUSTRIAL RELATIONS, 1917–32

Henry Ford, in his autobiography, outlined his position on trade union organisation:

> We have no antagonism to unions, but we participate in no arrangements with either employee or employer organizations. The wages paid are always higher than any reasonable union could think of demanding and the hours of work are always shorter. There is nothing that a union membership could do for our people ... We respect the unions, sympathize with their good aims and denounce their bad ones.[70]

Ford's attitude towards labour organisation was far harsher than his public writings suggest. He was, according to Huw Beynon, 'fundamentally and entirely opposed to trade unions. The idea of working men questioning his prerogatives as an owner was outrageous.'[71] The company's attitude was put into practice most dramatically in the River Rouge plant at Dearborn, through the Ford service department. The seemingly innocuous title of this internal organisation obscured the fact that the service department was a network of spies and thugs whose main purpose was to prevent union organisation within the vast facility. The everyday fear and violence that characterised being a Ford worker in Dearborn was revealed dramatically to the world in 1936 when union activists leafleting the Ford workforce were viciously attacked by the service department – events caught on camera by a reporter for the *Detroit Free Press* and immortalised as the 'Battle of the Overpass'.[72]

This attitude towards trade unions was imported into Ireland. As late as 1949, several years after the organisation of unions in American and British Ford factories, Gus McLoughlin, an active trade unionist involved in the unionisation of both the Dagenham and Cork plants, recalls being told by manager John O'Neill: 'Well, you can go back to Connolly Hall [the regional headquarters of the ITGWU] tomorrow and tell them that there'll be no shop steward ever stand in this company.'[73] Bob Elliott explained that he hid his union allegiances in the same period for fear of management reprisals.[74]

One incident that demonstrated the Fordist disdain for trade unions occurred in January 1923. That month saw the outbreak of a strike by the Dockers section of the ITGWU in response to an attempt to reduce wages by local employers. Edward Grace reported that the Ford plant was

> not affected by the strike in any way, except that as we have always in the past shipped our goods out by the regular service steamers of the City of Cork Steam Packet Company, which were loaded at the quay by the Dockers, and consequently, when the strike took place it was either necessary for us to get our materials in and our goods away or else close down.[75]

In the short term, Grace arranged for Steam Packet Company ships to dock instead at the Ford wharf, where they would handle Ford material only, allowing the company to transport materials while avoiding direct involvement in the dispute. The steamship *Cumbria* was loaded with material and ready to sail when the crew informed the captain they had been intimidated by the strikers, and 'as they were residents of Cork, they would not be able to sail the ship'.[76] To overcome this hurdle, Grace assembled a team of volunteers from the factory to sail the ship in place of the original crew. On discovering that the Steam Packet Company had not provided the replacement crew with blankets, Grace travelled to the company offices and tried to board another ship, the *Glengariff*, to collect bedding for his hastily conscripted volunteers.[77]

The Cork Examiner reported that Grace arrived at the docks around 11 a.m. in a Ford lorry. He was 'at once surrounded by a strong picket of the strikers and the driver of the lorry was meanwhile threatened against assisting in the removal of any goods from the steamer'.[78] Despite a 'very heated and animated discussion', Grace forced his way through the picket onto the *Glengariff*.[79] When he returned a few minutes later with the bedding he was held up on the gangway, where, he claimed, the strikers began throwing stones and bricks.[80] Grace then produced a revolver while he ordered his driver to find a National Army patrol to intervene. There was a tense stand-off, during which the dockers taunted the manager: 'Fire, and down you will go as sure as your name is Grace.'[81] Meanwhile, Grace's driver was surrounded by picketers, and the motor lorry was turned over and set alight in the street. Grace himself was eventually forced to pass the picket and take refuge in the Steam Packet Company, and was able to leave only under armed military escort.[82] The Ford Motor Company's first encounter with organised labour in Ireland had taken the form of an armed stand-off.

However, Fordism did not rely solely on coercion to prevent the establishment of trade unions. The high wages paid by the firm were among the most potent weapons wielded by the company in its battle against unionisation. The *Fordson Worker* demonstrates that maintaining positive relations between workers and management was a primary concern of the Irish plant from an early stage. The newspaper's own stated purpose was to 'cultivate and establish the broadest fellowship amongst Fordson workers through understanding each other'.[83] The editorial was devoted to this very theme:

> Frequently the men in the shops will tell you that those who labour in the executive offices have an easy time. Do they realise the heavy obligations and responsibilities carried by the executives ... Remember we are all workers here, employees and employers. Henry Ford is one of the greatest workers the world has ever known.[84]

The article concludes with a quote from the great industrialist himself: 'Remove misunderstandings and there will be no trouble between labour and capital, between employee and employer.'[85]

The newspaper was clearly intended to serve the function of removing these 'misunderstandings'. Other initiatives taken in the factory, such as a labour representation committee, sought to ensure that disputes between management and labour could be resolved without the involvement of trade unions and without recourse to industrial action.

Unlike Manchester, there is little evidence of pressure for trade union recognition in Cork. No major efforts to unionise the Marina workforce were made until the late 1940s, which is surprising in some respects. During the revolutionary period of 1917–23, Irish trade unions expanded massively and were increasingly radicalised.[86] Despite this expansion and radicalisation, the Ford plant remained off-limits. Ford's seeming imperviousness to trade unions was not unique. The immediate post-war years saw a 'rout' of the British trade union movement's strongholds in the fledgling motor industry, resulting in a series of devastating contractions and defeats.[87]

However, the absence of trade unions did not mean unquestioning deference and obedience on the part of workers. As Joan Sangster argues, workers engage in resistance to, or accommodation with, employers based on their actual material circumstances.[88] Numerous aspects of the Ford factory made resistance difficult, including the high levels of unemployment in the city, the hire-and-fire nature of employment in the plant and the lack of a tradition of trade unionism among the workforce. On at least one occasion, Ford employees even held a mass protest supporting the company during a dispute with Cork Corporation, informing executives that the firm's position was 'appreciated and endorsed by workers'.[89] However, there were at least two significant cases in which the inter-war Ford workforce conducted mass resistance to management, displaying significant discipline and determination in doing so.

The first occurred in 1920, at the height of the Irish War of Independence. Cork was one of the most active centres of republican political and military activity throughout the conflict, and the city experienced pitched battles between state forces and republican volunteers. Much of the commercial centre was burnt down by occupying British soldiers in December 1920. By and large, the Ford factory weathered the conflict, continuing production and construction activity throughout the period. However, Ford workers were not unaffected by the independence struggle, and there were IRA volunteers among the workforce.[90]

Republican activism was multifaceted, with IRA membership representing just one aspect of revolutionary activity. Workers in Cork, politicised and radicalised by the events of the war, engaged in strike actions and mass protests supporting the independence movement. One of the most significant of these mobilisations surrounded the hunger strike of Sinn Féin Lord Mayor Terence MacSwiney, who was elected following the murder of his predecessor, local IRA leader Tomás MacCurtain. On 12 August 1920, the new lord mayor was caught in possession of seditious documents and sentenced to two years' incarceration in Brixton prison. Soon after his arrival he began a hunger strike, which quickly became the focus of international attention.

MacSwiney's imprisonment occurred at the height of the 'troubles', and there was considerable local support for his plight. Between August and October 1920, several masses were organised by the local trade union movement supporting MacSwiney and other hunger strikers. These masses had elements of both a political protest and a general strike, with local businesses closing during the service. Reporting on the first of these masses, *The Cork Examiner* describes how 'all work was at a complete standstill in the city while the mass lasted'.[91] Ford workers were present both at the initial mass and again when services were held on 22 September, 'marching in huge numbers' from the factory to the churches.

Michael V. O'Donoghue, an IRA volunteer and engineering student then employed in the Marina plant, recalls returning to work after the September mass, an event he accidentally conflates with MacSwiney's funeral in late October:

> Judge of our surprise on when we reported back at Ford's, we were called before the manager (an Englishman) reprimanded for leaving the factory without specific managerial permission and told that our services would be dispensed with if such unauthorised abstention ever occurred again. The men were furiously resentful but they suppressed their anger. It may be noted that none of Ford's workmen of any kind were organised in any trade union at that time, Henry Ford himself boasting that as he paid wages above the general union rate he could afford to ignore their existence. His management, apparently, were as antagonistic to any expression of patriotic feeling by his Irish workers as Ford himself was to trade unionism.[92]

Several local republicans, predominantly young men, were also on hunger strike in Cork prison at this time. By October 1920, MacSwiney's condition was deteriorating, as was that of the local hunger strikers. A visitor to Cork prison on 16 October, who had 'been in close touch with the prisoners for some time', reported that 'there was a distinct change for the worse in their condition since last week'.[93] Hunger striker Michael Fitzgerald's situation was stated to be 'very grave', while Joseph Kenny was described as being in a critical condition, 'for the most part in a semi-conscious state'.[94] MacSwiney entered into a coma on 20 October and died five days later. It was in this context of rising tensions that another hunger strike mass was scheduled for Friday, 15 October.

According to Thomas Grimes, Edward Grace was absent from the factory during the first two stoppages and was coming under considerable pressure from Sorensen to maintain production levels. Grace decided to put his foot down.[95] After the announcement of a third hunger strike mass was made, notices were sent to all foremen stating that the plant would operate as usual and that 'anyone disobeying would be dismissed'.[96] Ignoring this threat, the majority of the workforce attended the mass. On returning to the Marina they found themselves locked out. Grace claimed that he had initially intended 'to discharge every man' who left the factory but was convinced to relent by 'the pleading of two men, whose opinions I highly esteem'.[97] Following arbitration between a local Sinn Féin TD, workers and management, it was agreed that work would resume, with the assurance that stoppages would not occur again. What is significant about the events of that day is both the spontaneous nature of the walkout, which bypassed the authority of the Labour Representation Committee, and the determination of the workforce in defying Grace's instructions despite the threat of dismissal.

The one-day cessation of work in the plant resulted in the loss to the workers of £1,400 in wages.[98] Grace, briefing Sorensen on the incident, was proud of his actions:

> I think that we have won one of our biggest fights – not only for ourselves, but for every employer of labour in Cork, as well as Ireland ... We have gained the respect of every sound-thinking man in the community. As for the others, *I do not care*.[99]

After the hunger strike affair, there were no significant industrial actions in the plant for the remainder of the decade. Any resistance to management in this period occurred on the level of individuals or small groups of workers and is lost to the historical record. In early 1932, however, Ford workers in Ireland took strike action for the first time in the history of the Marina plant. The action was taken in response to an attempt by the company to introduce a 10 per cent wage cut for all employees in the factory.[100] On Monday, 4 April 1932, a 'very brief stoppage' occurred in response to the proposed wage cut.[101] Despite concessions made by the company and the 'intervention of some prominent citizens', workers again downed tools the following Friday. After leaving their stations, the strikers picketed outside the factory while 'a large force of Civic Guards' was deployed to the plant.[102] The men were joined by 'many former employees of the firm', suggesting that links had been maintained between the survivors and victims of the mass lay-offs of 1930.[103] Following the stoppage, management quickly capitulated to the strikers' demands, restricting the pay cut to only the highest grades in the plant.[104] The resolution of the strike represented an almost total victory for the workers and was the last bout of industrial action taken by Marina employees until the advent of union organisation in 1949.

At first glance, the victory appears surprising given the company's usually dogged resistance to labour pressure. However, unknown to the striking workers, the company had decided to cease assembly operations at Cork entirely in April 1932. This decision was reversed only when the introduction of tariffs in June of that year caused a change of heart among the directors.[105] The strike's apparent significance in forcing a concession from Ford at a time when such concessions were rare obscures the reality. The wage cut had been reversed because the company did not expect to be employing their manufacturing workforce for much longer either way.

EMERGENCY AND EMIGRATION, 1932–47

Following the company's sudden adaptation of the Marina plant to assembly operations in 1932, the firm experienced stability for the remainder of the decade thanks to the significant protections the Fianna Fáil-led government had introduced for the industry. Although the numbers employed were now a mere fraction of what they had been previously, the fact that even a few hundred were engaged was a boon considering that the company had been on the verge of ceasing all assembly operations at Cork. This quiet prosperity was shattered by the outbreak of the Second World War, however, when Henry Ford and Sons and the rest of the Irish car-assembly industry suffered at the hands of wartime austerity, with the introduction of petrol rationing having a particularly severe impact. The number of new private car registrations between September 1939 and October 1940 dropped by over 50 per cent compared with the 1938-9 period.[106] The numbers employed in car assembly dropped from 1,500 in March 1939 to 744 in September 1940.[107] Ford, the largest employer in the industry by some margin, saw its workforce reduced from 567 to 372 in the same period.[108] Finally, as supplies of raw materials and fuel dried up, the factory was forced to cease producing cars completely. Operations were cut to the bare minimum. Some skilled workers were retained to maintain the plant and machinery, and the engine exchange remained in operation to supply the company's network of dealerships and garages. The numbers employed remained at low levels until 1947, when car assembly resumed and began approaching pre-war production and employment levels.

The effect of the war on Henry Ford and Sons contrasted with the experience of Ford in Britain. The United Kingdom's isolation from the continent necessitated that British agriculture provide for the country's needs and led to a huge demand for Ford tractors.[109]

Ford's British plants were also utilised for military production. The absence of men called up for military service and the increase in production meant a high demand for labour in Dagenham, Leamington Spa and other Ford plants. In Dagenham, the wartime shortage of labour was so severe that it led to the reversal of the company's previous policy of employing only male labour, so that by 1945 some 10 per cent of the Dagenham workforce was female.[110]

The British labour shortage provided a safety valve for the Marina workforce. During the war, the migration of Ford workers from Cork to Britain, which had begun with the transfer of Irish foundry employees in the early 1930s, intensified. A letter from manager John O'Neill to the Department of Industry and Commerce shows the extent of this migration:

> At our request the Ford Motor Company, England, have agreed to accept for employment at their various phases of activity, up to 500 of our men, provided that a full and clear explanation of living conditions in England is given to each prospective employee. This has been done and a very large number of our men have accepted and arrangements for the necessary Travelling Permits are under way.[111]

Correspondence between the company and the passport office in July 1941 reveals that 164 workers had applied for travel permits to take up employment in Dagenham, while ninety-five were seeking documentation for positions in Leamington Spa.[112] This migration from Cork to Ford centres in Britain continued throughout the war, with letters from the Marina plant employment department throughout 1943 indicating a steady stream of workers taking up positions in Ford plants in Britain.[113] The shortage of labour in Dagenham was such that Ford recruiters extended their net beyond those already employed in the Cork plant. Vaunie Downey recalls that Ford men recruited openly in Blackrock, paying the transport fares for those who agreed to accept jobs in Dagenham. Vaunie's husband left his job in a local bakery to take advantage of the high wages available in the gargantuan Ford factory on the banks of the Thames. Thousands of others did the same.[114]

The outbreak of war merely represented a new phase of a process that had begun many years earlier with the transfer of the Cork foundry to Dagenham. The establishment of the Dagenham foundry had involved the relocation of some 2,000 foundry labourers from other Ford centres.[115] Although the majority of these men were sourced from the Manchester plant, it was also the case that 'Irishmen ... began migrating to Dagenham to work in the Foundry'.[116] Additionally, the sudden contraction of the Marina's labour force in 1930 meant there was a pool of several thousand men in Cork who had experience in foundry labour and vehicle assembly, as well as a history of employment with the Ford company. For them, attracted by the high wages and other benefits of working in England, crossing the Irish Sea to take up work in Dagenham, Manchester and elsewhere was a logical move in the context of an Irish working class for whom periodic migration was already an established part of working life.[117] A ballad written by Gus McLoughlin illustrates the number of Irishmen (particularly Corkonians) employed in the Dagenham factory:

> At seventeen years, I had no fears as I sailed from Penrose Quay,
> Nor did I shirk the strong man's work in the Dagenham factory,
> There were men from every nation in the 20,000 force
> You can take it from me, the foundry were all Irishmen of course,

> From the office door to the furnace floor, the accent, as a rule,
> Was the one you'd meet down Patrick Street, Blackrock or sweet Blackpool.[118]

While most Ford workers featured in the current study were too young to recall this period of work in the factory, it is clear that a migratory employment pattern was a defining feature of work in Ford factories for a previous generation of employees. The fathers of Gus McLoughlin, Denis Forde and Patrick Dunlea all spent time abroad in British Ford factories. Denis himself began his career with Ford in Dagenham before returning to Cork, and he later spent time in the Leamington Spa plant.

This migration pattern had an important effect on both Cork and Dagenham. The effects of the conflict with Germany created new possibilities for unionisation in Britain as high labour demand and a sympathetic state facilitated the organisation of industrial workers.[119] Despite these new conditions, Ford remained resistant to trade unions, necessitating workplace militancy by employees at Dagenham. The available evidence suggests that Irish migrants were crucial to this increasing agitation for trade union recognition. Sheila Cohen highlights a significant strike in the Dagenham plant during the summer of 1944 related to the sacking of an Irish shop steward named Sweetman. The strike received 'great support from Sweetman's fellow-Irishmen in the foundry' who, Cohen notes, 'had become pillars of the union at Fords'.[120] The increasingly tumultuous industrial relations in the Dagenham plant inculcated trade union traditions among Irish migrant workers and demonstrated that Ford could be forced to concede trade union recognition. Gus McLoughlin's first introduction to trade unionism came during the period he spent working in the Dagenham plant in the war years, playing a significant role in the battle for recognition there. On his return to

Cork, he once again became an active participant in the campaign to unionise the Marina plant.[121]

The war period represented a high point in migration from Cork to Dagenham. When production in the Marina plant began to return to pre-war levels in 1947, many Cork workers returned to their hometown, while others remained in Dagenham. However, migration to Dagenham during times of 'slack' in the Marina plant continued after the resumption of vehicle production in Cork. Liam Downey moved to Dagenham in 1948, just as employment levels in Henry Ford and Sons were improving, and Dominic Carey recalled that brief stints of work in the English factory remained the norm for nearly a decade after the war.[122] Others chose to remain in England. Such was the case with Kerry-born Domhnall Mac an tSíthigh:

> When I was working in Fords I got to know a lot of people, mostly Irishmen. Fords came from Cork to Dagenham in the early 1930s. A lot of Ford workers from Cork went working in Dagenham. I met a share of them. When they were working in Fords in Cork they had been young men. By the time I met them they were getting old.[123]

There were still enough Irish athletes in Dagenham in 1965 that a hurling match between the Marina plant and the British facility could be organised, an annual tradition that had begun in the previous decade.[124]

WORK AND INDUSTRIAL RELATIONS, 1947–84

As the war came to an end, the difficulties that had beset the Marina plant lessened. The company announced in November 1945 that production in Cork would return to full levels in the new year. The re-opening provided 'a healthy stimulus to employment, necessitating the recall of many employees who had been transferred to the immense Dagenham factory during the war, and the engagement of other workers'.[125] Despite the increasing trend of unionisation within the Ford Motor Company internationally, the Marina management continued to resist the organisation of the plant. The available contemporary oral testimony confirms that the company retained a highly antagonistic attitude towards unions until the eventual success of the recognition strike.

In addition to the recognition of trade unions granted by the Ford Motor Company in both Britain and America during the war, there were also purely domestic factors that facilitated organisation in the Marina plant. Pre-war trade unionism in Ireland was an uphill struggle, with more defeats than victories.[126] However, after the war, legislative changes facilitated its expansion and consolidation. These changes included the creation of a labour court to arbitrate disputes between workers and employers and the introduction of joint agreements on wages. These new measures facilitated the organisation of workers.[127]

In 1949, Ford workers took serious action to garner recognition. The ITGWU announced in August that it was 'invoking the machinery of the Labour Court in our dispute with Messrs. Henry Ford and Sons Limited, of Cork, who, consequent on a big number of the employees becoming members, have adopted an attitude of non-recognition of the union'.[128] However, the company's continued refusal to agree to a conference with representatives of the ITGWU led to the unionised sections of the workforce threatening strike action in late September. It was estimated by *The Irish Times* that some 300 of the 800 workers employed in the plant were members of the ITGWU.[129] When the company refused to comply with the demands made by the union, the result was a strike that involved the vast majority of the manual workforce and completely halted production in the factory.[130]

The limited oral testimony relating to the strike suggests that the dispute, while brief, was characterised by unprecedented militancy on the part of the newly unionised workforce. Max Hayes, a Marina plant security guard, was not a member of the union, and he and the other security men continued to work after pickets had been placed. The situation was so tense that the security guards took the precaution of meeting up before the beginning of their shift so as to avoid facing the pickets alone.[131] Charge-hand Arthur Owens recalled being threatened that he would be tossed into the river Lee.[132] The picketing by Ford employees was aggressive and extensive. Eddie Cleary was a teenager when his father, an active trade unionist in the plant, became involved in the strike. Eddie stated that strike-breakers were verbally and physically intimidated by large groups of the organised labour force.[133] Such tactics appear to have been effective. Both Max Hayes and Arthur Owens were instructed by management not to continue crossing the picket, for their own safety.

The strike continued until 10 October 1949, when management finally agreed to negotiate with trade union representatives, resulting in victory for the workers. In the ITGWU'S *Liberty* Christmas special of that year, congratulations were issued to its members in Ford for achieving full union recognition.[134] This recognition was won only with aggressive strike action.[135] By contrast, Irish Steel and Sunbeam both accepted trade unions quietly, and workers there were not compelled to strike for union acceptance.

For the first few years of the union's existence in the plant, the militancy that had accompanied the initial recognition strikes seems to have continued. The fact, for example, that Fords competed with Gouldings (a large fertiliser factory in Cork) and CIÉ for most copies of *Liberty* sold indicates a high level of individual activism within the ITGWU.[136] This early militancy is corroborated by Eddie Mullins, who recalled high strike levels in the early years of union presence.[137] These strikes were frequent and usually unofficial. Of the large number of strikes in the early 1950s, the most memorable occurred in August 1954. In that month, Henry Ford II visited the Cork plant. The visit was significant, representing the first time a member of the Ford family had ever seen the completed factory. Two months prior to the visit, 500 workers had gone out on strike in pursuit of a wage claim. When Henry Ford II arrived on 29 August he found himself unable to visit the plant. That morning, a demand for a general raise of 3d had been denied by management. Reacting swiftly, the workers downed tools and occupied the factory premises. Later that afternoon, the strikers formed a parade that marched to the Imperial Hotel, where Ford was being received by management and the city's elite. The workers carried banners which proclaimed: 'Bosses feast while workers starve'. Whatever the effect these actions had on public opinion, it did not deter the workers, who continued their strike action for another week, despite strong condemnation from official labour bodies.[138]

Despite unionisation, the insecure 'hire and fire' nature of vehicle assembly in Ireland remained commonplace until at least the early 1960s. A CIO report in 1962 remarked on this seasonal variation. It noted that the number of manual workers fell from 2,571 to 1,722 between June and November 1960.[139] Ford's market share and superior plant meant that such seasonal variations were not as pronounced in percentage terms as those in the smaller assemblers. In 1956, between the on-season and off-season, the Marina plant saw its workforce contract from 745 to 525. Buckley Motors Ltd saw a much more dramatic reduction, from 164 during the high point of 1956, to just 18 during the following year's slump.[140] Such seasonal contractions and lay-offs remained the norm in the Marina plant for decades.

4.2 Michael Lenihan installing a window at the Ford Marina plant, 1984. Photo reproduced with the kind permission of Michael Lenihan.

The high wages paid by the Ford company meant that only breadwinners were considered appropriate recruits, reflecting prevailing attitudes to male labour.[141] Denis Forde (born 1928 in Greenmount, Cork city; general operative and later film unit projectionist at Dagenham, Leamington Spa and Cork Ford plants, 1942–84), who claimed to be the youngest worker ever to be employed at the Marina plant, recalled his first day at work in the factory:

> So, I was sent down outside the gate anyway. I started at eight o'clock. I was there at about ten past seven, sitting on the kerb. And the next thing one of the security came down the stairs, opened the gate and said: 'What are you doing there young fella? You should be at school!' … I said: 'I'm waiting to start work, sir.' And he started laughing. He said: 'We don't take on any young fellas,' he said. 'You should be in school!'[142]

The exception for Denis Forde was only made because his father (a long-time employee of the company) had died on the job in the Leamington Spa plant, leaving the family deprived of a breadwinner. Nyhan notes the existence of another young worker hired under similar circumstances.[143] Indeed, it was factory policy in earlier years that only one member of a single family be employed in the Marina plant, although this seems to have been abandoned over time.

The basis of this policy was that Ford remained among the premier industrial employers in the city and county in terms of wages and conditions throughout its existence. Michael Lenihan (born 1958 in the Blarney Street area of Cork city; general operative at Fords, 1980–84) expressed the high esteem in which working in Fords was regarded:

> You were on good wages, you were on good conditions, I mean you got a job in Fords, because Fords have been in Cork since 1917 and at that time he was paying above the odds, he always paid above the odds. So, getting a job in Henry Fords was definitely the place to work. There were certain places where you got a job and, oh Jesus, you couldn't go wrong, you were made for life. And like I say, these were pensionable jobs, good jobs, and there was no reason to see why a place would close. Dunlops was the same, you were in a very good job; Verolme, these were good jobs like, good money, security of employment. So yeah, if you were working in Fords, yeah, you had a very good job, you certainly had a lot more money than anybody else out there … Even at that time, my wife didn't work for a very long time, it was on the one wage really that we survived. It was a very good job.[144]

Those such as Michael Costelloe (born 1940 in Duagh, County Kerry; warehouse operative in Ford, 1960s–1989) who came to the plant in earlier years expressed much the same sentiments:

> I doubled my wages in Fords from the job I was in ... I always remember that ... It was some fecking jump like ... you could live in comfort. It made the difference between comfort and scraping, you know?[145]

A sense of pride, and a perception that to be a Ford worker was a source of privilege, runs through the oral testimony. Despite the frequent strikes, a discernible sense of loyalty to the company permeates the narratives, a feature also noted by Miriam Nyhan.[146]

LABOUR PROCESS

A recurrent theme in the narratives of car assembly workers internationally is the monotony and tedium of the job. Huw Beynon provides an evocative description of Ford's Liverpool Halewood plant:

> If you stand on the catwalk at the end of the plant you can look down over the whole assembly floor. Few people do, for to stand there and look at the endless, perpetual tedium of it all is to be threatened by the overwhelming insanity of it. The sheer audacious madness of a system based upon those wishing their lives away. I was never able, even remotely, to come to terms with the line. Mind you, I never worked on it.[147]

Similarly, Paul Thompson, in his interviews with Coventry car workers, notes that a recurrent phrase used by the men to describe the assembly line process was 'soul-destroying'.[148] Ford workers in Cork were less inclined to use such emotive language. While terms such as 'monotonous' were employed, phrases such as 'soul-destroying', 'perpetual tedium', etc. were rare. Several reasons can be offered to explain the different experiences of Cork workers compared with their British counterparts. First, the function of the Cork plant, supplying all Ford products, from family cars to commercial vans, meant there was a much greater variety of tasks to be performed, lessening the drudgery of repetitive labour. Second, production demands in Cork were less onerous than those of factories located elsewhere. It is perhaps because of this that the alleged 'speed-up' (a recurrent complaint of car workers in other countries) was only mentioned once by the narrators as a source of conflict.[149]

While the narrators did not describe working for Ford in the severe and dramatic terms of their British counterparts, many, such as Gus McLoughlin, did complain about the strain and monotony of the labour process:

> It was tough. There was no doubt about it. One might consider that doing a certain job, we'll say if you were doing it in the garage, you might get an hour to do it. You'd be expected to perform that operation in production in minutes, because minutes is all you got to perform any operation, no matter how difficult it was. You just had to find a way of doing that within a certain time. You know?[150]

Michael Lenihan expressed similar sentiments:

> It was a hard job. It wasn't easy, like … The sheer amount you have to do and it was repetitive, like … I mean, can you imagine saying to someone, 'You're going to fit 160 screens in one day'?[151]

However, while the workers disliked the monotony and discipline of assembly line car production, it appears they were willing to tolerate this form of production. To reduce monotony, they would work 'up the line' and distract themselves with activities such as chess, draughts, singing, pranks and cards. Such activities were highly popular among the workforce.

In contrast to post-war Dagenham, the Marina plant was far from a stronghold of militancy. Miriam Nyhan found that most of the Ford employees she interviewed only reluctantly used the term 'strike'.[152] My own interviews corroborate her findings. Narrators usually opted for terms such as 'stoppages' or 'walkouts'. Similarly, almost all the narrators were dismissive of the minor disputes that did occur and often attributed the causes to hangovers or boredom, rather than serious industrial conflict. Michael Lenihan recalled that 'there used be kind of wildcat strikes and they ... every now and again it would happen, and I think the chassis line in particular were kind of noted for it'.[153] Michael was hard pressed to recall specific reasons why such strikes occurred but did jokingly claim that one strike was the result of the canteen providing plain biscuits rather than chocolate ones.[154] In a similarly dismissive tone, Tim Murphy said that a good deal of strike action in the plant was caused by a lone 'troublemaker' who 'was very fond of the strike and every Monday morning ... he'd have to cause a strike, to alleviate the pressure in his head, I suppose'.[155]

The nature of the assembly line process meant that strike action by a small group of workers, or even a single individual, could stop all activity in the production process. Tim Murphy explained that

> the pressure used [to] be great if any group stopped anywhere on the line, because the whole way back the track to the

building of the [car] body was all stopped. Once one line couldn't move, no line moved. So you had hundreds of workers then standing around doing nothing and the company would get very excited then, the management.[156]

The camaraderie of Ford workers on the production line and the 'sacrosanct' nature of the picket (a more general feature of trade unionism in Ireland) meant that the majority of workers respected any strike or stoppage, even if it only involved a small group of employees.[157] Michael Lenihan remembered that, even though he often 'couldn't fathom' the reasons for walkouts, the line was always respected:

> Some mornings you'd go in and there'd be a picket on the gate and no one would pass a picket, official or otherwise, it was a sacred cow, like … because I mean if one person had a grievance, the whole factory could come to a halt if there was an unofficial picket put on … But the men did wield a lot of power in that sense.[158]

Walkouts and stoppages can also be understood as a rebellion against the monotony of the line, with one former supervisor concluding that 'frustration on the line caused a lot of it, frustration in the line, and frustration in the discipline which a line imposes caused a lot of fellas to get excited'.[159] As Robert Bruno states of wildcat strikes in Ohio steel mills, such walkouts were a way for workers to control their own labour time and to liberate themselves temporarily from the tyranny of the assembly line.[160]

During the late 1970s, the possibility of Ford establishing a new £175 million engine plant in Cork was mooted. The company was examining its options as to where to locate the new plant, and there was considerable enthusiasm in Ireland at the possibility of the estimated 2,000 additional jobs that could be provided in the

4.3 Workers at the Ford Marina plant, 1984.
Photo reproduced with the kind permission of Michael Lenihan.

Cork area. One periodical claimed that extreme militancy in the factory was placing the project in jeopardy, and eventually Ford located the engine plant in Wales rather than Ireland.[161] Following this decision, the claim was again made that the company had opted for Wales over Ireland due to plant-level militancy.[162] However, this bore little relation to reality. When these claims were raised, they were quickly refuted by Ford management themselves: 'In all our 60 years we have never had an official strike and the longest unofficial stoppage was ten days.'[163] Similarly, far from being overpaid, wage rates in Ireland were much lower than those in Britain.[164] Contemporary commentators observed that the brief disputes characteristic of industrial relations in the Marina plant, but also common in the British motor industry, had little significant effect on output.[165] The post-war strike pattern at Fords was by no means unusual (either in an Irish context or in comparison with similar firms operating in Britain) nor did it have a significant overall effect on output, production or profitability. Wales had been chosen over Ireland due to its lower transport costs, larger supply of local skilled labour and the stronger negotiating power of the British government.[166]

The failure to acquire the engine facility dealt a significant blow to both the Marina plant and to Ireland. However, worse lay in store:

> It was in January 1984 we were told we'd be laid off. And we were given the date we'd be laid off, in July. Paddy Hayes sent out word that everyone was to gather in the canteen … Staff, hourly paid and salary paid, they all got the same message. We just didn't know what to do sort of thing. Many people just froze. They didn't see any way forward … so many fellows just froze on the day. A lot of them are froze to this day in the sense that a lot of them that weren't getting on didn't work anymore, you know?[167]

The closure was a huge blow for Cork, which was plunging into crisis levels of unemployment. This disappointment was, however, somewhat softened by the generous redundancy and pensions provided by Ford, who wished to retain goodwill to safeguard its position in Ireland, which remained an important market.[168] The closure of Fords represented a watershed for the working class of the city. The factory had been a beacon for more than half a century, offering hopes of social advancement and financial security. Now it lay empty and silent.

5

Working for Sunbeam Wolsey, 1927–90

INTRODUCTION

The figure of William Dwyer looms over the history of the Sunbeam plant, and is recalled strongly in the collective memory of the northside of Cork city.[1] During his stewardship of Sunbeam Wolsey, Dwyer pursued a policy of industrial paternalism in relation to the large, mostly female workforce employed at his factory. This strategy sought to ensure harmonious relations between management and staff and was (within Dwyer's lifetime) largely successful. In 1949 Dwyer bragged: 'I have spent a long life in business trying to avoid strikes and I am glad to say in the last twenty-one years no strike has occurred.'[2] This was no idle boast. A 1955 issue of *Liberty*, the magazine of the ITGWU, spoke in glowing terms of the company:

> When I go into a factory and, talking about a social service, hear a worker declare that their factory has 'one of the best' then I am certain that I'm in a happy factory – and there are 'happy factories' just as there are 'happy ships' in the navy. That kind of remark shows that labour and management [at Sunbeam] are both doing a good job.[3]

This state of affairs remained the norm after Dwyer's death in 1951 and until the early 1970s, when the cordial relations between staff and management at Sunbeam disintegrated in the face of several major strikes and Dwyer's 'happy ship' ran aground.

How did William Dwyer and his successors maintain such pacific relations in the workplace for four decades? What were the specific features of industrial paternalism as experienced in Sunbeam Wolsey? Why did those relations eventually break down so dramatically? This chapter addresses these questions in depth, examining the strategies employed by management to acquire and maintain consent in the workplace, the reasons for their success and eventual failure, and the 'material and cultural bases'[4] of the management regime that evolved at Sunbeam. First, however, we must define what we mean by industrial paternalism and the general features of the practice.

INDUSTRIAL PATERNALISM

Industrial paternalism is a form of management regime that developed in the nineteenth century. The practice was pursued by philanthropic manufacturers who sought to resolve the intense class polarisation of Victorian England. Paternalism was also practised by many Irish firms in the nineteenth and twentieth centuries but, with some exceptions, these examples have not been studied in detail.[5]

Paternalism, and the system of welfare capitalism that succeeded it, is described by Andrea Tone as being based on deference to the employer and an unspoken contract of mutual obligation.[6] Paternalist practices range from housing provision and profit-sharing to the construction of churches and libraries.[7] Most paternalist firms had some or more of these features but rarely included all of them. William Dwyer, for example, employed traditional paternalist policies but condemned profit-sharing with workers (a common feature of paternalist and welfare capitalist firms in the United States) as 'there was no mention of them sharing in the losses'.[8] Paternalism is, thus, a broad approach to industrial relations that varies in form depending on context. Firms that employed this system must be considered in their historical, political and social settings to be fully understood.

Finally, we must distinguish between 'industrial paternalism' and 'welfare capitalism'. While the terms are sometimes used interchangeably, there are notable and significant differences. Industrial paternalism emerged in the nineteenth century and was based on the cultivation of reciprocity, community and shared interest among employer and employees. Industrial paternalism was deeply local and based on links between owners and operatives who usually lived in the same area. The system could also be highly informal. The distribution of fringe benefits, housing, etc. was often left to the discretion of the industrialist. Welfare capitalism, by contrast, emerged in the United States during the 1920s in a more bureaucratic form among large firms. These bigger firms (such as Ford) were spread across multiple sites and possessed workforces that numbered in the tens of thousands. Like traditional paternalists, these firms also sought to create a sense of mutual obligation and reciprocity between employer and employee, but did so on a more rationalised basis. Fringe benefits and other employee provisions were organised through a modern, bureaucratic apparatus in which the company owner was a more distant figure. Industrial paternalism is best applied to firms in which a real or imaginary relationship with the business leader is at the centre of the employment relationship. Welfare capitalism more accurately describes firms in which the same sense of loyalty and mutual endeavour is achieved through a standardised system of rules and rewards.[9] Sunbeam fits firmly into the former category.

PATERNALIST MANAGEMENT AT SUNBEAM

Former Sunbeam workers are almost unanimous in their opinions of William and Declan Dwyer (William's son and successor as managing director). Workers recalled them as being 'excellent employers',[10] 'very good people',[11] 'marvellous'[12] and 'very respectful and very decent and nice to their ... employees'.[13] Such was the popularity of both men that this reputation survived their deaths and passed into popular memory. The recollections of workers present a narrative in which the era of paternalist management under the Dwyers is depicted as a 'golden age' for the factory. This 'golden age' is in contrast to the strife and insecurity of the 1970s and '80s, when control passed away from the Dwyer family and Sunbeam went into decline. Catherine O'Callaghan, who worked at Sunbeam from 1975 to 1984, attributed the 'fall of the Sunbeam empire' to distant shareholders and other interests 'only in there at the time to feather their own nest and [who] didn't really care about what happened the actual company at the end of the day'. She contrasts this to when the company was 'in their [the Dwyers'] own house'.[14] Madge Barry expressed the common opinion that 'they should have kept it as a Dwyer establishment and ... they'd still be going today if they had done that'.[15]

Such high praise is indicative of the success of the Dwyers' paternalist management. The provisions afforded to employees were indeed generous, including an on-site doctor, nurse, dentist and dispensary, baths for employee usage, sickness benefits, marriage and mortality grants, a canteen, social outings subsidised by the company, sports teams, housing provisions, tennis courts, better pay and working conditions than other firms, as well as extravagant grounds that included eighty plum and pear trees, a vegetable garden, 300 apple trees, a pitch-and-putt course, a fish pond, peacocks, cockatoos and glasshouses. Furthermore,

5.1 Workers in the half-hose knitting department, Sunbeam Wolsey, c.1944.
Photo reproduced with the kind permission of Cork City and County Archives.
B505 Sunbeam Photos Temp 75.

Sunbeam workers had access to a shop where they could buy clothing at a low price, including luxuries such as silk stockings. During the Second World War, the employees were even provided with an air-raid shelter capable of protecting the entire workforce in the unlikely event of Cork being bombed. As Madge Barry fondly recalled, 'We had everything.'[16]

In addition to these benefits, the working conditions at Sunbeam were considerably better than those of similar operators in the region. Rena McCarthy recalled her first job at the Lee Boot Factory on Western Road:

> Well, there was a good atmosphere, but the working conditions were shocking. I mean, there was the floor there, you'd be frozen, summer or winter. We were frozen! There

might be one heater up in the middle of the room to heat the whole lot of it, and it was a huge room.[17]

These conditions stood in sharp contrast to work at Sunbeam:

> Yeah, it was fabulous, the food was lovely out there. Hot food on a cold day. You know, it was very comfortable to go up there. The heaters were on for you. It was nice to go into work in the morning. I mean that time there was no central heating [in houses], of course. I mean it was just a fire down in your home, and you could be frozen at home. We'd be glad to get into work for a bit of heat.[18]

It was 'good work, and clean work, comfortable work'.[19] The generous pay at the Millfield factory also stood out in Rena's recollections:

> God, it was exceptionally good money out there ... Often we had to work Saturday and Sunday on orders that had to be got out. The money was fabulous ... I haven't a clue what we started with. 'Twas good, though, I know 'twas good money.[20]

However, paternalism goes beyond the simple provision of good pay and benefits. Paternalist employers attempt to create the feeling of a community of interest between workers and management. Loyalty and a sense of mutual endeavour were encouraged in other ways too. Sunbeam workers could participate in leisure activities based out of the factory, including choirs, soccer and basketball, but it was best known for its hurling and Gaelic football teams, which made history in 1957 when they became the first to win both the hurling and football inter-firm championships in the same year.[21] Sports teams were more than simply another fringe benefit for the workforce; they also created a sense of shared endeavour and identification with the firm.[22] Social gatherings and company events served a similar function. Peggy Payne recalled an excursion in the early years of Sunbeam:

> All the factory came. It was like a picnic lunch. It was marvellous and Mr Dwyer and all his family, a lot of his friends, they waited on us. We had chicken legs and everything, you know. They was really wonderful.[23]

Gatherings like this created a sense of mutuality and intimacy. Additionally, Dwyer's family would often visit the factory: 'His wife used to come in and a young daughter with her ... she used to come around. They were very good ... They'd come down and talk to you.'[24] After the business moved to the Millfield site, Dwyer initiated his famous garden parties. These events, held as part of the Kermesse charity fundraising drive, were opulent. On one occasion, the swimming pool on the grounds was bridged, so that the Cork symphony orchestra could play there. These garden parties involved both the city's elite and the factory workers themselves. Workers and management temporarily socialised as equals, while workers experienced another fringe benefit in being able to attend an event otherwise beyond their financial means. Other events were more formal and ritualised, including presentations and factory-wide Catholic masses that brought together management and staff. Regardless, the function of these events was the same: to obfuscate temporarily the gulf between management and labour and to create the impression of an 'organic partnership in a co-operative enterprise'.[25]

To analyse Dwyer paternalism without looking beyond the walls of the factory would be misguided. Cork's old bourgeoisie, the so-called 'merchant princes', were deeply embedded within the community. It is impossible to draw a clear line between paternalism in the workplace and within the wider area. Howard Newby identifies the locality as being highly significant in the maintenance of paternalism.[26] In the nineteenth century, paternalist employers had secured goodwill in their localities through local patronage and charitable works.[27] William Dwyer continued this tradition into the modern age.

The most famous example of Dwyer benevolence in the Blackpool area is the Church of the Annunciation, rebuilt and remodelled by William Dwyer before being presented to the parish. To this day, the church is still colloquially known as 'Billy Dwyer's Fire Escape'. However, the church was merely the tip of the iceberg. Dwyer was also a director of the Guild of Goodwill in Cork and an organiser of the Marsh Building Society.[28] Perhaps the most successful of his charitable endeavours was the Kermesse, an annual fundraising entertainments festival held on the grounds of Sunbeam itself, which raised £6,000 for local charities over a three-year period.[29] The significance of this philanthropy was its local nature. At a Kermesse in Youghal (where the Dwyer-owned Seafield Fabrics was located) the majority of the money raised was donated to the local St Vincent de Paul Society and District Nursing Association.[30] Even those local people not directly employed by the Dwyers could still be recipients of paternalist benevolence. The success of William Dwyer in establishing influence, power and respect within the community was reflected in the result of the 1944 general election, when he ran as an independent and topped the poll with an astounding 11,241 first-preference votes.[31] This result was considerably better than the respectable vote he had garnered in the previous election, in which he had run under the banner of Fine Gael and failed to take a seat. Without a party machine and largely relying on his own reputation, William Dwyer's electoral success was a singular achievement.

RECRUITMENT

An important factor in the cementing of ties of loyalty and obligation between management and labour was the construction of kin networks within the factory. Joan Sangster notes that when family connections led to job acquisition, kin networks both assisted acculturation into the factory and provided an informal form of supervision.[32] The memories of Sunbeam workers suggest that recruitment to the company through kin and personal connections was common. Billy Foley described how

> you had a control, Sunbeam always had a class of a control, if you were a good worker, and you had a daughter or something and you were guaranteed to get your daughter into it, or your son into it, or your husband into it if he had no job ... If you were working here and you were a good worker, you were always guaranteed to get in here.[33]

The Dwyers often handled recruitment personally. Peggy Payne recalled how she was leaving the factory one day when William Dwyer asked if her brother was working. When she told him he wasn't, Dwyer saw to it that her brother was hired the following day.[34] This method of recruitment reinforced the personal relationship between workers and their employer.

While personal, community and family contacts were a common way for people to gain employment in all three factories, it was much more prevalent at Sunbeam. Many narrators emphasised the number of relatives they had in the factory. In 1990, when Sunbeam closed, Linda McCarthy recalled, 'it was whole families [who lost their jobs], yeah, it was whole families and whole extended families'.[35] The large numbers of family members employed by Sunbeam at any particular time contrasts sharply with the policy at the Ford Marina plant, in its early years, of only employing one (male) person per family. By the 1960s, Sunbeam had introduced a modern personnel apparatus, including a welfare officer. The personnel manager's duties included recruitment, dismissals and dealing with the trade unions, but also 'dealing with employees who may request advice on their private affairs'.[36] However, Billy Foley suggested that a modern personnel department and discretionary family recruitment co-existed until the closure of the factory:

> That time say Paddy Madden, he was looking for someone in the dyehouse, you'd go up and say, 'Paddy, I've a son, he's idle' and he'd give him a start, bring him in in the morning … It went through the personnel [department] but the personnel was doing what it was told.[37]

This overlap between discretionary paternalism and modern management methods lends credence to Joan Sangster's suggestion that traditional nineteenth-century paternalism and modern welfare capitalism could co-exist within the same enterprise.[38]

The consequences of this style of recruitment on the workforce and their outlook were numerous. First, kin recruitment created a sense of loyalty to the company that could transcend generations, who viewed the boss as having done right, not simply by them but by their parents, siblings and other relatives. Second, kin recruitment when unemployment was rife could be considered a gift, as a worker chosen through kin connections had been offered an opportunity unavailable to other jobseekers. Billy Foley's narrative suggests that kin recruitment was available only to 'good' workers. As such, diligence and hard work could translate into much-needed employment for family members. Finally, a family tradition of loyalty and pride in the firm meant that workers were motivated to work hard and behave well lest they embarrass their older relatives and soil the family's good reputation with the firm.

However, there were also consequences that could not have been foreseen by the Dwyers. Kin connections and family networks within the factory also created bonds of solidarity between workers when conflict arose with management. In the early 1980s, Linda McCarthy, like all Sunbeam office workers at the time, was in a different branch of the ITGWU to that of the manufacturing workers:

> I remember thinking there was a strike nearly came off at one stage, that, like, there was no way, we were told we'd have to pass the picket and we were saying there was no way, like, that we were all the same union, but our branch were telling us at the time that we would have to pass the picket line. I remember thinking, imagine! I'd have to stay out sick, like, there's no way I'd have passed the picket, like. I lived up near most of the people – my own brothers would have been on the other side nearly, like, and have to pass it – no way, like! Me own mother would nearly have been there, you know?[39]

The popular memory of the Sunbeam factory tends to focus primarily on the women who worked there. In 1968, for example, women comprised 1,075 of the 1,655-strong labour force in the company,[40] a situation that affected the nature of paternalism at the firm. Paternalist measures reflected the gendered division of labour and that of Irish society in general. Many of the benefits provided by Dwyer were clearly directed towards his female employees. In this era, women's time in the workforce was generally expected to be brief, filling the gap between school and marriage, when women would leave the factory for the family home.[41] Accordingly, women in Sunbeam who wished to 'better' themselves could go to the 'one-day week' provision for domestic education.[42] In addition, the company's Social Services Society's provision of marriage grants as a gift to betrothed workers was an implicit recognition of the loss of income that would occur when the wife would have to forsake her job. Like other paternalist firms, Sunbeam provided small tokens of femininity in the design of the factory, which sought to soften the harshness of industrial life. A company pamphlet, for example, displayed a picture of the factory canteen where 'gay check cloths on the table give a cheerful continental air to the kitchen'.[43] Similarly, official pictures taken by the company showed clean, prim, smiling female employees working in bright, clean rooms to project a workplace compatible with traditional femininity.

PATERNALISM AND TRADE UNIONISM

Early examinations of paternalism concluded that the practice was nothing more than an anti-union ploy.[44] This was clearly not the case at Sunbeam. The ITGWU commanded the loyalties of most of the Sunbeam workforce and was well-established there by the outbreak of the Second World War. Supervisory, maintenance and warehouse staff were also unionised. While many firms saw paternalism as a way of holding off the challenge of trade unions and ensuring greater control over their employees, others 'accepted unionism in principle and in practice'.[45] Sunbeam was not unique in this regard, even in an Irish context. Guinness, another paternalistic employer, had accepted the principle of a closed shop for craft unions since the late nineteenth century, and general workers were unionised there with little fuss in the 1950s.[46] Dwyer fell into the same category and sought to include trade unions within the paternalist ethos of the factory, once even claiming that he was a 'trade unionist dyed in the wool'.[47] This attitude contrasts with Ford's visceral anti-unionism.

Whatever Dwyer's own opinions regarding trade unionism, he would likely have been unable to resist the unionisation of the workforce that occurred with little significant fanfare in the first decade of the factory's existence. Protectionism in the 1930s meant that business was weaker than labour. The result was increased trade union membership for workers and less autonomy for capitalists who depended on tariff protections for their existence.[48] Rather than fight unionisation, Dwyer sought to accommodate trade unions and ensure good relations with them. Kathleen Fitzgibbon recalled how these relations played out on the factory floor. When asked how her employers viewed the union, she replied that Dwyer

> always listened when they went with complaints about anything. Other places, there used be war, like ... They didn't want to give in to this and give in to that ... There wasn't that much hassle with the union and the employer out there [Sunbeam].[49]

She also suggested that the deferential relationship with Dwyer extended to the ITGWU: 'Things were slow and they [the union] didn't want to ruffle them, you got that feeling, they didn't want to ruffle the bosses.'[50] Beyond the factory, Dwyer's good relations with the local trade union movement were reflected in the tributes paid to him by the Cork Workers' Council on his death. The council described him as 'one of the most progressive men in the country' and noted that 'Cork would be the poorer by his passing'.[51] *Liberty*, the ITGWU magazine, frequently carried advertisements for Sunbeam, Seafield Fabrics and other companies owned by the Dwyers. Advertising space in the magazine was a privilege reserved only for firms that were positively regarded by the trade union movement.

However, while trade unionism was accepted practice within Sunbeam Wolsey, it was challenged when it impinged on the perceived rights of the owner-operator. The employment relationship is (by its very nature) an unequal and hierarchical one. Paternalism, as Alessandro Portelli puts it, masks the reality of exploitation inherent in the employment relationship.[52] Despite Dwyer's 1949 claim that the firm had been strike-free since its inception, there was a significant industrial dispute involving the firm's travelling salesmen in 1936. In 1935, the Commercial Travellers Federation (CTF) approached the Cork Workers' Council, stating its intention to resume activities in the council and to engage in a major recruitment drive.[53] The CTF representative described himself as 'eager to organise all the travellers in the Cork area'.[54] In April 1936, the CTF received word that three of its members in Sunbeam Wolsey had been threatened with dismissal. With the backing of the Workers' Council, the union decided to resist. Dwyer was obstinate in his battle with the CTF men. To combat the travellers, he employed blacklegging, convincing nine members of staff to do the work of the striking salesmen, and consistently rebuffed arbitration attempts by University College Cork (UCC) professor and Catholic intellectual Alfred O'Rahilly until he was finally forced to give in to the demands of the workers.[55]

Dwyer's behaviour in the dispute was not simply a matter of business expediency. The dispute cost the company more than making concessions to the workers would have done. In an unsent press statement, Dwyer revealed that 'since this dispute started our sales have fallen to such an extent that over one hundred workers have been disemployed.'[56] Similarly, the board of Sunbeam unanimously agreed that, 'should the managing director, after taking legal opinion on the matter, consider it in the company's interest not to compromise in any way with the travellers, the Board would support him *regardless of loss to the company*'.[57] The real reasoning behind Dwyer's resolute and obstinate behaviour with regard to the commercial travellers is revealed in a letter to business partner C.O. Stanley:

> It is my opinion that ... this firm should not give in, as I think it is a matter of vital importance that an employer *would have the right* to dismiss surplus hands or hands who are not suitable for the particular jobs they are doing.[58]

The dispute was, therefore, primarily a question surrounding the rights and authority of Dwyer as the capitalist owner, whose power over employment and dismissal had been challenged by the commercial travellers. Ultimately, the situation was resolved to the satisfaction of the CTF members at Sunbeam. Although Dwyer was prepared to accept the existence of trade unions, he was unwilling to allow them to challenge the perceived rights and authority of the managing director. When trade unions stepped outside of their prescribed limits, William Dwyer was more than willing to take them on. However, the company's defeat in the CTF dispute demonstrated the power of the resurgent trade union movement in the 1930s. Like other contemporary employers, Dwyer was forced to accept limitations on his power and authority.

PATERNALIST TRADITIONS AND CATHOLICISM

William Dwyer was not the first paternalist employer to exist in Ireland. Quaker industrialists, for example, had been well known in the country for paternalist business practices since the nineteenth century. Betty Messenger's research on women workers in the Belfast linen industry also notes the presence of several paternalist workplaces.[59] Cork was no exception. An article in *The Irish Times* in 1963 describes the city's business tradition as being characterised by a 'blend of initiative and paternalism'.[60] Paternalism seems to have been a more general feature of the city's woollen industry. Edward Lahiff notes of Blarney Woollen Mills, which in 1890 was the largest such concern in the county, that, *'like the other large woollen works* in the area ... it was a paternalistic company, building cottages, a dining hall, reading rooms and a school for the workers and their families'.[61] Similarly, D.J. Coakley, describing the woollen manufacturers in Cork city and county in 1919, writes that 'the cheap land surrounding the factories has enabled the employers to carry out proper housing schemes for their workers'.[62] Indeed, the previous occupant of the Millfield factory, James Ogilvie's Cork Spinning and Weaving Company, was a paternalistic enterprise also, as evidenced by the firm's construction of labourers' dwellings.[63] William Dwyer, therefore, inherited a pre-existing tradition of paternalist labour relations that was already an established trend in local and national business practices.

William and Declan Dwyer's employment policies were also influenced by religion. Máire Leane and Elizabeth Kiely state that 'William Dwyer was ... a devout Catholic, who embraced Catholic social teaching on the duty of employers to workers, as enunciated in the papal encyclical *Quadragesimo Anno*', which 'advised of the need to cultivate greater solidarity between capitalist employers and workers'.[64] His piety and commitment to Catholic social teaching appears to have been sincere. In 1950, for example, he organised two staff pilgrimages to Rome, chartering several planes and covering half the cost of the expedition.[65] While in Rome, he was even granted an audience with the pope.[66] Although Sunbeam had always been a generous employer, it was during the Second World War that this generosity was institutionalised by the setting up of the Sunbeam Social Services Society. The society was a voluntary body within the factory, which workers could join with a small subscription, and included both managers and workers on its committee.[67] The society was responsible for many of the facilities available at Sunbeam, including the expansion of the existing medical amenities, the construction of employee baths and the establishment of a lending library.[68] The introduction of such schemes, in which both management and workers participated in aspects of the running of the company, was suggested in *Quadragesimo Anno*:

> We consider it more advisable, however, in the present condition of human society that, so far as is possible, the work-contract be somewhat modified by a partnership-contract, as is already being done in various ways and with no small advantage to workers and owners. Workers and other employees thus become sharers in ownership or management or participate in some fashion in the profits received.[69]

Dwyer's introduction of a Social Services Society received the support of the clergy when the local bishop 'gave his cordial approval and blessing' to the undertaking, noting that, 'in the last fifty years especially, the Church had exercised a very important influence on the relations between employer and employee'.[70] Similarly, Reverend O'Donnell, a member of An Ríoghacht (a lay Catholic organisation dedicated to implementing the papal encyclicals) noted that it was 'gratifying to see that Irish companies, like Sunbeam Wolsey, were showing that a Catholic country was putting into practice the principles of their sociology'.[71]

Dwyer's adoption of Catholic social teaching in practice formed part of a more general tendency within Irish society during and after the Second World War. From the 1920s onwards, initiatives to put Catholic social teaching into practice were intensified. The Catholic Action movement became a major force in Ireland, founding influential and long-lasting organisations, such as

Muintir na Tíre (established in 1931).[72] *Liberty* magazine reflected the commitment to Catholic social teaching in the trade union movement. A 1952 article, for example, called on management to 'look upon its shops as social institutions in which the employees are entitled to citizenship'.[73] In line with its commitment to Catholic principles of industrial relations, the magazine included a regular feature on firms that implemented these in practice. An examination of various issues of *Liberty* in this period indicates that paternalist measures, similar to those at Sunbeam, were introduced in a significant number of firms across the country in the post-war period.[74] Dwyer's Catholic paternalism reflected a more general ideological hegemony enjoyed by Catholic social teaching within Irish society in the 1940s and '50s.

Dwyer's Catholicism was an important factor in Sunbeam's employee welfare policies, but there was also a more pragmatic element. Dwyer noted that the introduction of medical facilities had led to a 30 per cent decrease in the amount spent on sickness benefit.[75] Similarly, company publications expressed the hope that the provision of fringe benefits would aid productivity, commenting that 'the feeling that good work will get grateful recognition is itself a powerful incentive to greater efforts'.[76] The same pamphlet also noted that 'the pleasant human relations which exist between the management and its employees' were its greatest asset and that initiatives bridging the gap between employers and workers gave them a 'personal interest in the wellbeing of the firm that employs them'.[77] Dwyer also hoped that the cultivation of ties of loyalty between workers and management would be a safeguard against industrial unrest, declaring that, 'what will settle all strikes is the absolute loyalty … of the Staff and the Workers here to their Capitalist managing director'.[78]

However, whatever the ideological or cultural bases of paternalism, a profitable company in an economically favourable environment was necessary for capitalists to choose the strategy of industrial paternalism in the first place. Morris and Smyth note that paternalism necessitates considerable capital and expenditure to be established and maintained.[79] It was Fianna Fáil's protectionist economic policies that shielded Sunbeam from competition and gave the company its cutting edge within the industry. When these policies were later rescinded, paternalism ceased to be a viable policy for the company.

THE SINKING OF THE 'HAPPY SHIP', 1965–80

As late as 1966, the Cork Economic Development Council was using Sunbeam as an example of friendly labour relations in the city in order to attract foreign investment.[80] Within just a few years, however, this situation had changed drastically, coinciding with the challenges the company faced in the late 1960s (see Chapter Two). There were rumblings as early as 1968, when members of the National Electrical and Engineering Trade Union (NEETU) picketed the premises. Even though the dispute only concerned the hosiery mechanical workers (a small minority of the total workforce), between 800 and 900 workers refused to pass the picket.[81] One local newspaper commented that the strike was 'believed to be the first major shutdown at the Sunbeam factory for many years though there have been minor disputes and unofficial stoppages'.[82] Three years later, an even larger stoppage occurred when 1,200 workers took unofficial strike action over the dismissal of a technician. A company spokesman commented at the time that 'it was difficult to believe that a union of the size and stature of the ITGWU could not effectively control its members' and that 'this type of tactic had become prevalent of late in the company'.[83]

These clashes, however, were mere preludes to the 'big strike' of 1975. The dispute began when the company attempted to introduce a three-day working week in three departments at Millfield and to make redundancies on the basis of department rather than the factory as a whole. The ITGWU rejected this proposal and demanded redundancies on a factory-wide 'first-in, last-out' basis instead. However, when workers in the half-hose, nylon-knitting and underwear divisions arrived at the plant on Monday, 6 January 1975 they found the departments shut.[84] ITGWU members in the plant voted 'overwhelmingly' in favour of strike action,[85] and the following Monday there was a complete stoppage at the factory when 700 workers in the affected sections withdrew their labour.[86] One hundred clerical workers were also put out of work due to the effects of the dispute. Two aspects of the strike that stand out were the militancy of the workers and the intransigence of management. The strikers organised a march from the city centre to the plant, where they occupied the boardroom and remained there for the following two nights.[87] When office staff attempted to access the building, the workers barricaded the corridors to prevent them from entering.[88] On the management side, the board had repeatedly ignored Labour Court recommendations and consistently insisted that the ITGWU meet with departmental managers rather than company representatives.[89] On 21 February 1975, the strikers voted to return to work in exchange for some concessions from management. The strike had lasted nearly six weeks.[90] From an island of industrial peace, Sunbeam had become one of the most strike-afflicted factories in the city.

Few could have imagined that the tranquil labour relations enjoyed previously at Sunbeam could have fallen apart as quickly and as dramatically as they did. How had this state of affairs come about? The key factor was the introduction of free trade. Scranton writes that since not all firms are paternalist, those that are become vulnerable to competition from more ruthless competitors.[91] Prior to the 1960s, Sunbeam's monopolistic domination of Irish textiles had allowed the company to offer generous wages and benefits to its staff. Manager Tom Scott was headhunted by Sunbeam in the late 1950s. Having been involved in the textile and clothing industries in Nottingham, he found the generous employment conditions at Sunbeam to be a 'culture shock', noting that the paternalist management practices he experienced there, 'protected from the harsh, cruel world of competition', were a world away from the free trade conditions he had known in Britain.[92]

During the 1970s and '80s, the liberalisation of the Irish economy saw the end of Sunbeam's isolation. As discussed in Chapter Two, the textile and clothing industries suffered particularly harshly at the hands of foreign competition. The Sunbeam Group's 1975 annual report reveals how devastating this period was for the company:

> A recession has occurred at international level in clothing and textiles, making competition so intense that we could not sell profitably in most of our Companies ... Some of our activities had to be closed or severely curtailed involving losses over and above normal trading losses ... This Company [Sunbeam Ltd, the Millfield factory rather than the Sunbeam Group] producing knitwear, underwear, half-hose and tights had an extremely bad year, due to decreased demand, labour difficulties and high operating expenses.[93]

The new economic climate meant the introduction of redundancies and short-time working. Between 1973 and 1975, 340 jobs were lost in the outerwear department alone.[94] Similarly, the company was forced to 'cut back' on many of the fringe benefits previously provided to Sunbeam employees.[95] The new, more aggressive approach to be adopted by company management was spelt out by new Sunbeam Group Director William Kiley in 1971:

You are going to have to face 7-day working on four shifts. Why should Irish people work 7 days 4-shifts for foreign firms and not for us? Restrictions will have to go on the hours of employment of female labour. I have been in textile factories in France where the female labour actually works on night shifts. I am not saying it is right, but, gentlemen, we are going into a Free Trade area and this is what it means, that the people who work the hardest are the people who are going to survive. The people who do not want to work are not going to survive. The companies who do not will go under.[96]

In addition to these factory-specific factors, other developments were important in the outbreak of militancy at Sunbeam Wolsey. The crisis in the textile industry took place against a backdrop of unprecedented industrial strength on the part of the trade union movement, which had a total membership of 576,000 by 1975.[97] The relatively high employment levels in Ireland during the first half of the 1970s increased labour's bargaining power dramatically. This superior bargaining power was reflected in the victories won by the workforce in the 1968 and 1971 strikes.

The increased militancy of Sunbeam workers was not unique within the industry in this period. Between 1972 and 1975, there were significant strikes in Westport Textiles, the Danus Clothing Company in Limerick and Blarney Woollen Mills.[98] Sunbeam business documents reflect a more generalised industrial unrest within the wider Sunbeam Group. There were strikes within five subsidiaries in 1975 alone as workers sought to either maintain wages or restore them to earlier levels.[99]

The extent of the changes that occurred in Sunbeam in the post-1965 era was articulated by shop steward Frank Wallace (born 1933 in Blackpool, Cork city; general operative/presser at Sunbeam Wolsey from c.1950). Like other Sunbeam workers, he described the history of the company in terms of a 'golden era' under William Dwyer, which then degenerated under his successors:

> Sunbeam ... they were a major company ... The welfare that William Dwyer brought in ... that was unknown at the time, but they were very good. He was miles ahead of everyone in his thinking about the welfare of the workers. He ensured as far as he possibly could that working conditions were excellent in comparison to what was happening on the outside. He was unique in his foresight, in his thinking. There was nothing like it in Cork ... he was outstanding ... Everyone respected him ... His son took over then, Declan, he was no William. He had a very hard act to follow, and he couldn't.[100]

Compared with his glowing description of Sunbeam under the elder Dwyer, Frank's impressions of the company's behaviour during the 1970s were highly critical. He even suggested that management 'were out to break the union' at that time.[101] Frank described the 1975 dispute as a 'lockout' rather than a strike, and regarded the six-week industrial conflict as a watershed in the history of the company: 'Things were never the same after that. There was a lot of tension.'[102] However, while also employing the 'golden age' narrative, Frank attributed the negative changes in the company to the effects of free trade. Indeed, while some narrators attributed Sunbeam's decline and deteriorating industrial relations to declining standards of management under William Dwyer's successors, these changes in ownership merely coincided with the ending of protectionism. It was the changes wrought by free trade, not the end of Dwyer control, that led to the rapid and unhappy transformation of industrial relations at Sunbeam.

QUIESCENCE AND DECLINE, 1980-90

After the mid-1970s high point of labour unrest in the factory, the 1980s was an era of industrial peace, and industrial decline, for the Millfield factory. This reduction in strike activity was a more general feature of the textile and clothing industry at the time. One 1983 report noted that industrial relations in the textile and clothing trades were less conflictual than in other sectors in terms of days lost to industrial action or absenteeism.[103] In the broader context of redundancies and closures within the declining industry, and a generalised economic recession, workers were poorly placed to act in defence of jobs and conditions. This reduction in bargaining power had been noted as early as 1973 by *Liberty*, which remarked that future redundancies in the textiles and clothing sectors meant that workers in those industries were less likely to 'discriminate between the good and the bad employer'.[104] In the more specific case of Sunbeam, the fact that the Millfield factory was a poor performer within the wider Sunbeam Group gave management the upper hand in negotiations.

A threatened strike by Sunbeam knitters in 1982 demonstrated this altered power relationship. During the lengthy negotiations, management discussed what actions to take. Among the options discussed was to

> threaten closure to get ultimate agreement on terms acceptable to us. The strategy around this proposal would need very detailed consideration as it would be very difficult to do without causing widespread disruption and possible irrecoverable losses to the company.[105]

These threats were not idle. Another option considered was simply to 'close the division/company as with employee attitudes and other problems it has no prospects now or in the future of making profit'.[106] Management's casual consideration of either threatened or actual closure reflects the poor bargaining position that Sunbeam workers faced in the context of a declining industry. Marian Hickey (born c.1950 in Cork city; general operative at Sunbeam, 1960s–1972; returned part-time during the 1980s), who came back to work at Sunbeam during this period of economic turbulence, described how the interplay of economic hardship and aggressive management led to the decline of pay and working conditions:

> Then the work got scarce ... it wasn't a nice place then. The girls would be fighting over work ... There was no work there ... The work got harder. You really had to work because they cut the devil out of all the time, so you really weren't making a big load of money ... They cut the minutes on everything. Cut everything so it was different ... Things were harder and the orders weren't there.[107]

The picture painted by Marian, of a decline in solidarity and an increase in competition over scarce work, is corroborated by June Hickey, who worked in the underwear department in the same period:

> There was all different departments and that was it. The underwear stuck together, the knitwear stuck together and any time anything happened there and you asked someone out of the department to stick in, they never done it. They never, ever, anyone out there stuck together ... they'd never actually stand up together.[108]

This apparent atomisation stands in contrast to the solidarity shown during unofficial, wildcat strikes at Sunbeam during the late 1960s and early 1970s. In the same interview, June mentioned that she once engaged in a one-woman strike over unpaid holiday money. Though told in a joking manner, this humour masks her frustrations – as a shop steward – over the lack of worker solidarity in the factory:

> Catherine Fray: Did you remember a strike? Do you ever remember any strike and if there was a strike or even a fall out would you think the people would stick together?
> June Hickey: No.
> CF: No way?
> JH: No way. I was the only one that went out on strike on me own (laugh) I did me.
> CF: You?
> JH: I did, yeah.
> CF: And what happened then?
> JH: I got no wages.
> CF: Ah June, come on, this is serious now.
> JH: I got no wages. They wouldn't pay me no holiday money, so I sat on the machine on my own.
> CF: Right.
> JH: Yeah, and then I got what I wanted.
> CF: And whose fault was it? Management?
> JH: Management of course.[109]

Linda McCarthy's account of the same period also depicts a significant change in the employment relationship at Sunbeam, suggesting a breakdown in trust between workers and union representatives, as well as management taking advantage of fears regarding the future of the plant (particularly its less profitable sections) to assert its authority:

> There was always a threat hanging over the underwear division that it was going to close … One of the top union

reps that at the time when, when the union weren't strong anymore – through doing the wages I knew what was going on – there was a man in the knitting floor, and ... he wouldn't have been now a hundred percent mentally, but he was there for years and years and years ... And anyway he ... they were trying to get rid of him off the knitting floor, they were really starting to tighten up now at this stage ... it was kinda gone from being the *nice* management and the *nice* Sunbeam ... it was really now work and sorta stuff, so they, they were trying to get rid of him, and there was no budging. The knitters were saying 'no way!' and this and that, and the union rep actually in charge of the section he was in and the knitting floor section, got around all the knitters ... The man was left go, and the union rep got a [slaps her hand to illustrate] backhander onto his wages.[110]

Living fearfully in the shadow of closure, the workforce at Millfield remained largely quiescent until their fears were finally realised in 1990.

Sunbeam's remaining workers did not quietly accept this closure; they launched a brief but vigorous campaign to save the factory. When Sunbeam went into receivership the workforce relied on political and trade union officials to negotiate a satisfactory redundancy agreement. When the workers felt that their interests were not being represented well in the negotiations, sixty employees staged a three-week sit-in during March 1990.[111] The workers also mobilised community support by organising a protest march in support of the occupation.[112] When the occupiers were persuaded to call off their sit-in later that month, the secured agreement was highly disappointing, with minimal redundancy payments and the dismissal of the majority of the workforce. Jim Cronin, a Services, Industrial, Professional and Technical Union (SIPTU) shop steward and leading figure in the campaign to save the factory, regarded the deal as a betrayal.[113] The workers even threatened to run their own candidates in the forthcoming general election, either to pressure the community's political representatives or to punish them for their failure to secure adequate terms.[114]

However, little came of these threats. The ending of the sit-in had deprived the workforce of their last major bargaining chip: the plant and its machinery. The campaign was a failure. While a small firm continued trading in the Millfield premises under the name 'Sunbeam Industries' into the 1990s, the redundancies announcement of 1990 marked the end of Sunbeam as a major employer in Cork.

CONCLUSION

One scholar has noted that 'workers do not simply enter work and then seek means of resistance. Instead, they find means of living with the system as they find it.'[115] The workers who entered Sunbeam in the 1940s and '50s chose the route of accommodation to reap the benefits in terms of wages and conditions that paternalism provided. Those who entered, or remained in the firm in the 1970s chose instead the route of resistance in the face of threats to their jobs, wages and conditions. In the 1980s, Cork's transformation into an unemployment black spot and the constant threat of closure blunted the industrial edge of the much-reduced Sunbeam workforce. In the next chapter, we observe how a broadly similar pattern – pacific labour relations established under the rubric of protectionism, followed by industrial conflict during the transition to free trade conditions and, finally, a gradual consolidation of managerial power in those new conditions – also characterised the labour history of Irish Steel, albeit with important and significant differences.

6

Working for Irish Steel, 1939–2001

INTRODUCTION

In September 2006, a local newsletter in Cobh reported on the recent demolition of the Irish Steel plant on Haulbowline Island:

> After providing seventy years of employment to generations of Cobh people, the last big structure of what once was the great Irish Steel plant was brought down last Thursday evening ... the people of Cobh gathered at various points around the town in anticipation of the historic event ... While many of those who looked on might have harboured mixed memories about their old work place, all who watched the final curtain close on the plant were left in no doubt that they were witnessing a significant historical event.[1]

The article accurately summarises the complicated legacy of the steel mill for both its workforce and the town that had relied heavily on it for so long. A few decades earlier, a reporter from *The Irish Press* had interviewed Irish Steel employees and Cobh residents about the importance of the factory to the town. According to the newspaper, the workers of Irish Steel were men who 'have worked all their life, some of them straight from school, at Haulbowline: they have never known unemployment'.[2] For these local workers, Irish Steel was an integral 'part of Cobh'.[3] The centrality of the steelworks to the small seaside town was spelt out by locals:

Before Verolme and the Dockyard, before gas and NET, the one and only constant in the industrial life of the town was the steelworks. Wages here were good, management was good. Cobh, which had been drained by emigration, became a place in which a worker and his family could live in dignity.[4]

While the Irish Steel plant had provided long-term and significant employment for three-quarters of a century, its legacy was mixed. In the later years of its existence it had a tumultuous industrial relations record, marked by militancy among the plant's craftworkers. In those years, the firm's dogged battle to survive saw drastic changes, culminating in privatisation, closure, and what many Irish Steel workers saw as betrayal at the hands of the Irish state and Ispat (the Indian multinational that operated the factory for the last five years of its existence). Moreover, the secure and highly paid employment in the plant came at a cost to the health and lives of many of its employees in what was widely acknowledged to be a physically demanding and dangerous workplace.

This chapter examines the history of work in Irish Steel from its inception in 1939 to its eventual closure in 2001. We begin by examining occupational health at Irish Steel, providing a descriptive account of the dangerous and demanding conditions of labour there. We then examine the changing industrial relations of the company over the course of its existence. This latter section pays particular attention to the six-month strike that occurred at Irish Steel in 1977 and the gradual decline of militancy among the plant workforce.

'IT WAS A TOUGH, HARD JOB': WORKING CONDITIONS AND OCCUPATIONAL SAFETY

A 1938 visitor to the (then-unfinished) Irish Steel plant was deeply impressed by the modernity of the industry and was of the opinion that the Haulbowline facility was going to defy the popular perception of the steel mill as a brutal and demanding place of work:

> All steel mills are much the same, little worlds full of hot metal, sometimes glowing, sometimes black, but always hot and creating an atmosphere in which it seems men should shrivel and fade away. But they don't; the steel mills develop hardy, wiry men, greatly skilled in the control of machinery and of somewhat sedentary habits, just because of their occupations. There was a time in steel production when only hulking giants were regarded as qualified for steel works, but modern power methods have made a vast difference.[5]

The visitor's impression was more than a little naïve. One of the most notable aspects of Irish Steel (especially when compared with Sunbeam Wolsey and the Ford Marina plant) was the dangerous and arduous nature of work at the factory.[6]

Before major changes were introduced in the early 1980s, conditions at Irish Steel were recalled as being less than desirable. Jim Shealy (born 1950 in Cobh; tongsman at Irish Steel rolling mills, *c.*1973–80) remembered:

> There were lockers, there was no place to change your clothes, you went to work and worked in the same clothes that you went home in so you effectively went into work with your clothes wringing with sweat and there was no place that you had a shower, toilets were there but they were primitive ... And 'twas really very backward.[7]

However, the spartan conditions of the plant were less significant than the dangers of working there. While there are no exact records or statistics for the number of deaths and injuries in Irish

Steel, newspaper evidence and the recollections of narrators make it clear that Irish Steel was an especially dangerous place. To take just two of the recorded examples, the earliest death reported at the plant was that of Michael O'Riordan, who in 1950 was crushed to death when an overhead trolley slipped from its platform and fell on top on of him from a height of twenty feet.[8] One particular death, notable for its extreme nature rather than the fact that it occurred, saw a worker die from burns received when he found himself suspended waist-high in sulphuric acid.[9]

When asked about the dangers of working for Irish Steel, former employees were frank in their assessment. Despite the benefits of job security and good wages provided by the company, Jim Shealy recalled that many new employees in the 1970s were put off by the harshness of the conditions there:

> You were thrown in at the deep end straight away. Immediately. There was no training. There was no health and safety. You were there. It was very, very labour-intensive. And you either did it … If you stuck the first couple of shifts you were okay, if you didn't, you just left. It's what a lot of people just did. Fear or otherwise.[10]

Despite having worked in construction, engineering and heavy industry, Jim considered Irish Steel to be a particularly demanding place:

> The conditions of employment, they were really bad there because, from a health and safety point of view, there wasn't any … I don't even think you were given a … you were given a pair of gloves alright. You were given really rough, crude gloves and the gloves themselves would actually cut your hands, there was some material that was … you were given, if you were working in and around the really hot areas

by the furnaces, you were given clogs, wooden clogs, that were absolutely, totally uncomfortable. The heat was just unimaginable.[11]

The furnace was by far the most physically demanding part of the facility, and workers' descriptions of it echo the hellish depictions of the Ford foundry discussed in Chapter One. According to Billy McMurty (born 1938 in south Armagh; crane driver and security guard at Irish Steel, 1960s to 1990s), foundry work was a 'horrible job … it was a tough job. They were men of steel as a matter of fact. I didn't envy them at all.'[12] Christy Buckley (born 1930 in Cobh; foundry operative at Irish Steel, 1950s–90s) simply described it as 'a madhouse'.[13] The intense heat and brutal working conditions of the foundry meant that employees would try to avoid being placed there if they possibly could. For example, Robert Walsh (born 1950 in the Lower Harbour area; fitter's mate at Irish Steel, 1960s–1980s) was initially taken on as a worker in the furnace. However, when a relative heard that he was to be sent to the foundry, he personally intervened to ensure that Robert was given a different position.[14] Christy Buckley, a long-term employee of Irish Steel, well-acquainted with the dangers of the plant, discouraged his sons from seeking employment there.[15]

DEATHS AND INJURIES

Former employees of Irish Steel were understandably reluctant to discuss individual deaths and injuries. This reticence can be attributed to the emotional effect of serious accidents on the workers themselves. Friends, relatives and spouses of workers who experienced death and injury in the plant were often still living with the personal impact of such accidents. Nevertheless, while ensuring the anonymity of those who died or were injured,

6.1 Irish Steel tongsmen at work, 1951.
Photo reproduced with the kind permission of the *Irish Examiner.*

many workers described the hazards of life in the steelworks and the human consequences of such a dangerous environment. Jim Shealy recalled one of his colleagues, a tongsman,[16] in the rolling mills:

> He'd have been working there longer than me. He would have had more experience. But, in spite of that, all the experience in the world wouldn't have stood to him for what happened. It was in the rolling mills and ... a cobble was when the bar was fed into the wrong channel. The channels, the bars, would be ... calibrated. And if, by any chance, in the positioning of the bars going into the rolls, that the bar went into the wrong channel, maybe the one on the right or the one on the left of the particular channel they should have gone into, it came out in a distorted shape and it was known as a cobble. But when it came out in a distorted shape ... it was out of control, and it was ... driven out by the power of the rolls and the motors but ... the reaction of the people on the floor when

this happened, and it happened very regularly, was that – you were always aware that it could happen – that you just ran and got out of there ... and left it be fed through. But it appears that ah, the person who was killed had their back turned to it and I think it clipped one of the steel plates on the floor and it flipped the plate up on top of the individual, trapping him underneath, and the bar itself when it came out of the roll, it rested on top of the plate that he was trapped under. It was pretty horrific.[17]

Robert Walsh estimated that there were five deaths at the plant during the 1970s:

I remember walking past the scrapyard one day. And I walked past a girder, the girder holding up the scrapyard crane. And I heard a thump and I went around the girder and 'twas a chap after falling off. He was welding up on the rail and he fell off it and he was dead obviously, like ... So I ran and got the ambulance, got him into it, up to St Finbarr's hospital ... he was dead obviously on arrival ... Another chap got burned to death ... [Another] got two legs taken off by a bulldozer. There was another chap fell off a building ... another chap lost his leg ... he got squashed between a crane and a trailer.[18]

Placing this anecdotal evidence within a broader domestic context is a difficult task due to the paucity of official data on occupational safety in post-war Ireland.[19] The 1983 Barrington Commission on workplace safety, for example, found itself frustrated by the lack of reliable data on workplace injuries in general: 'Not a great deal is known about the state of occupational health in Ireland. There is little published data on the topic, poor statistics and few specialists.'[20] The best sources available are the annual reports of the Factory Inspectorate.[21] These reports, however, possess some flaws, not least due to the meagre resources of the inspectorate. In 1968, for example, the authority employed just twenty-four inspectors, who were responsible for monitoring some 13,000 premises (of which 9,637 were visited).[22] The inspectors complained of being 'under very severe and sustained pressure to meet the demands being made upon them'.[23] Additionally, the accidents recounted in the reports are only referred to with regard to broad industrial groupings and in such a way as to make it difficult to identify specific factories. In the case of Irish Steel, accident and fatality rates are considered, until 1972, under the broad category of 'Metal Manufacture and Engineering', a heading that includes primary metal manufacturing, secondary industries (such as steel wire concerns) and unrelated engineering firms. After this date, the category was narrowed to 'General Iron and Steel Manufacture', which we can take to refer only to Irish Steel and several iron foundries, allowing more precise analysis.

Accepting the limitations described above, we can still go some way towards placing occupational safety in Irish Steel within a broader context. Taking 1966, and cross-referencing the Industrial Inspectorate report for that year with the 1966 census, we obtain a broad picture of accident and fatality rates.[24] Comparing the annual accident rates for several industrial groupings, including the highly dangerous construction industry and the category of 'Metal Manufacture and Engineering', we find some telling figures.[25] Even allowing for some flaws in the collection process, the data clearly demonstrate that the broad category of 'Metal Manufacture and Engineering' (employing only 13,044 people) had a notably high incidence of accidents (2.62 per cent), especially when compared with the other larger industries (Textiles: 0.9 per cent, Food: 1.38 per cent and Construction: 0.24 per cent) included in the results.[26] This rate is nearly three times the 1961 average accident rate of 0.96 per cent given by Francis Devine.[27]

Moving ahead a few years, comparing the 1969 inspectorate report with the 1966 census, narrowing our categories and including fatality rates, we see that the 'Metal Manufacture and Engineering' category, despite the relatively low numbers employed, remained a particularly dangerous industry, with a death rate of 0.03 per cent (compared with 0.01 per cent in construction) and an accident rate of 2.5 per cent (compared with 0.38 per cent in construction).[28] Once again, a picture of an industry characterised by high accident and mortality rates emerges. Even when compared with the notoriously dangerous construction sector, we discover that a worker was three times more likely to lose their life in the 'Metal Manufacture and Engineering' sector than on a building site. The accident and mortality rates are particularly noteworthy when compared with Francis Devine's estimates for 1971, which had a general accident rate of 1.06 per cent and a mortality rate of 0.01 per cent for all industry.[29]

Finally, the inspectorate's narrowing of the category of 'Metal Manufacture and Engineering' to 'General Iron and Steel Manufacture' (representing just 3,774 workers in the 1971 census) is highly revealing due in its greater precision. 'General Iron and Steel Manufacture' suffered accident rates of 2.65 per cent and 3.2 per cent in 1973 and 1974, respectively.[30] The lack of substantial change in accident and death rates between the 1960s reports (with their substantially broader categorisation) tallies with the perception that foundry work was particularly dangerous and responsible for a disproportionate number of accidents and fatalities. Moreover, within the narrowed category, the same high mortality rates observed in previous decades are replicated, reaching a brutal nadir of 0.05 per cent in 1973.[31] Thus, even allowing for under-reporting and other potential flaws regarding the data collected, the statistical evidence supports the oral evidence presented by former Irish Steel workers of a highly dangerous (even life-threatening) industry.

Given the evidence presented thus far in relation to the hazardous conditions of work at Irish Steel, an interesting feature of the oral testimony was the extent to which deaths and injuries were simply considered an accepted part of life on Haulbowline:

> Jim Shealy: It could be very frightening, looking back on it, it was terrifying. But we didn't realise that at the time.[32]
>
> Fionnán Kerrigan (born 1967 in 'The Lough', Cork city; general operative and later production manager at Irish Steel, 1987–2001): I got out of there without having a major accident, but there was guys there missing fingers, buckled legs, bad burns, that was a common occurrence … But it was like everywhere else, you got used to it.[33]

The hardships and dangers of Irish Steel were typical of steelmaking more generally. Martin Upham, for example, notes that in 1957 one out of every sixteen steelworkers in the British industry suffered some kind of accident, despite the fact that UK safety legislation was generally regarded as second to none.[34] David Hall suggests that, regardless of legislation, heavy industries in the post-war era remained inherently dangerous.[35] Robert Bruno, describing the American industry, concurs. He writes that a steel mill is 'a dangerous place to make a living and produce a good product. Every worker knew the dangers of mill work … Accidents and injuries were … common', but this was 'a contradiction that workers had to accept, it was the source of livelihood and the most threatening part of life'.[36]

The perilous and arduous nature of steelmaking, and similar industries, was therefore a much wider phenomenon. Indeed, Irish Steel workers often seemed to demonstrate an acceptance of the dangers they faced and rationalised them as being integral to the nature of the industry:

> Billy McMurty: There was always accidents, small and big. There was bound to be, a heavy industry like that.[37]
>
> Tony Cummins (born 1944 in Cobh; rolling mill operative at Irish Steel, 1966–2001): It [the danger] is part and parcel of steelmaking.[38]

As Robert Walsh laconically put it: 'That was the nature of the job.'[39] These comments reflect Arthur McIvor's observation that dangerous work was regarded as a normal feature of life among men in working-class communities.[40] These dangers do not seem to have been seriously questioned by the workers themselves, except during the process of reflection engendered by the oral history interview. The resigned and accepting attitude of Irish Steel employees to the danger they faced can in part be attributed to the social construction of male working identity described in Chapter Eight. To face danger and to endure hardship was to manifest 'manly' virtues.[41]

As we discuss in Chapter Seven, the main motivating factors for male jobseekers were pay and employment security. This attitude was reflected in the fact that every recorded strike at Irish Steel was taken in response either to wage disputes, work practices or dismissals. Safety and personal security were often of secondary importance to male aspirations to be a respected worker and breadwinner. Narrators suggested that the security and high pay available in Irish Steel was viewed as adequate recompense for the toughness and danger of the factory. Fionnán Kerrigan, for example, complained that it was a 'dirty, filthy job' but that 'the money was the end of the day for me'.[42] Billy McMurty expressed similar sentiments: 'If you're in a dangerous job, you're entitled to be compensated for it.'[43] Jim Shealy, when asked why working at the plant was considered desirable despite the dangers, explained that 'they weren't exactly a beneficial employer other than that they wanted their pound of flesh ... but they had to pay for it'.[44] The importance of the breadwinner ideology in influencing decisions relating to work and the centrality of wages often meant that the availability of a steady income took precedence over potential risks to the body. Billy McMurty highlighted this feature when he spoke of the risks faced by workers at Haulbowline: 'A lot of people wouldn't go in there ... [but] you'd no option if you had a family really.'[45]

The narrators were unanimous in their opinions that health, safety and working conditions all improved greatly from the late 1970s onwards. Even after these changes, however, the steel mill remained a dangerous workplace. For example, between 1993 and 2001 alone, three workers lost their lives at Irish Steel.[46] In one incident – the death of a worker who fell from a crane – the company faced prosecution from the Health and Safety Authority, who accused it of breaching safety legislation. Pleading guilty to the charges, the company was forced to pay a fine for its failure to observe the law.[47] Even until its final days, Irish Steel remained a workplace where the danger of injury and death was a permanent feature.

The overall evidence for Irish industry suggests that occupational safety was not given adequate consideration by either workers or employers. The Industrial Inspectorate, the sole organisation dedicated entirely to protecting the body at work, frequently complained that this dedication was not shared by others. The authority's 1968 report, for example, outlined how most fatal accidents that year

> would not have happened if adequate attention had been given to the observance of the minimum safety standards laid

down by law ... All of them could have been prevented if the recognised safety precautions had been taken.[48]

The previous year, the inspectorate had complained of 'carelessness and indifference to statutory safety provisions'.[49] One indication of the lack of importance attributed to occupational safety, in an area in which worker agency could have been exercised successfully, was in relation to safety committees established as a statutory right for workers through the 1955 Factories Act. Devine writes that, despite constant urging from the minister for labour, the Industrial Inspectorate and some individual activists to establish safety committees in unionised workplaces (which they were legally entitled to do), the trade union response was lacklustre to non-existent.[50] By 1980, only 1.47 per cent of premises registered with the Industrial Inspectorate possessed such committees.[51]

It appears that an apparent indifference to occupational safety was characteristic of both Irish Steel and Irish industry in general. We have some indications as to why this situation prevailed. Both the evidence presented in the preceding pages and our examination of male working identities in Chapter Eight suggest that masculinity and risk-taking were intimately connected. This connection is expressed by Christy Buckley's preference for working 'with a bunch of men' in the foundry over less demanding areas of employment at Haulbowline, and Billy McMurty's admiring description of foundry workers as 'men of steel'. Irish Steel workers were willing to tolerate poor working conditions and the perennial danger of death and injury in exchange for high pay and employment security. When confronted with the brutal reality of the plant, these dangers could be simply ignored and dismissed as part and parcel of the steelmaking industry. As Johnston and McIvor note of post-war Scotland, 'the prevailing ethos incorporated a widespread acceptance of very high levels of risk, of dirt, fumes, dust and danger. This was part of the customary order of things – the way work had always been done.'[52] This workplace culture was replicated at Irish Steel.

Nevertheless, while masculinist work cultures can explain how danger and risk were understood, articulated and even accepted by workers, this factor alone is insufficient to explain the causes of occupational danger and, moreover, threatens to assign blame to the victims of occupational risk themselves. Johnston and McIvor note that only very rarely were workers themselves to blame for contributing to their own ill-health and mortality.[53] Masculinist work cultures 'provided an environment conducive to the incubation' of accidents and ill-health.[54] This work culture, when combined with the structural context of the innate inequality of the employment relationship, as well as a managerial focus on capital, profit and production to the neglect of the health and wellbeing of labour, made for a dangerous combination. Furthermore, the broader context of an Irish approach to health and safety that until 1980 was characterised by loose voluntarism rather than compulsion and regulation, as well as the apparent inaction of important actors in the state and the trade union movement, created a situation in which workers were subject to unnecessary risks to their lives and their bodies, both at Irish Steel and other dangerous industries in the Republic.[55]

INDUSTRIAL RELATIONS AT IRISH STEEL, 1939–77

If the safety record of Irish Steel was worthy of note, so too was its often dramatic history of industrial relations. In the early years of Irish Steel, the lack of a steelmaking tradition in Ireland meant that the workforce consisted of a mixture of unskilled local labour and foreign technicians with backgrounds in the industry. Management experienced trouble with these predominantly British employees in the early years of the firm. In their 1949 annual report, the directors complained that the foreign experts were 'arrogant', 'insubordinate' and 'not disposed to pass on their knowledge to local workers'.[56] Poor relations between these foreign technicians and management meant that 'the Directors had to intensify their efforts to loosen the grip which these non-Irish workers have over the industry'.[57] The matter came to a head in December 1948 when one of the English workers was fired for malicious damage and most of the foreign personnel left the company with him. Most of the skilled positions were quickly filled by Irishmen trained at local technical schools, and the number of non-national technicians in the firm fell from fifty to just eight.[58]

When Irish Steel came under state control in 1947 it inherited the union structures of the private company. Most of the workforce were organised in the ITGWU, while the tradesmen employed in the factory belonged to small craft unions catering for each individual trade. This structure remained in operation with little change until closure in 2001. In the early years of the firm, management often adopted a hard line that contrasted sharply with the approach developed in later years. In 1954, for example, there was an unofficial strike in the merchant mill. The general manager responded by sacking the strikers and used a mixture of non-unionised mill labour and 'gallant volunteers' from the unorganised office staff to break the strike. No sympathetic action emerged from the other sections of the plant, and the strikers were forced to capitulate after ten days.[59] Most of the workers were re-employed, but the ringleaders were immediately dismissed. Sarsfield Hogan, recalling the incident in 1980, noted that it was memorable only because 'in the light of present-day management/labour attitudes, it seems incredible that it ever could have happened'.[60]

Despite this tough management attitude, the ITGWU consolidated its position greatly during the 1950s, culminating in the recognition of a 'closed shop' in 1957.[61] The strengthening of the ITGWU's hand, combined with the power of the craft unions (representing fitters, plumbers, electricians and other skilled workers), led to a steady increase in the wages paid at the firm. Hogan believes that, 'on many grounds, the company would have preferred to deal with a single well-organised union'.[62] The multiplicity of craft unions, combined with strong ITGWU organisation in the plant, led to leapfrogging in wage negotiations. The tradesmen at Irish Steel possessed considerable industrial strength. They were primarily employed in maintenance, and without them the furnaces could not be kept in operation. Thus, despite representing a small minority of the total workforce, the craftworkers could halt production entirely. While the craft unions consistently negotiated significant pay increases, the ITGWU ensured that the pay of their unskilled members would mirror those increases in what Hogan describes as a 'tug of war'.[63] The maintenance of differentials meant that a pay increase for any section of the workforce would be immediately followed by claims from other sections. As such, the wages of both the skilled and unskilled workers in the plant rose consistently. In the early years of the firm, the wages of unskilled workers were tied to those of builders' labourers in the Cork area, a sum lower than the generally higher-than-average wages received by workers in larger manufacturing concerns.[64] By the end of the 1950s, the general workforce was receiving the average industrial wage, and by the mid-1980s the average wage in Irish Steel was nearly a third higher than that of an average manufacturing worker.[65]

The industrial relations record in Irish Steel prior to the 1977 strike was not especially dramatic. Hogan recalled only one instance of official strike action in the history of the plant: a brief strike by electricians in 1952. The narrators, when asked about strike activity, generally spoke immediately and solely about the long strike of 1977. Other disputes were mentioned, but were described as brief and of relatively little importance:

> Donal Brady (born 1932 in Shanbally; electrician at Irish Steel, 1960–94): There was a few small strikes there [over] small, niggly little things.[66]
>
> Robert Walsh: In all the years that I was there, a strike might last for two or three hours, might last for a day. I don't think there was ever any strike, any other strike that lasted more than a day, maybe forty-eight hours at the most.[67]
>
> Jim Shealy: There had been other strikes, lightning strikes, they would have been over, you know, some minor issue that could be, ah, resolved within twenty-four or forty-eight hours.[68]

This strike pattern corresponds broadly with the type of strike activity we describe in Chapter Eight and was typical of post-war Irish industry. The lack of significant strike action in Irish Steel prior to 1977, combined with the consistent increase in wages for both skilled and unskilled workers, suggests that management policy at the company was to avoid industrial action by acceding to the demands made by the unions. Since the industry was buffered by significant protective legislation, it could afford to make these concessions. When Ireland voted in favour of joining the EEC in 1972, however, it became clear that the status quo could not be maintained. The warm front of worker militancy met the cold front of a more aggressive management and a storm ensued.

THE 1977 STRIKE

1977 saw a major departure from the established pattern of industrial relations at Haulbowline. In March of that year, eighty-seven craftsmen placed two pickets at the Irish Steel plant. The craftsmen sought full implementation of a pay increase agreement made in 1972 and to ensure relativity of 20 per cent with the unskilled workers in the factory.[69] The remainder of the workforce (700 general operatives and office staff) were instructed by their unions to ignore the picket and did so.[70] That the pickets were passed was unusual. At both Sunbeam Wolsey and Henry Ford and Sons, there is abundant evidence to suggest that picket lines were almost never crossed by most workers, regardless of the nature of the dispute or the number of workers involved. The pickets placed by the Irish Steel craftsmen marked the beginning of a strike that would last for six months, inflict £5 million in losses on the company and cause significant divisions among the 800 or so men and women who worked for Ireland's only steel mill.

Lengthy and severe strike actions were not unusual in Ireland during the late 1970s. Indeed, the entire decade saw extremely high levels of strike activity within Irish industry. High employment levels combined with the introduction of redundancies, short-time working and pay freezes in the formerly protected industries led to increased industrial militancy across the country. Craft unions were particularly active during these years as tradesmen experienced nearly full employment within a broader context of rising trade union membership.[71]

Contemporary craft militancy was linked to the fact that, while Irish trade unions had increasingly become tied into corporatist structures such as national wage agreements, craft unions were generally opposed to centralised bargaining and were confident of winning pay increases due to their own industrial muscle.[72] This militancy was reflected in the number and severity of disputes involving craftworkers between the late 1960s and early 1980s. In 1974, for example, seventy craftsmen in the employ of Dublin Corporation took strike action, resulting in a dispute that lasted nearly two months and burdened the capital with some 30,000 tonnes of uncollected refuse.[73] In the summer of 1976, a six-week strike of craftsmen in Bord na Móna inflicted significant damage to the company and resulted in the laying off of 1,200 non-craft employees.[74] A seven-month strike by 149 craftworkers in the Tara Zinc mines in 1982 completely halted all production and resulted in the laying-off of 1,200 clerical workers and general operatives. Furthermore, in April 1974 a craft strike in the Guinness brewery raised the chilling prospect that 'the majority of public houses' would be unable to provide Guinness on draught.[75]

The power of Irish craft unions was demonstrated most clearly in the 1969 maintenance workers strike, the 'largest and most costly strike in the history of the state', between an alliance of craft unions and the Federated Union of Employers (FUE).[76] Although fewer than 2,000 men were 'directly on strike', the dispute shut down 142 firms, left over 31,000 workers idle, caused the loss of 636,000 man days and resulted in losses of £13.4 million in industrial production nationally.[77] All these disputes made it clear to government, industry and the craftworkers themselves what the latter were capable of when they flexed their muscles. Additionally, the Irish taboo of crossing picket lines under almost any circumstances meant that small numbers of tradesmen could often rely on the broader workforce to withdraw their labour in the event of strike action. Even in the highly divisive maintenance strike, a government investigation noted that strikers 'sought and got observance' of most of the pickets it placed, although this solidarity did not materialise in the case of the 1977 Irish Steel strike.[78]

While the specific factor of Irish craft militancy in the 1970s is crucial for understanding the 1977 Irish Steel strike, it should be noted that the industrial power and militancy of craftworkers was a more general phenomenon within certain industries. As contemporary craft disputes demonstrated, those industries most reliant on the maintenance of heavy machinery (the responsibility of craftsmen) were most vulnerable to strike action undertaken by tradesmen. The severity of the 1974 Dublin binmen's strike was primarily because the entire fleet of refuse trucks had broken down and could not be repaired due to the dispute, while the 1982 Tara Mines strike succeeded because the heavy machinery required for mining operations became unusable in the absence of the tradesmen.[79]

In this context, the 1977 Irish Steel strike was not especially significant in terms of its occurrence. What was most notable about the dispute, even compared with the most determined examples of contemporary craft militancy, was its duration. Of the three workplaces under examination, the 1977 Irish Steel strike was the longest by a wide margin. The second longest strike to occur in the three plants was the 1975 Sunbeam strike, which lasted for only six weeks.

An important reason for the prolonged nature of the dispute was the structure of craft organisation within the plant. The tradesmen were spread across six unions, which created immense problems in resolving the strike.[80] This multiplicity of unions meant that power was in the hands of the strike committee (the only body that represented all the strikers), which allowed militant shop stewards (rather than more conservative union officials) to direct the strike. For a resolution to be reached, it had to be agreed upon by each union, no matter how few workers it represented. In particular, the fact that the largest single craft union, the Amalgamated Union of Engineering Workers (AUEW), representing forty-one of the eighty-seven strikers, was British-based, and therefore outside of the Irish Congress of Trade Unions, presented major difficulties. For example, during one round of negotiations, held under the auspices of the Congress, the AUEW did not attend, were not immediately informed of the settlement proposals, and did not discuss them until long after the proposals were presented by management.[81] Andrew Pendleton notes that negotiating with multiple unions can be a slow process; sometimes, it could be positively glacial.[82] The convoluted and lengthy negotiations ended in September 1977, with the craft unions accepting a productivity package that provided pay increases ranging from £8 to £12 a week. This agreement was, on balance, a victory for the strikers.[83]

The impact of such a lengthy strike on the Cobh area was considerable. According to the *Evening Echo*, some fifty of the eighty-seven striking craftworkers were from Cobh, and based on estimates from former employees, a similar ratio can be assumed for the whole of the plant's manufacturing workforce.[84] In a town with a population of fewer than 7,000 people, the loss of nearly 800 workers had a drastic effect on the local economy. One journalist described how 'the strike had a shattering effect on the business and social life of the town ... Food suppliers were badly hit while hotels, lounges and places of entertainment also suffered severely'.[85] According to the chairman of Cobh Urban District Council, the area was 'on its knees'.[86]

An article by Jean Sheridan appeared in *The Irish Press* in August 1977, the fifth month of the strike. Based on extensive consultation with 'a large representative group' of general operatives, the article revealed the extent of the hardship inflicted by the stoppage. Sheridan estimated that the majority of the workforce were breadwinners for families ranging from two children to seven, and that 2,000 workers and dependants were directly affected.[87] The average dole payment received by the men was about £44, about half the wages they would have received had they been working in the plant.[88] The high rent and mortgage rates that prevailed in Cobh at the time meant the laid-off operatives were particularly concerned about their homes. Workers who had availed themselves of an EEC scheme to purchase houses faced repayments of £60 per month, while those with county council loans faced monthly repayments of £45. Rental prices, mainly applicable to young couples, were particularly expensive, averaging between £20 and £30 per week.[89] While the ITGWU did what it could to sustain these workers, the financial impact of the strike was severe, with one magazine noting that, 'in a number of cases, workers have cashed in their insurance policies. Three of them have been forced to sell furniture. In only two certain cases have ITGWU members got other work to tide them over.'[90]

While the strike was divisive both within the town of Cobh and among the workforce, the craftsmen took advantage of solidarity networks that stretched beyond Haulbowline. Donal Brady recalled that:

> we got help from other factories like Dunlops and Fords and the dockyards ... We made collections there and we ... [would] go to ... those factories for collections, and we, any fella that was badly off, some fellas weren't as badly off as others, we'd look after them.[91]

In addition to providing money to supplement strike pay, organised employees in the county assisted in more concrete ways. Electricity Supply Board (ESB) workers guaranteed that none of those affected at Irish Steel would have their electricity cut off due to inability to pay, and on one occasion the dockers, assisted by striking craftsmen, attacked a consignment of imported steel and dumped it. On 20 June 1977, the Irish Steel strike committee organised a one-day stoppage of craftworkers across Cork city and county.[92] There was a mixed response to the strike demand, but several hundred workers heeded the call and took unofficial industrial action in support of their comrades at Irish Steel. The most important group to take action was the dockers, who successfully shut down the port of Cork for twenty-four hours.[93] Maritime Industries and the Ford Marina plant were forced to close as a result of action taken by their own employees, and two large workplaces in Cobh (Verolme dockyard and Nítrigin Éireann Teoranta) operated at 50 per cent capacity.[94] Electricity services were severely restricted as a result of linesmen and other skilled workers in the ESB respecting the pickets.[95] In total, nearly 1,000 workers across Cork city and county either could not enter work or refused to cross the pickets placed by the craftsmen and their allies.

The solidarity demonstrated by craftworkers in Fords, the ESB and other plants contrasted sharply with the divisive effects of the dispute within Irish Steel itself. Tensions remained high throughout the dispute. At the peak of the strike, Donal Brady received a bullet through the post: 'Oh, I was gonna be shot ... I was supposed to be the ringleader.'[96] One letter from the wife of a laid-off worker to the Taoiseach, Jack Lynch, complained that the strikers were doing contract work in secret and were 'mad with money'.[97] James Cronin compared the bitterness of the strike to the Irish Civil War, with its undertones of brother fighting against brother:

> It created a lot of hardship for the people out on strike, and some of the people that were on strike, their brothers were general operatives and they were on the dole so it kind of ate into families in Cobh, so it was a bit like the Civil War.[98]

An operative interviewed at the height of the strike offered contemporary evidence of these divisions. He was quoted as saying of the strikers:

> There's a strange situation here as some of them are friends or neighbours or even relations. One man is the father of a

craftworker who is on the picket at the pier head from seven o'clock in the morning until one o'clock the next.[99]

Fitter's mate Robert Walsh commented that 'there was a few of them [tradesmen and general operatives] never spoke to each other again'.[100]

Why did the strike occur in the first place? A central factor in explaining the outbreak of such a major and lengthy stoppage following years of relative quiescence was the changing economic context of Irish Steel. As described earlier in this chapter, the generous tariff protections extended to the firm in the 1940s, '50s and '60s allowed the workforce to ensure high wages for both craftsmen and general operatives. Trade unions in the plant had become used to easy concessions from management. The militancy of the Irish Steel craftworkers was recounted by one former worker: 'They did have several strikes over there, and it wasn't us, it was the tradesmen.'[101] Another narrator told an anecdote that seems to illustrate the pre-1977 position of trade unions in the plant. A shop steward representing the tradesmen received a complaint that the payment of wages had been delayed. He took this grievance to the personnel manager:

> 'The tradesmen aren't too happy. If they don't get ...' (they got paid on a Thursday, I think) ... 'If they don't get their money, they, do you know, there's going to be something done. There could be a ban on overtime. Maybe going on strike even.' So this guy called the phone and he called down the chap who was in charge of the wages department. And he said, 'Is there anything, you know, about the shortage of money and so many fellas' wages?'
>
> 'Oh yeah ... there's a shortage this way. We'll fix it up next week.'
>
> 'You won't,' he said. 'You'll fix it up today,' he said.

'And tomorrow,' he said, 'is Friday. And those men had better be paid by tomorrow night, before they leave here tomorrow evening because remember ... it's they're keeping you in the job. You're not keeping them in a job ... Without these men working out there and making steel and all that we wouldn't have any business for you in here.'

So, your man went away with his tail between his legs and he had the money ready for them the next day.[102]

Whether the details of this story are recalled accurately is of only minor importance. As Alessandro Portelli writes, 'oral narrators ... have a tendency to couch their ideas in narrative form'.[103] Robert's story is not told to reconstruct a particular historical episode, but to demonstrate the power and influence of the craft unions and their representatives, and the willingness of management to concede in order to prevent strike action.

By 1977, Irish Steel was in the process of re-inventing itself to survive without the protections it had previously enjoyed. In particular, the vital scrap monopoly was due to be removed in December of that year.[104] The status quo of wage negotiations and industrial relations at Irish Steel was based on both plant-level militancy and the ability of management to make concessions in the context of a heavily protected market. Irish Steel was now facing real competition for the first time in its history (not to mention a global steel recession) and was under pressure to reduce labour costs. The company was forced to take a firm line against the demands of the tradesmen. This sudden change in management attitudes surprised the craftworkers, who were unused to management resistance and expected a quick settlement. The result was a long and devastating industrial dispute which ended with a pyrrhic victory for the craftsmen.

INDUSTRIAL RELATIONS, 1978-2001

The 1977 strike was the high-water mark of militancy at Irish Steel. Tony Cummins remembered the gradual decline in the power of the unions in the 1980s: 'The trade union was strong in its day. Very early on it was fairly strong. But towards the end then, Irish Steel had a union, but they had very little input really.'[105] There were both internal and external reasons for this changing situation. In the case of the latter, the 1980s were a fraught decade for Irish trade unionism in general. Recession and mass unemployment reduced the bargaining power of workers and their unions, militating against the industrial power of the trade union movement and inhibiting strike action. Emmet O'Connor notes that the annual average of strike days across all industries in Ireland fell from 719,000 in the late 1970s to just 237,000 in the last four years of the 1980s.[106] Trade union density within the national labour force also declined, falling from a high of 55 per cent in 1980 to 43 per cent by 1997.[107] We have already discussed the impact of these changes on plant-level industrial relations at Sunbeam Wolsey in Chapter Five.

The massive losses experienced by Irish Steel in the 1980s (see Chapter Three) created a precarious position for workers and their unions when it came to negotiations with management. There were frequent calls in the media for the company to be abandoned, in the context of the vast amounts of state money being invested without returns. On the other hand, the government feared the political consequences of closure. During union negotiations in 1985, for example, one newspaper noted that,

> the Government has done its homework, both on what a continuation of the Company at its present size would mean in drawing off millions for the taxpayer without establishing

viability, *and in electoral terms* ... Cork is a key voting cockpit in a general election and a shaping influence in the make-up of the next government.[108]

In the aftermath of the high-profile closures of Verolme, Fords and Dunlop, the political consequences of another lost industry in the Cork region would have been drastic. This importance was underlined at a 1985 meeting of Fianna Fáil in Carrigaline (one of the plant's main sources of labour), when branch president Pearse Wyse declared that 'we in Cork have only one major industry left and that is Irish Steel' and insisted that their [Fianna Fáil's] 'representatives in the Dáil will do everything in their power to keep Irish Steel open'.[109]

Despite political commitments to maintain the plant, the company was in constant danger of closure. The threat of the industry being scrapped gave the government and senior management the upper hand in negotiations with the Irish Steel trade unions. In 1985, following several years of losses, the government proposed a rationalisation plan to the unions. This plan coincided with a state infusion of £89 million into the plant. Director Kevin McCourt, speaking to trade union leaders, proposed a stringent set of cost-cutting measures as a requirement for government support of the plant to continue. These measures included one hundred redundancies, an eighteen-month pay freeze and unspecified changes to 'restrictive' work practices.[110] The deal was narrowly rejected by the trade unions in the plant, sparking a series of tense negotiations that dragged on for months. While management did make some minor concessions to the workforce, the 'demoralised' plant unions eventually lost the game of brinksmanship that followed and accepted the draconian terms by a large majority.[111]

Trade union acceptance of the conditions imposed was largely due to the government making acceptance of the rationalisation plan a condition of the £18 million in state aid needed to keep the firm afloat.[112] As one employee remembered of the period: 'We were always in trouble, though. Every so often, the headlines in the paper ... "Irish Steel Problems".'[113] The danger of closure and the need for government assistance blunted the industrial edge possessed by the plant's workforce. The stringent conditions imposed in the 1985 deal were accepted without recourse to industrial action, contrasting sharply with the relatively minor demands made by management that had precipitated the 1977 craftsmen's strike.

Strike action became increasingly rare, and industrial disputes tended to be resolved in favour of a more aggressive management. In 1987, a dispute over the hiring of contractors led to the company laying off some 200 workers until the ITGWU accepted a labour court recommendation in favour of plant management.[114] In 1991, the trade unions accepted a redundancy package that saw the loss of 100 jobs without resistance.[115] The tense negotiations that had occurred in 1985 were repeated nine years later, when the company again found itself in need of state aid. In 1993, the government offered the company a loan of £10 million on the condition that the firm implement a significant cost-cutting plan.[116] The plan demanded that the workforce forego a 3.75 per cent pay increase.[117] The following year, the trade unions clashed with new Irish Steel chairman Pat Dineen over the cost-cutting plan. While a majority of the SIPTU-organised general workers voted to accept the proposal, the craft unions voted by a three to one majority to reject the package in July 1994.[118] Dineen played hardball, refusing to make concessions to, or even meet with, the craft unions. The stand-off reached crisis point in September, when 412 of the 530 workers in the plan were laid off.[119] Neither Dineen nor the chief executive Lesley Buckley responded to calls by the craft unions for an urgent meeting to rescue the stalled negotiations.[120]

Finally, on 21 September, Dineen and the government brought the game of brinksmanship to an end. Minister for Enterprise and Employment Ruairí Quinn announced that 'there was no hope for further negotiations' and that a liquidator was being sought for the company's assets.[121] The following morning, the Irish Steel workforce found the plant shut.[122] The closure appeared to be final, and was the main story in all national media outlets.

To the surprise of most observers, a last-minute turnaround did occur due to the divine (or at least clerical) intervention of John Magee, Bishop of Cloyne. Magee had been central to the cost-cutting negotiations throughout 1994, acting as an intermediary between the craft unions and management.[123] It is difficult to ascertain whether Dineen's decision to seek a liquidator represented a genuine abandonment of his attempts to reform Irish Steel and ensure its continuation or a dramatic calling of the craft unions' bluff. However, the effect of the closure was to force the tradesmen to finally capitulate to the government's demands. All ninety craftworkers reversed their decision to reject the cost-cutting plans within twenty-four hours of the factory's closure.[124] The government initially dismissed the reversal as a case of 'too little, too late'. However, soon afterwards, the government contacted John Magee to issue a series of further demands to the unions. These conditions were reluctantly accepted. On Monday, 26 September 1994, the same newspapers that had proclaimed the end of Irish Steel just a few days earlier carried headlines announcing that the 520 Irish Steel jobs were to be saved.[125] The tradesmen must surely have had complex feelings about the plant's resurrection; their jobs had been secured but at the cost of major concessions.

CLOSURE, REDUNDANCIES AND DE-INDUSTRIALISATION

Following the sale of Irish Steel to Ispat in 1995, the Haulbowline plant entered a period of controversy and decline. Employment levels had been reduced to 350 by then, meaning that the industry was already a 'slimmed-down' operation by the time the Indian multinational took the firm off the hands of the government.[126] The six years of Ispat ownership were controversial, not least because the company was accused of 'quietly' storing radioactive scrap on the island, placing the health of the entire Lower Harbour population in jeopardy.[127] Workers recalled the final years of the plant's existence with bitterness. Fionnán Kerrigan believed that Ispat had a 'hidden agenda ... The Indians walked away with the money ... not the workers ... There is a bitter taste in my mouth about that, I must say.'[128] Donal Brady echoed his colleague:

> They sold the plant off for a pound to the Indians and they ran the plant down ... All they wanted to do was split whatever custom they had and he [Lakshmi Mittal, owner of Ispat] ran the plant down, because he had several plants in England and in India and everywhere, they were all over the world. He left a massive debt after him here when he went away.[129]

Controversy followed what one Cobh newsletter described as 'a less than credible company'.[130] After the closure of the plant in 2001, it was claimed that Ispat had failed to make capital investments in the firm in contravention of the original contract of sale, which compelled Ispat to invest £50 million into the plant.[131] Local councillor and former Irish Steel worker John Mulvihill accused Ispat of asset-stripping the plant.[132] Memos leaked in 2002 confirmed the darkest suspicions of commentators. Ispat had already stripped the plant of its assets by the time it closed in

2001. The company left a trail of debt, owing £2 million to the ESB, £100,000 to Iarnród Éireann, £100,000 to Bord Gáis, and over a million to Customs and Excise and the Revenue Commissioners.[133] Moreover, in a final insult to the workers sacked by the firm, the leaked memos revealed that Ispat had considered dismissing all Irish Steel employees with less than two years' service to avoid paying them redundancy.[134] The redundancy money proved to be the most significant issue for the workers, who were owed £7 million by Ispat when Irish Steel was liquidated in 2001.[135] The issue proved highly controversial and resulted in a lengthy campaign by former Irish Steel workers to retrieve the money they were owed. Fionnán Kerrigan believed that the government

> didn't have the balls to stand up and say, 'It's not viable.' It is viable or it isn't viable. Pour the money [if it's viable]. If it wasn't viable then they should have stood up and said, 'Right, we're going to give these people a decent redundancy' rather than prolonging the agony for five years ... At the time it closed, I think for fifteen or sixteen years' service – now I'd been on decent money as I said – now when the place closed I think my redundancy at the time, because I was young when it closed ... under forty ... I got 200 euros statutory redundancy for every year of service ... which was crazy ... We were basically cut loose.[136]

The controversies over Ispat's behaviour, and the Irish Steel workers' struggle for fair redundancy payments, acquired greater significance because they coincided with the industrial and economic decline of Cobh itself. From a point of seemingly terminal decline in the earlier half of the twentieth century, Cobh's fortunes had turned sharply upwards by the 1960s. In 1953, Cobh was suffering the highest unemployment levels in all of east Cork, but just ten years later the town clerk boasted of 'virtually full employment', including 600 employed in the steel industry, 1,100 in the dockyards and a further 200 in harbour services, in addition to those employed in naval services and in areas of employment that depended on the income of those in manufacturing.[137] Christy Buckley recalled that, 'between the dockyards and the steelworks, Cobh was booming that time [the 1960s]'.[138] By 2001, however, the town had suffered the loss of almost all of its major industrial employers.

Many narrators, particularly those living in Cobh, spoke of this decline:

> Jim Shealy: The town was decimated really. There was no replacements really. Young people in the town at the moment, like … have no conception of what it was like to get out of your bed in the morning, get on your bike or walk to work. Ah, you know, in twenty minutes you could walk to work … there isn't any employment in any type of industry in Cobh, we don't even have an industrial estate. The biggest employer I think at the moment in the town is SuperValu, which is in retail. And the hotel. So we're depending on, sad to say, yellow-pack jobs. They wouldn't be anything like … in no way could they compare to the security and the employment and the wages that were earned in these [manufacturing] jobs. There's no comparison.[139]

> James Cronin (born 1945 in Cobh; payroll clerk and manager at Irish Steel, 1958–2001): 'Twas a kind of a place that in Cobh, you either got into the dockyards or into the steel and there was plenty apprenticeships back along, whereas now it's only the army or the navy available … there's no industry in Cobh now, Nitrigin Éireann or IFI as it later became, are gone. So there's a big change … There's people in Irish Steel who haven't worked since 2001 and they're still not old age …

there's a lot of emigration, there is, and this all goes back now to the younger people that were just out of their trades, they had to move away, especially the electricians.[140]

These narratives of de-industrialisation were only employed by Irish Steel workers with strong connections to the town of Cobh. Cork city largely recovered from the plant closures of the early 1980s after the establishment of multinational manufacturing concerns in commuter towns and suburbs, such as Little Island and Ringaskiddy. In contrast, Cobh failed to attract significant foreign or manufacturing investment to the area and became increasingly reliant on a precarious tourism industry to provide local employment.

The trauma that the loss of Irish Steel and other industrial concerns led to in Cobh is indicative of the importance of the workplace within the lives of ordinary people. Irish Steel, Sunbeam Wolsey and Fords were all noteworthy and important workplaces in their own right. Accordingly, the previous three chapters have focused on the specific nature of life in each firm. However, life and work in these factories cannot be examined in isolation from the broader context of working lives in Ireland. It is this broader context that our final two chapters address.

7

Employment, Inequality and Emigration

INTRODUCTION

Working lives at Irish Steel, Sunbeam Wolsey and the Ford Marina plant did not play out in a vacuum but in the context of economic performance and of inequality between classes. Perry Share, Hilary Tovey and Mary Corcoran remark that, in the early twentieth century, economic opportunities for Irish people were limited and predicated on property ownership. Those lacking businesses or farms were often forced to emigrate unless they were lucky enough to chance upon one of the limited job opportunities available in Ireland.[1] Both the persistent economic underdevelopment of Ireland and the limitations imposed by one's social class combined to create a labour market that offered restricted opportunities for those without access to wealth and education. Richard Breen and Christopher T. Whelan argue that, 'contrary to popular belief, class barriers in Ireland are substantially more rigid than in other countries'.[2]

The situation prevailing in the earlier part of the twentieth century, as described by Tovey and others, was not static. The gradual expansion of educational opportunities allowed a degree of social mobility (beginning in the 1960s and expanding thereafter) inconceivable for working-class Irish people who grew up in the 1930s, '40s and '50s. However, while there is abundant evidence of change in this regard, there are also significant signs of continuity. An Economic and Social Research Institute (ESRI) report published in 1982, for example, found that class remained central in defining the job opportunities and expectations of working-class people. The report notes that 'a clear social class base exists in the allocation of students to either a secondary or a vocational school ... with considerable career consequences'.[3] The authors were forced to conclude that 'social class differences are so deeply implanted in Irish society as to be self-perpetuating'.[4] It is the nature of these 'deeply implanted' and 'self-perpetuating' class differences, how they affected the lives of narrators, and how narrators negotiated, understood and experienced limitations imposed by class origin on their working lives that the first half of this chapter addresses.

Given the limitations imposed both by economic weakness and a rigid class structure, many Irish people simply decided to leave Ireland in search of greater opportunities elsewhere, mostly in Britain. While emigration occurred across all social classes, it was particularly evident among the working class and lower middle class.[5] Emigration was a well-established fact of life for working-class people in twentieth-century Ireland. During the 1950s, an estimated 50,000 people were leaving the country annually, giving rise to fears of a 'vanishing Ireland'.[6] Even after this high point, emigration remained a constant, especially for those in rural areas. A 1967 study of Skibbereen, County Cork found few families without at least one member currently living (or who had previously spent time) abroad.[7] A survey of Drogheda released the same year found that 19 per cent of the men and 10 per cent of the women interviewed had concrete plans to migrate in the near future.[8] Given that emigration was such a defining feature of the lives of working-class Irishmen and women, and the fact that eight of the twenty primary narrators interviewed for this project emigrated at some point in their lives, it would be a remarkable oversight if the experience of these narrators, seen in the light of the existing literature, were not examined. As such, the second half of this chapter addresses these questions in detail.

INEQUALITY AND OPPORTUNITY

The testimonies of the older working-class narrators in this study (those born in the 1930s and 1940s) tend to emphasise the limited opportunities for employment and advancement that existed for them. Generally, these narrators indicate that steady and well-paid work was difficult to secure. This perspective is borne out by the high unemployment levels in Cork during the period immediately before and after the Second World War. In 1936, for example, 19.5 per cent of males in the Cork borough area were out of work.[9] During the war, unemployment remained high but was alleviated by massive labour demand in nearby Britain. Between 1936 and 1951, the number of unemployed men fell from 4,461 to 4,186, a minor reduction that must be understood in the context of high levels of emigration in the post-war period.[10]

Despite the high levels of unemployment in Cork in the 1940s and '50s, the narrators suggested that work was available but that much of it was inconsistent and undesirable. Despite mass unemployment, John O'Shea (born 1932 in Ballymacthomas, Cork city; general operative at Sunbeam Wolsey c.1951–5) recalled that 'everybody worked'.[11] This work, however, was semi-official labour characterised by short-term and poorly paid employment, often seasonal agricultural work, 'picking spuds, and working with the farmers, and here and there'.[12] Michael Costelloe (born 1940), who grew up in a rural area of north Kerry in the 1950s and '60s, described a similar situation. Despite a lack of any major industry and high rates of emigration, he noted that 'there was a lot of casual work. Farmers employed people, maybe not on a full-time basis, but maybe on an on-and-off basis. There was quite a lot of that. Local council. Again, that used to come into the picture a lot, casual work you know.'[13] Michael briefly worked as an agricultural labourer, and while he described the farmer as a good employer, he stated that this type of employment was irregular and unreliable: 'I wouldn't say we were there full-time now, like, but for the busy times of the year, cutting the hay, saving the turf, those kind of jobs, you know?'[14] John O'Shea's first paid employment was assisting with the driving of cattle from outside the city to the *Inisfallen* ferryboat, on which the animals were exported to Britain. While this work provided a welcome source of income, it was far from pleasant or reliable: 'We were in between the cattle sliding in the shite and dirt, you know? And when we got to the quays we had to keep our eye on the fella we were working for or he'd be gone with our money!'[15] Later, he worked in a succession of jobs, mostly for different farmers in the vicinity of the city: 'There was full and plenty employment, but frugal. I mean the wages were laughable, you know?'[16] While John was consistently able to secure this type of employment, he was, nevertheless, unsatisfied with it:

> I was keeping company with Patsy [his future wife] that time. And she worked in Dunlops at a job she hated. And I worked for the farmers. But I was forever smelling, you know? If I was working pigs or cattle or sheep I mean, you could run a drag-hunt with me ... We ... both decided to emigrate.[17]

It was only the sudden and unexpected offer of a job in the Sunbeam factory that compelled John to reconsider his plan to seek work in England. It is significant that he mentioned his future wife in connection with this period in his life. Christy Buckley (born 1930), who, like John, worked a succession of low-paying agricultural jobs before acquiring a post at Irish Steel, also connected his move to the steelworks to his future wife: 'I went to the Steel then when I got tied up to my little woman.'[18] In both cases, it seems to be the case that the prospect of marriage compelled the narrators to seek more secure, stable and well-paid employment than the irregular labour they had engaged in up to that point in their lives. While the type of low-quality work described by John and Christy was sufficient for young, single men, it was neither adequately secure nor well-paid enough for those on the verge of married life, with the increased financial burden of supporting a family. As mentioned in previous chapters, the comparatively stable, long-term and secure employment offered by large, tariff-protected industries such as Irish Steel, Sunbeam Wolsey and the Ford Marina plant was particularly desirable in the context of the unstable and limited employment opportunities in the rest of the economy.

Nevertheless, while some people were lucky enough to find employment in a secure, well-paying establishment such as Fords, opportunities generally remained very limited for young working-class people. Gus McLoughlin (born 1924), describing the 1930s and '40s, clarified that class was a central determinant in the choice and quality of work available to young people in Cork:

> Most working-class people finished school at 14 and then they either went to join the British Army or went to work in whatever line that their fathers could produce for them ... if their father was a tradesman, they'd get into a trade, or maybe gardening work or menial work like working on the docks or working on the buildings, which was a terrible job in those days, with no conditions.[19]

It was, however, accepted by the working-class narrators that their work and career choices were limited. These limitations were questioned only in the reflective context of the oral history interviews, via implicit comparisons to the wider educational and career opportunities available in contemporary Ireland. Lack of social mobility was simply accepted as part of a constricted horizon of expectations. Tim Murphy (born 1940s), for example, when asked what jobs were considered the most desirable in his youth, responded:

> The professions would be the most thing, but shall I say *ordinary people didn't aspire to that because they weren't qualified for it*. All the professionals, teaching and all that sort of thing, well, of course, the jobs in City Hall, government jobs, they were all the jobs aspired to, in my estimation. They're the jobs I'd like to have worked my way into if I could. But it didn't happen for me.[20]

This passive acceptance is echoed in the autobiography of Gene Kerrigan, who commented about growing up in working-class Cabra in the 1950s: 'hardly anyone from our neighbourhood went to third level, not a lot went to second level, and many of us never got much beyond primary. *There was no sense of deprivation, just that this was how things were.*'[21]

These recollections are supported by other evidence. A series of articles in *The Irish Press* in late 1949 and early 1950 entitled 'Any Jobs Going?' offers career advice to teenagers about entering the workforce and paints a frank picture of the highly stratified and limited labour market that existed at the time. Professions such as medicine or law were far beyond the reach of working-class people. The cost of becoming a doctor, for example, was estimated to be between £1,500 and £2,000 at a time when even a relatively good job, such as a glass worker, had an income of just £8 to £10 per week.[22] Even within the sphere of traditional crafts, options were often limited. Carpentry, for example, a well-paid and high-status craft, was effectively closed to those without relatives in the trade: 'If you are not a carpenter's son or do not have relatives who are engaged in the industry, your chances are not so bright.'[23] Similarly, the majority of those involved in the confectionery business were 'closely connected to the trade by family ties and preference is given to those who have relations in the trade'.[24] Apprenticeships in Ireland were exceptionally long by international standards. To be a bartender required an apprenticeship of four years, and even the relatively humble trade of grocer's assistant called for a training period of at least three years.[25] These long apprenticeship periods meant half a decade of underpaid labour, at the end of which lay only low or moderate incomes.[26] There were some exceptions to this general pattern. The relatively new trade of electrician, for example, was comparatively open and highly desirable: 'Rural electrification alone absorbs the vast majority of electricians turned out from our technical schools each year. With good working conditions, a forty-four-hour week at 3/3 an hour, who wouldn't be an electrician?'[27] Despite such bright spots, the articles contained in 'Any Jobs Going?' paint a picture of a very limited labour market for young working-class people, who generally could not access the educational opportunities required for the professions, and for whom access to crafts was highly restricted.

As 'Any Jobs Going?' indicates, tradesmen occupied a more privileged position in terms of working-class employment opportunities. Possessing a valuable commodity – a set of skills available only through apprenticeships zealously guarded by those who possessed them – tradesmen occupied a more fluid position within the labour market. On the one hand, this position offered them greater bargaining power within the workplace. The maintenance of demarcation and pay relativity with the 'unskilled' mass of general workers was a central concern of craftworkers, reflected in the fact that, until the 1980s, most tradesmen organised in their own unions, which were distinct from the larger, 'general' unions such as the ITGWU. The higher demand for skilled labour meant that tradesmen could move more easily from job to job and were less likely to face long periods of unemployment or be compelled to engage in the type of casual and insecure labour described by John O'Shea and Michael Costelloe. Electrician Donal Brady (born 1932), for example, recalled that, 'I never drew the dole. I never signed on. I was never idle ... I could change from job to job.'[28] However, access to apprenticeships was tightly controlled, and even the comparatively open trade of electrician was a difficult one to break into:

> Liam Cullinane: In those days ... how would you get into an apprenticeship ... what was your way into that?
> Donal: You'd have to have the Group Cert 'twas called. Ah, now, what would you call it, you'd qualify after, the Inter Cert, and then you had another means of getting in there if your parents were rich enough, you could pay a fee, I think 'twas about a hundred quid ... for an apprentice. They'd go in and pay. So there was an awful lot of, in the electrical business, there was an awful lot of farmer's sons, because the farmers had the money and they paid the fees in for their sons, you know? They hadn't the qualifications at all ... There was another way in then. If your father was an electrician – we'll just talk about electricians – he was entitled if there was a vacancy. An employer for every three electricians he employed, he was entitled to take on an apprentice ... And if your father, or in my case an uncle, was an electrician, I qualified then under the union rules.[29]

As Donal's testimony reveals, even becoming a tradesman, a comparatively privileged, yet essentially working-class occupation, was off-limits to those without the financial resources to complete a technical education or to purchase a paid apprenticeship, unless one already possessed family connections within the trade itself.[30] Tradesmen formed part of the working class, and (as we discuss in the next chapter) were considered such by both themselves and by general operatives. However, their distinctive economic position, bargaining power and separate trade union structures had important consequences for industrial relations. Chapter Six demonstrated how these distinctive features of tradesmen and craft-unionism played out in dramatic fashion at Irish Steel during the late 1970s, when there was a significant divergence between the tactics and perceived interests of craftworkers and general operatives.

James Cronin (born 1945), in a poem describing his own neighbourhood in the 1960s, emphasises the limitations in life choices based on class still evident in this period: 'Education for the poor past primary school, did not exist / Physical work, emigration to Britain, mainly to enlist.'[31] The confluence highlighted by James, between class structure and educational opportunity, was also made manifest in Michael Costelloe's (born 1940) recollections, in which he commented that, while most working-class young people left school at fourteen, strong farming families typically sent their children to college.[32] Similarly, Gus McLoughlin explained how, for a young man to gain access to a third-level education, his father 'would have to be a grocer, or a TD [Teachta Dála, member of the Irish parliament] or a publican or a teacher or working in Inland Revenue or something like that'.[33] In addition to these pressures, it remained the case that structural opportunities for employment remained limited until a period of economic boom in the 1960s. Great Islander Jim Shealy (born 1950), who finished his education in the earlier part of that decade, recalled that there were few opportunities for young working-class people in and around Cobh. Aside from a number of highly sought-after apprenticeships in Irish Steel or the dockyards, there was not 'any other option, other than to emigrate'.[34] Billy McMurty (born 1938), describing the area in roughly the same period, commented that 'most of the lads, their fathers were working in England'.[35]

Michael Costelloe, recalling his schooldays in the late 1950s, offered a concrete example of the pressures faced by young working-class men who wished to continue their education, but who were also faced with the necessity of contributing to the family income and establishing a secure financial base for themselves in order to buy a home and start their own family:

> Now, if I say so myself, I was fairly bright, especially at the tech, and they were anxious for me to keep going there, for another year at least. As I say, there was costs involved that time as well, with books and everything like that, and they left it up to me, the parents. They said, 'Look, we'll manage, if you want to keep going.' And I had a think about it. I had an offer of a job as well, an apprenticeship in the motor trade. And I was agonising over it, you know? And I was visualising the parents being under pressure, and having the job would keep me in pocket money. Anyway, you know, so I opted to go with the job, and that was the end of my education, my formal education anyway.[36]

In Michael's case, the financial pressures associated with being part of a large working-class family, particularly knowing the sacrifices his parents would have to make to ensure his continued education, were the primary factors in his opting for an apprenticeship despite his success in school and the fact that he

> dearly would have loved to keep going ... and I had a great thirst for going further ... But, you know, costs and fees, as well as that the lack of earning power, were all factors, so that's why I never really got any more formal education.[37]

Similarly, Billy McMurty, who attended technical school for one year after finishing his initial education, remembered that there was only a dozen or so people in his class. He attributed the small numbers to the fact that 'there was no money. You had to pay that time. People just didn't have the money.'[38]

Tony Cummins (born 1944), who was able to take advantage of the new opportunities made available to working-class pupils in the 1960s, completed his Leaving Certificate. However, he was only able to do so while working a demanding job in a local cinema:

> I did part-time work while I was studying for the Leaving Cert ... I remember I used to come home, maybe half past eleven at night, when the films used be over, and I'd have sat through two separate shows at that time, maybe one from seven until nine, and the second show from nine until eleven and I'd be down there around half past six, and I'd often get home and get started on the homework at half eleven and up for school the following morning.[39]

Working-class pupils, unlike their middle-class peers, were often compelled to work to support their education. The importance of securing regular work and a reliable income often took precedence over schooling. Despite possessing his Leaving Certificate, Tony opted for the position of a general operative at Irish Steel as soon as one became available, a decision he did not regret:

> So I got those two exams and, at that time then, there wasn't that much opportunities for, you know, that type of work, so even though I went through it then, I never really pursued anything in that line. When I did go to take up employment in Irish Steel ... I spent most of my working life there ... it was more on the manual side, but I was quite happy with that, I was quite happy with that.[40]

The late 1960s and much of the 1970s saw some changes to the previous dispensation, some due to an increase in access to education and training, others due to improving economic circumstances. According to Emmet O'Connor, industrial output more than doubled between 1958 and 1973, and by 1972, 30 per cent of the labour force worked in manufacturing.[41] In the context of increased employment opportunities and the introduction of free secondary education, regional technical colleges and other measures designed to increase social mobility, opportunities for working-class people expanded. The younger narrators were able to avail of these new opportunities. Tony Cummins, as mentioned above, managed to complete his Leaving Certificate, while Fionnán Kerrigan (born 1967) received an advanced education in a technical school, contrasting sharply with the earlier generation of narrators, most of whom left school at fourteen or soon afterwards. Those who entered education in the 1960s and '70s did so in the midst of a changing class structure, with free secondary education and greater opportunities in skilled manual and lower non-manual employment, which created new, albeit limited, opportunities for social mobility.[42]

But despite the introduction of free secondary education in 1968, opportunities for social mobility and employment choice remained constrained by class and wealth. According to a 1982 report by the ESRI, based on the 1973 Household Budget Survey, Irish society was,

> by the 1970s, differentiated sharply according to class-linked packages of skills and qualifications attained mainly through education. The newer and more advantaged opportunities in white collar or skilled manual employment were disproportionately assumed by the already privileged middle-class and substantial farm families. Those unable to

secure such positions emigrated or remained in marginal farming or labouring categories.[43]

Third-level education remained 'a virtual middle-class monopoly' and, despite the advent of free secondary education, there had not been a corresponding equalisation. Inequalities of access to education actually increased between 1961 and 1971.[44] Bertram Hutchinson, in a study published in 1973, complains of a 'failure to provide educational access equally to those of all status levels (or class origin)' and concludes 'that a man's future depends as much, and perhaps more, upon his origin as upon his potentiality of skill and intelligence'.[45]

Class was a central determinant of expectations and opportunities in independent Ireland, all of which were highly dependent on access to educational and financial resources. These resources were distributed unevenly due to the recognised and rigidly maintained class system in the country, which ensured that one's future was closely connected to one's origins, particularly parental economic and social status. McIvor's conclusion in relation to post-war Britain, that social class was the primary determinant of employment choice, can be applied with little reservation to Ireland.[46] However, to this must be added the caveat that this situation, while remaining deeply entrenched, was not static, and economic and social changes were opening new opportunities for advancement, at least for certain sections of the Irish working class.

Economic factors were also important in determining the course of working lives. Economic contractions diminished the opportunities available to working-class people while periods of boom saw their ability to advance in social and material terms expand significantly. However, given the persistent weaknesses in the Irish economy throughout the twentieth century, many chose simply to seek greater opportunities in other countries, particularly Britain.

EMIGRATION

Enda Delaney estimates that, between the early 1920s and the end of the twentieth century, about 1.5 million people left independent Ireland.[47] Out of the twenty-four narrators in this project, eight spent time working abroad.[48] It should be remembered that several factors militated against a more significant presence of emigrants within the interview sample. First, all the interviewees were contacted by snowball sampling in Ireland, meaning that any emigrants who had remained abroad to this day were absent from the sample. Second, Fords, Irish Steel and, to a lesser extent, Sunbeam Wolsey provided comparatively secure and long-term employment. This security meant that former employees of these companies were less likely to emigrate in search of work than those who were unable to find employment in such stable industries.

Delaney suggests that those in the lower middle class and working class were more likely to emigrate because of their vulnerability during economic contractions and the lack of opportunities for advancement at home.[49] Despite a lack of systematic analysis of the class origins of emigrants, the oral testimony of the narrators tends to support Delaney's claim. Michael Costelloe recalled that emigration in his area was primarily a working-class phenomenon and that the children of strong farming families were less likely to leave because of the greater educational and career opportunities available to them in their home country.[50]

Given the significant unemployment levels that existed in Cork in the early part of the twentieth century, it is unsurprising that emigration was endemic. John O'Shea recounted that, immediately after the Second World War, emigration was the word that was on everyone's lips ... A lot of those finished at sixth standard, ah with their Primary Certificate, and they followed their brothers, their fathers across the water on the *Inisfallen*. I couldn't emphasise enough the exodus of the ... of all our friends. You could count on your two hands, the class of about forty, fifty I think who remained on after, you know?[51]

Michael Costelloe, recalling the same period, echoed these sentiments. Unlike Cork city-born John O'Shea, Michael grew up in the small village of Duagh, near Listowel, County Kerry. Emigration in rural areas, particularly in the west, was even more severe than in large towns and cities. Michael described emigration as the norm for rural working-class families in his area: 'The family, most of them emigrated really. England, 'twas literally ... automatically ... you literally went to England as a matter of course when you grew up.'[52] The fate of the Costelloes was far from unusual. As Sara Goek comments of the post-war period: 'The mechanisation of agriculture combined with little industrial or other economic development left few options for most raised in rural areas.'[53]

The pattern of emigration reported by the narrators broadly followed the contours of Irish economic performance in the twentieth century. Those narrators who grew up in the immediate post-war period, and during the 1950s, with its crisis levels of emigration, tended to emphasise mass emigration as a defining feature of life at that time. Frank Wallace (born 1933), part of the older cohort of narrators, recalled that

> a lot of people emigrated. I've a great memory of growing up in Spring Lane [a street on the northside of Cork city] ... The trains would come up under the tunnel. And there I saw my father going off to England ... There was mass emigration

then, like. There was a recession at that time, like now. The social welfare wasn't great, so he had to emigrate.[54]

Other narrators in this cohort, such as Donal Brady (born 1932), echoed his sentiments:

You see the war was over and there was people going over there [Britain], for after the war there was work there, you know? And we had construction work and that. But there was a good few people went from here, now. At that time. Now, you'd go into the post office, and the post office that time for this area was outside in Monkstown [a village just outside Cork city] ... my mother had a widow's pension. And I'd cycle in there of a Friday evening for the pension for her, and when I'd go in, the postmistress inside would give me a big bundle of telegrams to give out for her, all the people who were working in England, sending their monies home.[55]

Following the economic boom that began in the mid-1960s, the situation changed rapidly. Jim Shealy (born 1950), for example, who had left Cobh earlier in the decade due to a dearth of economic opportunities, explained why he decided to return:

I came back here in '72 because like everything else, I came back for a holiday and I saw there was opportunities. Interestingly enough, when I was leaving Ireland ... I think I came home around 1968 ... the dockyard was still really picking up ... when I came back on holidays ... I could see ... there were opportunities after arising and it was a chance to take a chance and come back. But ah, with that, I did. I'm here.[56]

Those narrators entering the working world in the same period (the 1970s), such as Michael Lenihan (born 1958), contrast sharply with the older cohort. They described emigration as being minor or even non-existent as Ireland became, over the course of that decade, a net importer of people for the first time in over a century. By the 1980s, however, a slump in the Irish economy had seen a return to mass emigration. Fionnán Kerrigan (born 1967), who went straight from secondary school into working for Irish Steel in 1985, recounted how

> the majority of the lads that I went to school with headed off at that stage … it was that time in the eighties … the majority of them headed off … There was very few of us in full-time jobs that stayed, that it would have paid for us to stay.[57]

As the correlation between economic performance and emigration reflected in the accounts of the narrators demonstrates, the economic factor was primary in determining whether narrators remained in their homeland or sought opportunities in Britain. Of the interviewees who emigrated, one did so for career development reasons (Denis Forde), five (Mary Cronin, Tim Murphy, Jim Shealy, Billy McMurty and Michael Costelloe) to find employment and one (Eleanor Ford) for social and cultural reasons. By and large, emigration was not regarded as a significant life event in the autobiographies of the narrators and was accorded less importance than other events, such as marriage or the purchase of a house. Delaney comments that many people who emigrated to Britain only did so as a short-term necessity during periods of high unemployment at home, intending to return once the situation improved.[58] Most of the emigrant-narrators' comments reflected the accuracy of this claim. Mary Cronin (born 1938 in Farranree, Cork city; 'runner' at Sunbeam Wolsey 1953–7) mentioned her emigration to England (where she remained for more than a decade) in an offhand, almost dismissive manner – the potentially intimidating move softened by the fact that she had already had a sister there who could ease the transition.

> Liam: And how did you find going over to England? Was that a big culture shock?
> Mary: I didn't mind it really. Yeah, I didn't mind.[59]

Jim Shealy's experience was somewhat different:

> It was, ah, it was a major experience, it was a major lifestyle change, it was about going from the small town to the big city. The big smoke. And I pretty soon integrated and I really, really have huge, great memories of that particular period.[60]

Significantly, however, Jim regarded the move as a 'major experience' not primarily because of the differences between Ireland and Britain, but because of the difference between the small town of Cobh and the cosmopolitan city of London. Moreover, like Mary Cronin, his transition from Ireland to Britain was eased by his family connections to London. Both his parents had lived there for a period and he already had a sister established in the city:

> I went to England because, as I said earlier, I had a sister living there and, like, that was [the way] normally, if you had a connection … that's still the same anyway, that's still anyone emigrating from the country today, the majority of them go to a relative or a connection or a friend.[61]

Much like the other emigrants, Michael Costelloe's period spent in England was eased by the presence of relatives and the existence of a large Irish community in London:

Of course, you had every nationality in London which was new to me, but the Irish were obviously in the ascendancy. Everywhere you went there was Irish. So even though it was London, it had a very big Irish influence. You could almost say you were in Ireland if you walked down Chiswick High Road or something like that, you know?[62]

It is largely in keeping with the patterns of Irish emigration to Britain that the destinations chosen by the emigrants in the study (Birmingham, Glasgow and London) were places with large, well-established Irish communities.[63]

The narrators tended to emphasise the positive aspects of their adopted homes, and the opportunities and luxuries available there. Michael Costelloe and Eleanor Ford (born c.1950; general operative at Sunbeam in the mid-1960s) emphasised the glamour and cultural activities of 1960s' London, while Mary Cronin, who emigrated in the same period, highlighted the advantages offered by the British welfare state and the facilities available to families:

Michael Costelloe: That's right, it was a huge culture shock. But I lapped it up, London. I explored the place, upside down, you know? There was an old friend there as well. He worked in the garage with me in London. And I was … I had him to fall back on in every way, we'd the same interest in music and we socialised a lot, so really I've great memories of that time, exploring London and doing all the touristy things, you know? Museums and art galleries. I lapped it all up, you know? I really did. And as I say, it fascinated me, to be honest. I never … I was really very stimulated by London, very stimulated by London and the people, like … It was a great aul spot. I mean it was a great place. No matter what you'd think of, you could find places in London that were big into it, regardless of what 'twould be, you know, music, painting, I dabbled in everything, you know? Yeah, I've great memories of London, really and truly, you know?[64]

Eleanor Ford: It was amazing. Going into the sixties. I mean, don't forget in the sixties we were right in the middle, right in the sixties era, which was fantastic … I headed off to London, right into Carnaby Street, right into the sixties and the place was absolutely alive.[65]

Mary Cronin: The facilities … were better … I mean the health system and everything. Everything was very good there [Birmingham] … For the children, dentists, everything like was spot-on, you know?[66]

While most of the narrators emphasised economic reasons for emigrating, Eleanor Ford proved the exception to the rule in terms of her motivations. In her narrative, Eleanor frequently characterised Cork and Ireland as being 'small': 'I mean we had a very, very small world, a tiny world. Very, very, very small.'[67] The meaning of smallness here is more akin to a limiting, constraining quality, as well as the 'small-mindedness' she complains of in relation to Cork in her youth. Similarly, when discussing the limited opportunities available to women of her generation in Ireland, Eleanor contrasted these limitations with the broader opportunities and freedoms available in London. Eleanor was keen to emphasise her agency in deciding to leave, mentioning, for example, that she had already 'ran away' to Britain at the age of sixteen before being caught at Fishguard and sent back home aboard the *Inisfallen*.[68] Her use of the term 'ran away' indicates a desire to escape what she perceived to be a claustrophobic society that she felt was working against her desire for freedom and autonomy. For her, emigration represented a form of liberation from what one narrator (James Cronin) characterised as a 'pay, pray and obey' society, as well as the limited opportunities for courtship for those women who had not begun to settle down at an early age:

> Eleanor: Well you see what happened in ... when you were seventeen in Cork then, you either got engaged or you were courting a fella strong, going out with somebody, what would you call it? Dating. So then you were talking about getting engaged. It was either that or there was nothing else for anybody else to do. Most people were going out with somebody else, so the dancehalls, we had had the dancehalls, and then you'd be turning into the age of seventeen and eighteen and by then your friends are with boyfriends. Boyfriends are with girlfriends so if you go to a dance there's nobody there, so then you're stuck. I went away before that ... I wanted more. I didn't want to stay here and get engaged and get married.[69]

Overall, the testimony here generally confirms other studies of twentieth-century Irish emigration, which focus on the normalisation of emigration and the central role of economic factors in explaining why so many left Ireland for Britain and elsewhere. For most of the narrators in this survey, emigration was temporary. This finding is unsurprising given that all the narrators were resident in Ireland at the time of the interviews, and those who emigrated and permanently remained abroad are therefore silent in the testimony. Time spent abroad did not form a significant narrative moment in oral testimony. The narrators in this project formed part of a working class that operated in a bi-national labour market and moved easily between Ireland and Britain. For the older cohort of narrators, there was a close connection between emigration and 'slackage', that is, periods when product demand was low and temporary lay-offs were introduced. Gus McLoughlin, for example, explained how he 'would always have [his] fare for the *Inisfallen* ... ready to take me over to England ... when things got slack in Fords'.[70] As discussed in Chapter Four, the periodic migration of Ford workers was softened by the company's active role in securing Irish employees work in British Ford branches. Similarly, it was after being laid off 'on slack' from Sunbeam Wolsey that Mary Cronin sought employment in Britain, and a 'slackage' in Blarney Woollen Mills compelled Tim Murphy to emigrate to Glasgow. In later decades, economic changes and advances in production management made such periods of slackage less common (the term disappearing altogether from the vocabularies of work from the late 1960s onwards), and emigration, following the return of economic hard times in the 1980s, became a comparatively long-term prospect, a decision taken in the absence of any employment options whatsoever.

This section concludes with a caveat. While the testimony presented here generally presents a normalised and largely positive view of the emigrant experience, it is important to remember that the limited nature of the sample militates against a more representative image of the complex and multifaceted subjective experience of emigration. Delaney notes that alienation and culture shock are common features in the testimony of Irish emigrants.[71] This is not the case in the testimony of the (mostly) temporary migrants examined here. For others, those who were either compelled to emigrate or who left for long periods, the experience could be far more harrowing. It is appropriate to consider one example of such an experience, that of Vaunie Downey, the wife of a Ford worker who was transferred to Dagenham during the war years, and who followed her husband to Essex in the 1940s. Despite a large community of Irish people in the area, many of whom were Corkonian Ford workers and their families, Vaunie recalled these years quite negatively, describing her time in England as heart-breaking.[72] Unlike other narrators, who chose to emigrate in search of better prospects and employment, Vaunie's decision was based on a sense of family duty, expressed by the belief that 'your place is with your husband'. For Vaunie, emigration was a sacrifice to be made for the good of the family unit[73] and represented a darker side of the complex and variable experience of Irish emigrants.[74]

CONCLUSION

Social class was an important, though not absolute, determinant of the direction and nature of working lives in twentieth-century Ireland. However, while class analysis remains necessary, recent labour history has stressed the importance of taking other factors into account, particularly gender, race and ethnicity. While the latter two categories were not particularly relevant in the context of a largely homogenous white, Catholic country, gender was a major determining factor, both in terms of working expectations and opportunities, as well as generating the meanings by which both men and women understood and negotiated their working lives. It is questions of gender, status and the 'meaning' of work that the next chapter addresses.

8

Gender, Status and Resistance

INTRODUCTION

Even for a single individual, the meaning of work and of working lives can be endlessly complex. Gus McLoughlin, who worked in the Marina plant, recalled how 'there were times in the morning when I woke up and I was thinking, "Perhaps with a bit of luck, the place might have burned down during the night."'[1] However, despite occasionally hoping for its incineration, the factory had become central to his own identity, especially as he was the middle of three generations of Fords workers and had worked there for nearly half a century: 'You could say I was reared on Ford money and still living on it … There's a drop of petrol and a drop of oil mixed in with my blood somewhere.'[2]

The previous chapter addressed the structural factors that shaped the overall contours of working lives. This chapter focuses more specifically on the experiences of work itself. These experiences did not occur in a vacuum. Societal attitudes towards work, particularly in terms of gender and status, provided the ideological context in which working lives were lived. Particularly important in this regard was gender. A patriarchal familial ideology in Ireland, which defined the man as breadwinner and the woman as homemaker, was internalised by the narrators and is reflected in their oral testimony. The first part of this chapter demonstrates the existence of this ideology and its acceptance by the narrators. The chapter then examines how both men and women defined themselves and their attitudes to work in terms of this broader ideology, and how gendered beliefs about the 'proper' roles of men and women combined with related structural forces to influence the working lives of each.

The second section discusses the primary status division among workers themselves, namely 'staff' (white-collar workers, clerical staff and junior management), 'workers' (general operatives) and 'tradesmen' (craftworkers such as electricians and fitters). Although these divisions were not impermeable, the categorisation of workers into these different roles, defined by perceived skill and status, was a significant theme in the oral testimony. In examining these divisions, we bear in mind the conclusions of the previous section and analyse status divisions in the context of broader societal attitudes regarding gender, work and class.

Work is not merely a means of earning a living, but also an arena of conflict, the stage of an endless struggle between capital and labour.[3] Central to this conflict are the trade unions that workers form to defend themselves. Reflecting the high level of trade union density in post-war Irish society, particularly in larger, tariff-protected industries, all the narrators were members of trade unions. Irish Steel was unionised from its inception, and Sunbeam Wolsey either from its establishment in 1928 or very soon afterwards. The Ford Marina plant was an exception to this, becoming organised in 1949 (see Chapter Four). However, while all the narrators were trade union members and had some experience of strikes and other forms of industrial resistance, their attitudes towards trade unions vary greatly. Gender also informed how workers engaged with trade unions. The various attitudes evident in the oral testimony are examined in detail.

GENDER IDEOLOGY

Máire Leane and Elizabeth Kiely, in their extensive research into the working lives of Irish women in the period 1930–60, note the existence of a 'strong familial ideology' that permeated Irish society.[4] They state that 'this ideology – characterised by subordination of personal desire for the good of the wider family, acceptance of parental direction and assumption of familial caretaking roles' – provided a common framework of understanding for Irish men and women and was reflected at all levels of a society in which women were expected to remain in the home caring for their husbands and children.[5]

These beliefs were placed at the heart of the state through its inclusion in the Irish constitution:

> The State recognises the family as the primary and fundamental unit group of society, and as a moral institution possessing inalienable and imprescriptible rights, antecedent and superior to all positive law ... In particular the state recognises that, by her life within the home, woman gives to the State a support, without which the common good cannot be achieved. The State shall, therefore, endeavour to ensure that *mothers shall not be obliged by economic necessity to engage in labour to the neglect of their duties in the home.*[6]

In the ideological context of twentieth-century Ireland, the division of labour within the household, with the man as breadwinner and the woman as homemaker, was largely accepted by both men and women:

> Tony Cummins (born 1944): And in those days now, back to my time, it was the accepted thing that when a couple got married that the wife, or the woman, she would just finish

up work. That was the accepted thing then. She would take on the role of mother in the house, it was just accepted at that stage and that's the way it was with us here. The man then went out and provided for the house. But I know in recent years, the way the cost of houses went and so forth, it was necessary for both husband and wife possibly to have a job if they could and, because of the high cost of living, but in my day, it was the thing that the husband would have went out and provided the living and the woman stayed at home and looked after the house and the family and that's the way it would have been with us too.[7]

Marian Hickey (born c.1950): When I got married first, you had to give up work. You couldn't work … You weren't allowed go to work.[8]

Kathleen Fitzgibbon (born 1925): It was expected that time that you left your job when you got married … There was no talk about going back. When you were married, you were married and that was it, like … I was reared: The man was the fella that went out to work.[9]

While the narrators did not recall questioning these widely accepted beliefs in their own day, the context of the oral history interview, conducted decades later in the light of drastic social changes, allowed them to reflect critically on beliefs that were once taken for granted. In an interview with Rita Sisk (born 1949 in Shandon, Cork city; general operative at Sunbeam, 1965–72) and Eleanor Ford, a mixture of criticism and nostalgia emerged. While Rita commented that both she and her young female contemporaries in the 1960s were 'very happy', Eleanor insisted that this happiness was because 'we knew nothing else':

> Rita Sisk: As soon as we got married, we thought that was it. In then, rear your children, your little apron on, making your apple tarts, cooking their dinner.
>
> Eleanor Ford: You did, yeah, you were trained, you were trained, as a person, domestically, you were trained to look after the husband, the children and we were very, very young wives, you know? You were trained. Especially here [Ireland].[10]

Elaborating further, Rita and Eleanor highlighted the material and ideological factors that limited women's participation in the workplace after marriage, including lack of affordable childcare and a more general acceptance of prescribed gender roles:

> Rita Sisk: Got married then and went back then for a couple of months. I was a year and a half married before Roy was born and I worked away then outside, then when he was born, a couple of weeks before he was born, there was no going back then because there was no one to mind the child. We bought a house here and then we lived in a flat in Pope's Quay when we got married first. And we were there for a couple of months and then we bought this house. And I didn't drive, and I still don't drive so there was no going back to the Sunbeam. Maybe if I had been nearer, but that time your mother … there was mothers wouldn't mind your children: 'you have to mind your own children.'
>
> Eleanor Ford: They'd say, 'You made your bed. You lie in it.'
>
> Rita: And you were quite happy then to be, you know your husband then would be the provider, bringing in the money, and you'd be waiting for your husband's wages every week.[11]

Rita and Eleanor were not exceptions. The hegemonic strength of such ideas permeated the views of working-class women in

Irish society. In 1966, for example, although women comprised a quarter of the working population, married women 'comprised less than 3 per cent of the total labour force'.[12] Leane and Kiely conclude that, 'the principle of the male breadwinner was widely accepted by women', who, whether or not there was an element of compulsion to do so (as in teaching and civil service positions), ended their working lives at a young age to devote themselves to household labour and the raising of children.[13]

BREADWINNERS

It was not unexpected, given the prevalence of an ideology that assumed and valorised a male breadwinner, that the male narrators tended to attach a high degree of importance to money and their ability to earn. John O'Shea (born 1932) spoke proudly of an incident that occurred just before his wedding, demonstrating the importance the male narrators attached to their success as financial providers.

> I remember my father saying to my wife, God be good to her, all of them now, he said, the morning that we got married … He said: 'He's there. There's a lot of rough edges to him but you'll never be short a shilling.' And 'twas a fact, 'twas a fact. I mean, she wasn't, thank God. 'Twas one of me better claims to life, you know? When times were very, very hard, she didn't have to worry about bills.[14]

Other narrators expressed similar sentiments. On working at Irish Steel, Christy Buckley (born 1930) commented: ''Twas tough, but I reared my family out of it.'[15] Similarly, Michael Lenihan (born 1958) emphasised the importance of working in Ford when he was starting a family:

It meant an awful lot to me because it gave me a great start. At the beginning when I started, I'd no children. And when Fords closed in '84, I'd two. Like that, we'd bought a house in Donnybrook and the world was our oyster, basically ... So it gave me a great start because it came into my life at the right time.[16]

The dominant ideology identified the sphere of work as male and the domestic sphere as female. Therefore, men tended to define themselves by their skills as workers. Tim Murphy (born 1940s), a former Ford employee, mentioned several ways in which his experience in the company benefited him, and it is clear that Tim's construction of his own identity is linked to his pride as a worker in terms of his skills and his career advancement. Like John, Michael and Christy, Tim's narrative emphasised his self-identity as a breadwinner and being financially responsible for his family.

> They [my twenty-four years in Fords] were very important to me. I built the career I had. I built my family. I built my house ... It made a better man out of you ... It disciplined me and rounded me and made me a better man ... It made me ... it made me financially too ... I didn't drink, I didn't smoke, I wasn't a wilder. I don't have a lot of money but I'm financially sound ... It made me a lot of friends, and they're friends for life ... It inspired me to educate myself more ... It gave me a discipline to live and a discipline to work.[17]

Such remarks, especially phrases like 'I built my house out of it', were common among the male narrators in the study and emphasise the importance they placed on earnings. This financial aspect of employment, which took precedence over other concerns, was encapsulated by Fionnán Kerrigan (born 1967) in his attitude towards his work at Irish Steel: 'I'm there for one reason, and one reason only, and that is to make money.'[18]

In contrast, labour did not form the principal identity in the narratives of the women interviewed but was just one self-conception alongside those of friend, mother, household manager and other sources of selfhood and pride. The other side of the male breadwinner's identity was that a working wife would undermine a husband's self-image as a respectable and consistent provider for his family. One working-class memoirist from Cork commented that a husband's inability to earn enough to support a wife was an implicit admission of failure and a blot on his masculine self-identity.[19] Marian Hickey described her feelings on returning to work in the early 1980s:

> Marian: It was a big thing at that time to go back to work and leave your children too, you know? It wouldn't have been as popular now in '84 now, and '83.
>
> Liam: Oh really? That late. In what kinda way?
>
> Marian: You'd feel guilty, like, you know? You'd go to work but I remember my husband now at the time, he'd be saying: 'You don't need to go to work. What are you going to work for?' But he got used to it. But you'd always be feeling very guilty that you went to work.[20]

Both women and men were socialised into their future roles from an early age through social conditioning in family, community and society. Women, for example, were often expected to contribute to the raising of children in the large households typical of Catholic Ireland. Leane and Kiely comment that 'young women's ambitions and understanding in relation to employment were shaped by the combined forces of home, school, church and community and were "gendered" well in advance of their actual involvement in paid work'.[21] Marian Hickey began to take on responsibility for raising her younger brothers and sisters from an early age:

> When we were children she [my mother] was in the Sunbeam. It was, like, she'd go to work for nine. We'd go to school. We all pitched in to mind, well I suppose it was me really, it was me minding the gang of them, the five of them younger than me, so I'd mind them and she came home, my father came home. Yeah, that was my job, to mind them five until Mam came in.[22]

Another example of socialisation into gender roles was the differing distribution of income within the household. Most female narrators explained that their pay packets were given over to their mothers (responsible for the financial organisation of the household) while they were still living at home:

> Marian Hickey: I'd give my mam the ten shillings then when I came home ... even when I started in the Sunbeam, you wouldn't be allowed open that pay packet, no way José! You got back then what she thought [you needed].[23]

> Rita Sisk: You'd give up your wages, then you'd be waiting for a loan back from your mother. You'd give your wages up, then you'd get a loan back to go dancing and then there'd be the loan out of the money that you'd given them.[24]

> Rena McCarthy: The mother got the wage packet. That was it.[25]

Whether or not a young working man living at home handed over his packet varied and appears to have depended largely on the economic situation of the household. While some among the oldest cohort of male narrators gave over their wage packet while living at home, later generations of male narrators did not do so, something that most likely can be attributed to rising incomes, social welfare benefits and standards of living over time. Pat Dunlea (born 1945; grew up in Ballyphehane, Cork city; general operative at Fords, 1963–84), however, emphasised the significance of gender in this regard when he remarked that, of his siblings, all of whom (except him) were girls, he was the only one not compelled to hand over his wages to his mother. Such treatment prepared him for his future as an independent breadwinner and reflected the subordination of female labour and earning capacity to the 'greater good' of the household and family.[26]

This devaluing of paid female labour was reflected in the labour market more generally. A series of articles in *The Irish Press*, 'Any Jobs Going?', reflects the highly gendered nature of employment in mid-century Ireland. The number of occupations covered that were geared towards women was minimal and concentrated in traditional 'feminine' spheres of work, such as hairdressing, millinery, poultry-keeping and waitressing. The series also paints a clear picture of the discriminatory practices that existed in relation to payment. In Cork in 1949, for example, a waiter earned 55/- per week compared with 33/- for his female counterpart, and after ten years working as an assistant in a grocer's or off-licence, a man would have a weekly wage of 105/- compared with the female rate of 75/-.[27] Professions and high-status jobs were almost exclusively male domains, with only a handful of female exceptions, such as hotel manageress. The series also provides an insight into the brevity of women's working lives. Better-paid and high-status jobs for women in state bodies or semi-state companies, such as national school teacher or railway clerk, were inevitably cut short at marriage: 'But girls, a word of warning, if you want to get married and still hold your job, national school teaching is not for you.'[28]

GENDERED WORK

This feature of the labour market was reproduced within the workplace. Ethel Crowley comments that power relations in the workplace reflected those in the household.[29] Similarly, Leane and Kiely state that strict gender segregation and hierarchy (in terms of pay and the ideological construction of 'skill') were common in the workplace.[30] A clear example of this hierarchy is apparent at Sunbeam Wolsey in the text of a 1968 agreement hashed out between the company's personnel manager and the Irish Union of Distributive and Clerical Workers regarding the employment of women in the warehouse (previously a male domain), which only accepted the presence of female workers on three conditions:

1. No male personnel will be made redundant as a result.
2. In the event of redundancy, females will be laid off first.
3. Promotional opportunities for male juniors will not be restricted.[31]

This subordination of female labour was recognised (and largely accepted) by the narrators who worked in factories with a mixed-gender labour force. Marian Hickey recalled of Sunbeam Wolsey:

> The men were on the knitting machines, the men were in the dyehouse. You'd never see a woman on a knitting machine. They were men's jobs ... You wouldn't see a man on a sewing machine in a fit, no way ... The men went in there with men's jobs, knitting machines, electricians, mechanics, the furnace, that kind of thing ... There was women's jobs and men's jobs.[32]

The societal division of labour also affected the general contours of working life more generally. Leane and Kiely remark that women's working lives were 'transitory', 'fractured' and 'meandering', and that their careers were 'hampered by gender discrimination, narrow opportunities and the prospect that they could marry someday'.[33] The brevity of women's paid working lives is illustrated starkly in a 1956 pension report conducted by the Sunbeam Wolsey personnel manager. Although women comprised the majority of the total workforce, the ratio of women to men changed considerably from the younger categories, with women representing a clear majority in the under-25 category, before becoming increasingly under-represented in the older categories of workers.[34] The manager casually noted that, 'as very few of the female staff will ever reach pensionable age, they do not, in my opinion, create a problem and I have accordingly only taken the male employees only into account'.[35] The pension report reflects the brevity of women's experience of paid work, a factor identified also by the 1967 Drogheda Manpower Survey, which found that 72 per cent of the women interviewed, when asked about future employment, replied that they intended to become homemakers. Some 53 per cent of the total female sample had no intention of seeking another job, but instead to get married.[36]

It must be remembered that, while women's paid working lives were brief and transitory, their engagement in domestic labour was generally lifelong. Many of the women interviewed in this study did return to work after marriage, but the types of work they engaged in were generally not permanent and were of secondary importance to 'duties' in the home, often consisting of semi-official or part-time 'caring' labour in keeping with a woman's perceived role. Rita Sisk (born 1949), for example, took up babysitting to augment the family income, which allowed her to carry out labour in the home and to remain within a traditional feminine sphere of employment. When Marian Hickey returned to work in the 1980s, she shared her job with her sister, which allowed both to engage in paid labour while also looking after their respective families. Mary Cronin (born 1938), after starting a family in Birmingham, worked in the evenings in an 'old folk's hospital', work she enjoyed because it could be easily balanced with raising her family: 'It was five o'clock in the evening [that the shift started]. You went [home] at eight o'clock. And everything just fitted in nicely, you know? With [my husband] being working and that. He'd be in in the evening. I'd be going out and he'd be coming in.'[37]

The experiences of the male narrators contrasted sharply with those of the female narrators. Men's working lives were both longer and more varied. John O'Shea, for example, first found part-time employment as a child, driving cattle from the markets of the Cork city area to the *Inisfallen* ferry boat. After completing his education, he worked at the small Siltona textile factory, did various stints as an agricultural labourer for local landlords and briefly worked as an assistant for a local butcher. He then worked for Sunbeam Wolsey for a few years before the Cork Fire Brigade hired him. He remained in that post for thirty-nine years until his retirement. Few female narrators could boast such a long and elaborate curriculum vitae. Men who acquired desirable and secure employment, such as that offered by Fords and Irish Steel, generally remained in those jobs for as long as they could. Many boasted of the decades of continuous service they had provided, often spending twenty, thirty or forty years in an individual workplace. Additionally, men with long service records, even if they did not have an advanced education, could climb the social ladder by means of internal promotion. Fionnán Kerrigan, for example, began work at Irish Steel as a general operative but was production manager by the time the factory closed in 2001. Donal Brady began his employment in the same workplace as an electrician, before becoming charge-hand, and, eventually, a foreman. Tim Murphy started as a general operative in Ford, but progressed to supervisor. The company even paid for him to attend a course at the Irish Management Institute to train for a management role. Fords was particularly well known for its internal promotion system, which was one reason why it was considered such a desirable employer by working-class men in Cork. In contrast, although female narrators did note the existence of 'foreladies' and female managers at Sunbeam, they did not aspire to these roles, or even consider them a realistic possibility.

Changes in the overall nature of women's labour became apparent during the 1970s and '80s as married women began to either return to work or continued working after marriage. Marian Hickey recalled of the period: 'Things changed ... There were loads coming back then. Everyone had children then ... we all went back.'[38] One commentator has explained how equality legislation and, more generally, economic growth saw the percentage of working-age women employed grow from 30 per cent in 1985 to just shy of 50 per cent in 2004.[39] New areas of employment opened up for women, and the possibility of having a career and promotion prospects increasingly became a reality, especially in the context of an expanding service sector. Additionally, the increased availability of contraception, among other factors, allowed women greater control over their own lives, including careers and employment, although only a few of the narrators in this study were of an age to experience any of these (relatively recent) benefits. For most of the female narrators, as in Irish society more generally, ideological and material factors militated against the exercise of choice and agency, both in terms of employment decisions and life choices.

WHITE-COLLAR AND BLUE-COLLAR WORKERS

In 1950, an article appeared in *Liberty*, the magazine of the ITGWU, concerning social attitudes towards different types of labour. Entitled 'The Dignity of Dirty Hands', the piece offered a spirited defence of the inherent value of manual work:

> Most people would resent being called snobs. Still there is a great deal of snobbishness, some of it shown unwittingly when the question arises of advising young people about choice of career. Far too many cherish the illusion that there is something 'respectable' in activity that is not likely to soil the hands ... Some people act on the belief that it is kindness to a young person to advise choice of what has come to be known as a 'white-collar' job. Yet is there not a nobility about dirty hands when the dirt was put on through honest toil?[40]

Despite the nobility of hands 'dirtied by honest toil', the beliefs criticised by *Liberty* reflected a broader social tendency, one that regarded clerical, white-collar jobs as more respectable and desirable than manual or 'blue-collar' employment:

> Gus McLoughlin: I always felt very conscious, when I was growing up, of my hands, they were workman's hands ... very dirty jobs ... I was always acutely aware of that now ... I'd be always aware that he was an office worker or a shop worker and I was just a factory worker. I was always acutely aware of it ... that would be always in the background.[41]

Workers recalled the internal workplace division between 'workers' (general operatives, tradesmen) and 'staff' as being highly significant.[42] Jim Shealy, for example, described travelling to the Irish Steel Plant on Haulbowline Island on the 'staff boat':

> I, going back referring to the ferry ... because I worked in the rolling shift, or the rolling mills, there was a certain shift of an unusual start on a Monday morning ... which entailed that we, the people who were working in the rolling mills ... didn't

go until the nine o'clock boat, which meant we travelled in on what was considered the staff boat. And even on the staff boat ... unless you had a really, very good friend who was also on staff that you'd speak to and you'd talk to, but otherwise they were on one side of the boat and we were on the other ... So that was very, very clear. That distinction.[43]

This distinction was often resented by ordinary workers. A frequent complaint in relation to the Ford plant was what Arthur O'Callaghan referred to as the 'canteen caste system', in which there were separate sections for general workers, staff, supervisors and senior management.[44] Such sentiments were widespread, though they became less important for workers over time. Donal Brady, an electrician at Irish Steel, described how status divisions became apparent during social events:

> Every Christmas they'd have big parties, you know, the annual dinner dance. And ... everyone would be there. But in the early days there was a bit of demarcation in their eyes, a bit of snobbery, the office staff kept clear of the general dogsbody on the foundry, on the factory floor. The manager, he wouldn't [tolerate staff socialising with manual workers]. He brought them in at different times starting and at different times finishing and if he saw them talking to an ordinary [worker] he nearly fired them ... But that all went in latter years then.[45]

The ambiguous position of the white-collar worker, beneath management but above the general operatives and tradesmen, was reflected in the role they played in strikes and trade union activity in the three factories over the course of the twentieth century. In August 1954, for example, Sarsfield Hogan, faced with an unofficial walkout at Irish Steel's merchant mill, broke the strike using non-unionised mill employees and volunteers from the office staff.[46]

Similarly, when the commercial travellers at Sunbeam Wolsey were involved in a dispute with management in 1936, staff sided with management to break the strike. Eight staff went on the road to replace the striking salesmen, while managing director William Dwyer boasted: 'I spoke to the whole staff last evening (about 100), and they are with us to a man so far and I think that we will be able to hold them.'[47] At the Ford Marina plant, several years after management had accepted the presence of trade unions for the manual workforce, an attempt was made to organise the office staff. This attempt was resisted fiercely and defeated, with the leaders of the union drive forced out of the company.[48] Even when the office staff were finally organised after a second, more successful recruitment drive, the status gap between workers and 'staff' remained, reflected in the fact that clerical worker and union activist Max Hayes was described carefully as a 'salaried staff representative' rather than a shop steward.[49]

This industrial divide remained even after the unionisation of office workers. Michael Costelloe described the differing attitudes towards strike activity displayed by white-collar and blue-collar workers in the Ford Marina plant during the 1970s and '80s:

> Michael: They were definitely a completely separate animal from the factory workers, you know? Now this was in the overall picture. For instance now, if there was a labour dispute, like, and the factory workers put on pickets, there was no such thing as an office worker observing the pickets or respecting the pickets.
>
> Liam: They'd break the pickets?
>
> Michael: Oh yeah. The office workers would definitely walk in past the picket and it was expected that they would, like, you know? It was the done thing. You know? 'Twas regarded as … There was nothing, there was no bad feeling about it,

it was just automatically assumed that the office worker had nothing to do with the factory, you know what I mean?

Liam: Mm.

Michael: So no way.

Liam: It wasn't considered the same as scabbing or blacklegging?

Michael: No, no. Nothing like that. They were expected to walk in, and they walked in. There was no hassle about that.[50]

A similar situation prevailed at Irish Steel. Robert Walsh recalled an incident that occurred in 1981:

> We all had a meeting in the canteen. All the unions got together and I know that the office union came in with us that time and then that created a bit of bad feelings because the office workers always crossed the pickets, never backed a picket in their life, like, official or unofficial. At that time then when the steelworks closed down they came in with us. And I know that one fella had a go off of the secretary of their union, gave a lovely speech at the start of it and this fella had a go off him about it. And he said, 'How is it,' he said, 'that down through the years he passed every picket we ever put up, official or unofficial, and now because it's affecting me as well he wants the strength of us now behind him?'[51]

Attitudes towards manual and white-collar work were explicitly gendered. The most valued jobs for men, as identified by the narrators, were workplaces such as the ESB, Fords and Dunlop. The prestige afforded these (predominately male) workplaces was due to their high levels of pay and skill. Similarly, tradesmen and craftworkers (almost exclusively men) were cited as being 'higher up' due to their good wages, job security and useful skills.[52]

White-collar employment and the prestige accorded to it also varied depending on gender. The high standing associated with male clerical work differed radically from that attributed to their female counterparts. Aidan Kelly describes the typical male white-collar worker in the early decades of the twentieth century as being defined by his prestige. The white-collar worker was well-paid, usually owned his own house and took annual holidays (sometimes abroad) – things his blue-collar counterparts could rarely afford. The white-collar worker identified more closely with his employer than with manual workers, and the boss rewarded and deepened this identification by providing both material benefits and tokens of status. Such benefits included pension plans, bonuses and relatively generous sick leave. Moreover, he received a 'salary' rather than wages and was called 'staff' rather than a 'worker'.[53]

Status for women was linked to perceptions of the type of work one was engaged in, rather than pay, skill or other indicators of prestige. Rena McCarthy described the various tiers of this female status hierarchy: 'Oh yes, I mean there was what was called a good job then, a secretary in a solicitor's office, that was called a good job. Or you work in one of the big shops in town – Woolworths now or the Moderne, Brown Thomas when 'twas Cash's … They were all what you called good jobs.'[54] Contemporary distinctions between clerical, service and manufacturing employment were of central importance and defined how working women perceived themselves and were perceived by others. Rena recalled the snobbery she experienced when encountering former schoolmates who had gone on to office or shop work:

> Oh yeah, if you worked in a factory, you were looked down on … I mean these people … worked in shops now, you know. They'd say, 'God, you work in a factory, God.' That was the attitude, like. As if you were something under their shoe, like.[55]

Although Rena recalled that she and her friends who also worked in factories would simply laugh off such remarks, she also remembered that other female workers were far more sensitive to this form of snobbery: 'You see you'd even get people, you know, they may not be friends of mine, but you'd get people that time, "Oh I don't work in a factory." They'd actually deny it.'[56]

The positive attributes associated with the male white-collar worker reflect gender ideology. The white-collar worker's high standing was determined primarily by his skill, independence, financial security and ability to provide for his family. Female white-collar employees were similarly afforded a high level of prestige but for different reasons. Mary Muldowney, in her research into working women in the Second World War, found that her interviewees generally considered factory work inferior to other types of employment.[57] The perceived inferiority of manufacturing employment for women was not related to income but to respectability. Muldowney suggests that employment in a socially desirable sector was considered preferable to factory or manual work, even if the latter paid better.[58]

This assertion is supported by the documentary evidence and the accounts of the female respondents. The 1967 Drogheda Manpower Survey, for example, found that 'secretarial positions were the usual goal' of most of the female workers in the town.[59] The same survey found that the women interviewed regarded the comparably low-paid position of typist as being as, or more, desirable than a well-paid job as a floor supervisor. At Sunbeam, the gap in wages between female office staff and workers on the factory floor was minimal, yet the difference in status was significant. Billy Foley recalled that

> the office girls and the workers in the Sunbeam, there was a massive difference that time between them. They wouldn't even speak to one another. They wouldn't sit at one another's

table. The girls in the office thought they were way above the workers ... There used to be war over that, like.[60]

Nancy Byrne worked at Sunbeam in the 1930s and observed a considerable gap between the office staff and the workers on the factory floor: 'The office workers' hours were nine to six, life being much easier for them. Firstly, the boss never frequently visited their place of employment like he did in the factory. Also, their lives being much more pleasant, a tennis court and other sports being provided for them.'[61] While Nancy's recollections suggest that staff received more benefits than workers on the floor, most of the narrators indicated that differences in status were not related to levels of pay, but rather to the image associated with different types of work. Rena McCarthy observed the following about female office and shop workers: 'But I don't know did they come out with as much money as we did. I think it was ... The image of the thing. That they weren't factory workers.'[62] This view is corroborated by Billy Foley: 'My own daughter actually started off in the office here and she left the office and went back down to the floor because she was getting more money on the floor. She was like her father. She didn't want a title, she wanted money.'[63]

This concern with 'image' and 'respectability' was clearly related to gender ideology. Most women, to one extent or another, viewed paid employment through the lens of their designated role in the household.[64] Manufacturing work was disdained because it was perceived to be dirty, masculine and physical. In addition, there was a perception that women in manufacturing employment were 'uncouth' and less respectable than their counterparts in more 'feminine' employment. Clerical and shop work, on the other hand, were perceived to be more feminine because such employment was clean, not primarily physical, and closer to the domestic ideal of the Irish woman. Women who worked in manual labour were implicitly seen as transgressive.[65] Of course, as essential contributors to household incomes, female workers had little choice other than to engage in less 'respectable' forms of labour.

As time went on, the status gap between office and manual workers gradually lessened as educational opportunities increased (see Chapter Seven) and the status and working conditions of office workers came to resemble that of their manual counterparts. While status divisions were of central importance to the older cohort of narrators, their significance had lessened greatly by the 1970s and '80s. Those narrators who began their working lives in these decades rarely recalled status distinctions. This change can best be explained by a convergence arising from the 'proletarianisation' of previously high-status and middle-class jobs in the context of a de-industrialising economy.[66]

TRADESMEN AND GENERAL OPERATIVES

In contrast to the important distinction between manual and office workers there was little such differentiation between 'skilled' and 'unskilled' manual workers, despite some important differences between the two groups. Craftworkers relied heavily on restricting and controlling entry to their craft as a means of maintaining their pay and conditions (see Chapter Seven). Tradesmen generally earned higher wages than their non-skilled counterparts and were less prone to unemployment due to their skillset. Tradesmen also maintained separate trade unions and fervently defended the principle of pay relativity with general operatives. One might assume that these differences would result in a significant gap between skilled manual workers and general operatives. However, this was not the case. While a significant portion of the interviewees referred to the importance of the blue collar/white collar distinction in the workplace, only two narrators in the sample regarded the differences between skilled and unskilled manual labourers as being in any way important.[67] Irish Steel experienced a long and divisive strike by craftworkers in 1977 (see Chapter Six) over the issue of pay relativity. That strike saw the majority of the non-skilled manual workforce cross pickets in defiance of the strike and being forced into involuntary unemployment as a result of the dispute. Nevertheless, despite the undeniably divisive nature of the strike, the distinction between general operatives and tradesmen at Irish Steel was mostly downplayed. Robert Walsh described relations between the general operatives and craftsmen as 'absolutely brilliant'.[68] Similarly, Tony Cummins did not recall differences in this regard, commenting that 'there was never that distinction, like ... even the tradesmen now, like, we were all one really, you know, there was never anything like that'.[69] Even in the wake of the long and bitter 1977 Irish Steel craft strike, which 'did cause a bit of aggravation in the sense that it was the tradesmen went out on strike', most of the narrators insisted that any bitterness left over from the dispute dissipated relatively quickly: 'I think everybody did realise that, shortly after we went back, that there was no point in holding grudges.'[70]

While tradesmen clearly represented a distinct, higher-status and somewhat privileged section of workers compared with the general operatives, this distinction did not produce a status gap comparable to that between the manual labour force and white-collar staff. Christopher Whelan, in an examination of occupational satisfaction and perception published in 1980, notes that, while 'they [craftsmen] can be distinguished from other manual workers in a number of important respects, and are likely to be seen as different both by themselves and others', skilled manual workers were 'little different from other manual workers in terms of fringe benefits available to them, the nature of the authority relationships in which they are involved, and, most significantly, the proportion of their fathers who were manual workers'.[71] Despite differences in bargaining power and levels of pay, both skilled and unskilled manual workers generally came from the same families and communities, socialised together and lived in the same types of neighbourhoods.[72] Indeed, several non-skilled manual narrators in this study mentioned fathers, brothers and so on being tradesmen.

Unlike the broadly homogenous social origins of both the skilled and non-skilled general operatives, non-manual employees were more likely to live in different neighbourhoods and communities to their manual counterparts.[73] Whelan's study broadly corroborates the testimony of the narrators and emphasises the 'continuing importance of the Manual/Non-Manual distinction' as opposed to the far less significant distinctions between different grades of manual workers, as evidenced in the case of Michael Costelloe:

> Liam: And in the factory would there have been any kind of gap between the unskilled workers and the craftsmen, the skilled workers that you remember?
>
> Michael: Certainly no gap. No. No way. Certainly skilled workers now I would consider to be electricians, fitters, all that maintenance work, you know? Absolutely no gap, you know? The only gap I would say ... was between the office workers and us, the factory workers ... But the office worker and the factory worker, well they were two different breeds, you know?[74]

ATTITUDES TOWARDS TRADE UNIONS

Frank Wallace (born 1933) recalled that, soon after joining the ITGWU at Sunbeam, he was walking to his post when the new manager of the dyehouse threw a brush at him and barked: 'Clean up the place!'

'Who's he? [I thought]. I'm not going to let him get away with that!' I just wouldn't put up with it … I went up to see the shop steward, Denis O'Mahony, his nickname was the sheriff, he had been a shop steward there for years … eventually I took over from him … In an election for shop-steward, I got an overwhelming majority, so I became a shop-steward and I gradually went from part-time shop steward to full-time. We had our problems of course, we had a couple of strikes on occasions, but all in all, we got on well. That was the start of my involvement with the union.[75]

Frank's account is typical of trade union activist narratives. He emphasised his discovery of his own agency (through a trade union) after the insult to his dignity by the new dyehouse manager. This initial confrontation became a stepping stone for his involvement in trade unionism. Frank, who spent decades as a full-time union official, clearly defined himself in terms of this role, emphasising the trust placed in him by his colleagues in terms of the 'overwhelming majority' of votes he received in his election as shop steward and the fact that he was the 'youngest full-time shop steward in Ireland'.[76] For Frank, his capability as a trade union activist was as important to his self-identity as the breadwinner identity was for most male narrators.

Frank's activism was not typical of the majority of the interviewees, most of whose involvement in trade unionism did not go nearly so far. Moreover, attitudes towards trade unions were complex. Like Frank, Gus McLoughlin's narrative emphasised his trade union activism. He described how he became involved in trade unionism through his membership of the Young Christian Workers, a lay Catholic organisation committed to evangelising workplaces and combating the perceived threat of communism within the trade union movement. He proudly described his involvement in the Ford Dagenham recognition strike (like Frank, emphasising his youth at the time of his initial active involvement in trade union activism), despite his perception that it hindered his later career advancement:

> I actually was one of those who was at the first meeting of the trade union branch and one of the organisers of a trade union in the Cork plant and also in the Dagenham plant, even though I was only, I was in my twenties at the time and I had to organise the complete walkout and the subsequent acceptance of the unions in the Dagenham plant, so that was a bit of a blight from the management point of view. In my career I never got the chance of any advancement ... with that background.[77]

Most of the narrators did not have this degree of involvement in trade union activism – nor did their union membership hold the same significance in terms of personal identity as it did for Gus and Frank – even if they were shop stewards or part of other union structures. Robert Walsh once attended a shop stewards' meeting in the plant but had little further involvement, recalling that it was 'something I never bothered about much'.[78] Michael Costelloe remembered that 'I'd go to all the meetings, like, alright. But I wouldn't be one of these guys who'd be talking up at meetings.'[79] Similarly, Tim Murphy was a member of the National Union of Vehicle Builders (NUVB) and a member of their factory committee for a period despite not being 'a trade unionist at heart. I really wasn't. I didn't believe in bickering over small things and all that.'[80] Irish Steel employee Jim Shealy commented that, 'when we were younger, we were a bit indifferent to the union and things like that. The shop steward would come weekly to collect the subs physically off you, and we'd be watching out for him and trying to avoid him.'[81] However, despite this initially indifferent attitude, he later became a section representative for the Irish Steel rolling mills. Nevertheless, he remained suspicious of some union activists, feeling that they became involved to 'enhance their profile in the eyes of the managers. They used it as a stepping stone to promotion. They had another agenda.'[82] At the extreme end of the spectrum was John O'Shea, who described himself as being 'anti-union' all his life, despite recalling that his father was a founder member of the ITGWU and a Labour Party activist.[83] Most narrators' attitudes, however, fell somewhere between those of full-time activists such as Frank Wallace and those of outright opponents of trade unionism such as John O'Shea.

RESISTANCE IN THE WORKPLACE

The most common form of industrial action in all three plants was unofficial, so-called 'wildcat' strikes. Such strikes were a recognised phenomenon within Irish industrial relations. Charles McCarthy, a right-wing trade union official, in his history of Irish trade unionism in the 1960s, complains of 'the sacrosanct nature of the picket' and the ability of small numbers of men to have almost any unofficial picket recognised and respected.[84] Such unofficial strikes were a source of frustration for both trade union officials and management and reached their peak in the late 1970s, when over two-thirds of strikes were considered 'unofficial'.[85] As discussed in previous chapters, unofficial strikes were the most common form of collective resistance at all three factories, with officially sanctioned strikes and lockouts of significant length or severity being relatively rare phenomena in the overall industrial relations record.

The narrators reflected different attitudes to these strikes, most of which were brief and quickly resolved, either dismissing their importance or complaining about their perceived inconvenience. Tony Cummins joked that, in those days, you know, they always reckoned a great day for a strike would probably be a Monday, because people went to work on a Monday morning … I don't know does it hold much today, but, you know, Monday morning blues. And if there was any bit of a problem at all, down tools, we all go home … In actual fact, the vast majority of them probably went to the pub.[86]

Tony contrasted this era of strike frequency with the quiescence of later decades:

Any particular problem was sorted out. You went over with your shop steward or the branch secretary as we called him and, you know, you went in and you negotiated your point. And a compromise would normally be reached. You know? There was very little strikes towards the end.[87]

Fionnán Kerrigan, a shop steward at Irish Steel, was ambivalent about more militant representatives in the factory, complaining about unnamed 'old-style' shop stewards who entertained trivial grievances and 'defended the un-defendable'.[88] Fionnán, like other narrators, dismissed what he regarded as pointless or unnecessary militancy but still held firmly enough to the principles of trade unionism to take on the role of shop steward.

Many of the narrators active in trade unionism considered their purpose as being to resolve grievances in an orderly and disciplined manner. Jim Shealy saw his role on the section committee as that of peacemaker. He recalled that the committee would meet fortnightly 'to consider work, conditions, pay, any grievances that employees might have, sort them' before they escalated into industrial action, 'keeping everything under control, in a way'.[89] Frank Wallace saw his role as shop steward in a similar vein:

> They [disputes] could be [about] anything, personalities, a manager might come in ... antagonising one or a couple of people ... I'd find out what's the problem and have a discussion with them ... I'd go with the personnel manager to the personnel department ... and we'd get a resolution ... generally I believe we resolved most [disputes] ... [management] didn't like me coming into the floor ... I didn't come to the floor, someone came to me, 'cause I was the person with the union.[90]

Women's relationship with, and involvement in, trade unionism differed markedly from that of men. Marian Elders et al. note that trade unions were often regarded as male domains with a 'masculinist' culture.[91] They were not mistaken. In 1967, there were only twelve women officials in the entire Irish trade union movement.[92] Additionally, the transitory nature of women's engagement in paid labour, examined earlier in this chapter, made involvement in trade union activism difficult.[93] In contrast to the male narrators, most of the women interviewed for this study had little involvement in trade unionism. Neither Patsy Corcoran (born c.1940 in the Bandon Road area of Cork city; half-hose operative at Sunbeam Wolsey, 1956–65) nor Mary Cronin could remember for certain if they had been members of a trade union at Sunbeam. Kathleen Fitzgibbon was a shop steward for a time but recalled that her role did not go beyond the collection of subscriptions. Kathleen dismissed her union role in this regard, commenting that she 'became a shop steward because no-one else would take it ... I didn't care a jot about it.'[94] However, while women's involvement in trade unions was often minimal, the female narrators often expressed sincere (albeit passive) support for trade unionism. Despite not caring 'a jot' about her position as shop steward, Kathleen still valued her membership of the

ITGWU: 'You felt someone's behind you and you weren't on your own ... a necessary evil if you like.'[95] Rena McCarthy concurred: 'Oh yes, you had to be in the union if you wanted your rights in the job then. If you weren't in the union, if something happened [to] you on the job, you were out.'[96]

Whatever the degree of individual activity or commitment on the part of the narrators, it was generally the case that commitment to basic trade union principles, and in particular the respecting of picket lines, was taken for granted by workers.[97] Michael Lenihan remembered that, 'no one would pass a picket, official or otherwise. It was a sacred cow, like.'[98] Even in the case of the divisive dispute by tradesmen at Irish Steel in 1977, fitter's mate Robert Walsh called in sick rather than pass the picket, even though his own union (ITGWU) had instructed their members to do so: 'I know they probably called me an eejit or maybe a fool that I'd lost two weeks wages but as I say I made no bad friends with it anyway.'[99] Even women, who were substantially less likely to be trade union members or activists, took trade union membership, and respect for both official and unofficial strikes, for granted. In the words of one Sunbeam worker, if you didn't join the union 'the girls could refuse to work with you ... you weren't allowed not [to] join ... Anyone who wasn't in a union, it was unheard of, nobody would work with you.'[100] Commitment to trade union principles was enforced particularly by family members. Marian Hickey remembered that her father encouraged her and her sister to make sure they were signed up to the union and that they always paid their subscription fee. Rita Sisk described a time when there was 'a strike out in the Sunbeam ... I remember my mother now saying: "Whatever you do now, don't pass the picket." Because you can't, it was a Sunbeam strike, you'd be called "blackleg".'[101]

While the variety of attitudes towards and degrees of involvement in trade unionism varied widely, the overwhelming majority of the narrators accepted and acted in accordance with trade union principles (such as observing pickets), which were enforced collectively within the workplace, family and community. Even if many workers had only a passive attitude towards trade unionism, they were still sufficiently committed to trade union principles that they would pay dues, observe picket lines and accept instructions given by shop stewards and full-time officials. This commitment enabled trade unions to limit and resist the powers of management within each workplace, even though, as previous chapters have demonstrated, the complicated relationship between management power and worker agency was never static, with the frontier of control shifting constantly throughout the existence of each firm.

One must be careful not to focus overly on trade unions and strikes to the neglect of other, less obvious examples of workplace resistance. The most common example of resistance was simply withdrawal from a job, although one's ability to exercise this power was determined by broader labour market conditions. Marian Hickey recalled that her father (a long-time Fords employee) secured her brother a position in the factory. Loathing the assembly-line process and the lack of freedom, he quickly left his job for a lower-paid position in the construction industry, much to his father's dismay.[102] Similarly, Jim Shealy said that many of those who started working at Irish Steel did not linger long in the dangerous and physically demanding industry: 'If you stuck the first couple of shifts you were okay. If you didn't, you just left. It's what a lot of people just did.'[103] Other forms of resistance took the form of exerting control over the work process and attempting to soften the regimented and tedious nature of the workday. At Ford, the humanisation of the workplace most often took the form of working back the line to secure a few brief minutes of leisure time away from the monotony of the assembly process. It was, perhaps, for this reason that the game of draughts was particularly popular in the factory:

> Michael Lenihan: There was great community spirit and, as well as that, the best draughts player in the country, I reckon, came from Fords.
>
> Liam: Why was that?
>
> Michael: An awful lot of people played draughts in Fords so if you had any kind of a bit of break or you were back the line a bit, you'd go upstairs to have a game of draughts with somebody. 'Twas a way of breaking the monotony really, you know?[104]

Activities such as those described by Michael, while unlikely to feature in quantitative analysis or in media discussions of industrial relations, were, nevertheless, of great importance to working people. Paul Thompson writes of Coventry car workers that workplace sociability was a way of humanising the drab and draconian world of the factory.[105] Other activities by workers sought to exert control over the work process itself. For example, one former Sunbeam worker expressed her pity for 'the poor aul timer[s]', the work-study men who were employed to record the time taken by employees to complete their tasks for the purposes of efficiency and incentive schemes:

> They timed you and, it's probably a joke in a way, because, like, somebody would sit down and they'd be told – 'right, start … overlocking one side of a garment now. See how many you can do in a minute' and, whoever was doing it obviously was going to do it slower … than they could do it, so as that by the time they were … maybe they could do it in half a minute … and then they were doubling their money straight away,

doubling their production so the money would go up. I could never understand how … they thought that they were doing any good, like … 'cause anyone with half a brain was going to do it slower than they'd normally do it, you know?[106]

By fooling the 'poor aul timer[s]', a worker could increase their pay or win over some extra time away from the labour process without incurring a financial penalty. Another form of unofficial resistance was the 'blacking' of cars at Ford, whereby extra vehicle bodies placed on the line would be collectively ignored by the workforce, preventing an increase in work demand without the necessity to resort to a full withdrawal of labour. Theft was another common, but frowned-upon, occurrence, particularly at Sunbeam and Ford. Other acts of resistance, such as smoking at Fords (the activity was banned until unionisation in 1949), are well attested to in the oral testimony. The spectrum of resistance and accommodation in all three firms was, thus, a broad one and cannot be reduced simply to strike activity.

WORKPLACE COMMUNITIES

Michael Lenihan: 'Twas a little community and I'd run back there in the morning if I could.[107]

Tim Murphy: But one thing of course you can't forget in a place where there's 800 people is there were so many organisations and associations, I mean there was a Gaelic football team, a hurling team, a soccer team. It didn't matter what interest you had in life, there was some association, there was a golf society, there was stamp collectors, there was coin collectors, there was tennis. Anything you want would have a team in Fords. And that was a great help at the camaraderie, fellas working together during the day, they had something in common to discuss with some fella further down or another department about something that was on that night or at the weekend, all that sort of thing, it created a sort of a close-knit community, and we were in that relation. There were a number of people who were older, and *Fords wasn't just their workplace, it was their social life as well. Their total social life.* They came in to work in the morning to meet friends. They wouldn't mix much, they would be non-drinkers, these would be mostly older fellas, but it was their social life and there's no doubt about that, that was a very strong life, that was a very strong point.[108]

A frequent point made by the narrators in this study was the importance of camaraderie, friendships, and the sense of community within their former workplaces. The processes that gave rise to this sense of camaraderie and community were manifold, including everyday interactions, pranks, nicknames and, significantly, the rich associational and leisure culture organised through the workplace. Nicknames at Irish Steel and the Ford Marina plant included, but were not limited to, 'Piss in the Bottle', 'Beat the World', 'Stab the Rashers', 'Kill the Rabbit', 'The Bird', 'The Bee', 'Baths of Iron', 'Jerry the Cock', his apprentice 'The Young Cock', and one lucky man known only as 'The Handsome Welder'. Initiation rituals were also an important path of entry into the internal culture of the factory, with innumerable Sunbeam 'runners' spending significant portions of their first day on the hunt for the elusive 'bucket of steam'.[109] The importance of such customs lies in the fact that joining a workforce also meant joining a community with its own distinct culture, through which workers could express their individuality.[110] Within this context, both the male and female narrators emphasised the importance of the friendship and community ties within their places of work.

Michael Lenihan, for example, assigned the same weight to these as he did to the considerable financial advantages at Ford: 'I suppose the best things were the pay and conditions and working with the men and getting on with people basically.'[111] Similarly, Eleanor Ford and Patsy Corcoran placed considerable emphasis on the friendships and female solidarity formed at the Sunbeam plant:

> Eleanor Ford: The main thing of the Sunbeam ... was the girls had an awful lot of pride. They would go to work with make-up, hair done and they would walk with their heads held high, nearly every one of them had that pride of working in the Sunbeam ... Thousands of blue overalls used to come out the gate at 6 o'clock and you'd see them going the different areas, everywhere you looked, walking here, walking there and very pally, you know? They'd be linking each other and chat, chat, chat.[112]
>
> Patsy Corcoran: I loved it out there. It was such a happy place to work. I'd great friends.[113]

Robert Bruno, writing about the Youngstown steel mills in Ohio, USA, claims that 'the plant was a social microcosm. Some workers went so far as to nearly recreate the neighbourhood inside their respective shops.'[114] The same examples of solidarity and networks of mutual aid that were typical of working-class neighbourhoods had their counterparts in the workplace. Two such examples were the 'manage' and the 'diddlum'. These were informal saving schemes operated mainly by women (as household financial managers) and were evident in both the neighbourhood and the workplace. Eleanor Ford described the 'diddlum' as follows:

> There was a thing ... in Sunbeam then, it was a thing in most factories but in Sunbeam they called it a diddlum. And what

you done is that the girls would pay ... a shilling every week ... And then we'd say there are fifty girls and then Rita'd be number two, I'd be number three. We'll say you'd be number one. Then I'd put, we'd put the numbers into a hat and then you'd pick out and whichever came out first would get the first week's diddlum which would be about £50.[115]

The 'manage' was similar, whereby money would be deposited with a trusted colleague who would hold on to the money until it was needed, an important facility before the advent of credit unions, when working-class people had limited access to credit. For male workers, workplace-level assistance and solidarity were typified by the sharing of work skills or covering for friends who might find themselves in trouble with management:

Tim Murphy: But another aspect of Fords was the number of people that worked there and the number of skills they had. I remember in 1973 ... central heating was becoming the big thing in every house, so I got the idea I'd put in central heating and I began it myself, but I couldn't begin it without Fords. Every day I went into Fords, I would get information. Every day I'd pick up a bit of information, how to advance, in a short time, it did take me about three months ... So I put in all my pipes and everything, the radiator, the boilers, put it in myself, set it up, got it going, the whole lot, and that's for a man with no knowledge, but all the knowledge was there for me, every bit of it, I could go to a different fella every day and he would know a different aspect of the job. But it was the same with everything else. If you had a car which gave trouble you could go round and ask anybody and they'd help you, woodwork, anything.[116]

Michael Lenihan: And it was a place too where a lot of people looked out for each other. For instance, there was one man now he worked in the trim line now and he was fond of the drink and as a result the security guards were told to keep an eye and if such and such was coming in and he was a bit unsteady to send him home. And of course everybody knew where that would end up ... The workers would be concerned then. Now such and such, if he doesn't get in, so we got him passed the security guards then he got into work.[117]

In addition to these examples of workplace solidarity, an important feature of all three factories was the existence of a rich and vibrant associational culture. Sports and leisure pursuits were an important aspect of working-class life in general.[118] Two surviving issues of *The Ingot*, the magazine of the Irish Steel Sports and Social Association, attest to the great variety of leisure activities organised through the factory. These activities included the Irish Steel Angling Sea Club, Trout Fishing Club and Shore Angling Club (all separate), a Golfing Society, an interdepartmental soccer tournament, inter-firm soccer team, male voice choir and basketball, darts, bowling, badminton and tennis clubs operating out of the factory. The newsletter provides pictorial evidence of social occasions (such as dinner dances) that were organised through the Sports and Social. Both Fords and Sunbeam possessed a comparably vibrant associational culture.[119] The origins and organisation of workplace-based leisure activities varied. In the early days of the Ford plant, for example, many of the formal sports and cultural outlets were organised by and through a management that saw its role in somewhat paternalistic terms. Similarly, many of the cultural opportunities (though far from all) at Sunbeam Wolsey were centred on the paternalism of founder William Dwyer. However, most workplace leisure and cultural organisations in all three firms resulted from worker initiative rather than managerial paternalism. The evidence from Ford,

Sunbeam and Irish Steel tends to support David Toms' argument in his examination of soccer in Munster that these activities were a 'result of the sociability of work rather than being the result of top-down benevolence'.[120]

The factories were, thus, not merely places of work, but also environments that provided opportunities for workers to create a space in which they could organise the leisure, cultural and sporting activities that were central features of their lives. The importance of these aspects of the workplace is reflected in the words of one former Sunbeam worker:

> Like the wool, nylon and cotton woven, meshed and knitted on its massive machines, the memories of Sunbeam are part of the very fabric of our being. It was more than a factory, a place of work – it was an institution, one that has become an integral part of the folklore of Cork, and also the matrix whence came myriad dreams, some sporting glory and, overall, an entire sub-culture.[121]

While specifically referring to Sunbeam, such sentiments could be equally applied to Irish Steel or the Ford Marina plant.

CONCLUSION

The various worker experiences of our three factories were complex and multifaceted. For Gus McLoughlin and Frank Wallace, the workplace was where they discovered their agency as workers in the struggle against the power of management. For Tim Murphy, it was where he learned the values of skill and discipline, and where he found an opportunity to advance himself through promotion. For others, it was a place to engage in meaningful leisure activities through associational culture. For the male narrators, it was where they realised their goals of financial security and the source of their ability to fulfil the role of provider and breadwinner. For most of the female narrators, their experience of the workplace was brief and transitory, but one that allowed them to develop meaningful and lasting friendships and to exercise their agency as workers and earners, even if both structural and ideological factors undervalued this agency. For most, however, the workplace was a rich combination of many of these things.

Conclusion

The point of local histories, to deploy a cliché, is to ask big questions about small places. By answering these big questions at the analytical level of the locality, we can address the larger concerns of Irish labour history on a manageable scale and point towards future research avenues. In this light, it is worth taking a moment to review some of the questions introduced previously in this book.

What were the factors that determined the overall pattern of working lives in Ireland? Economic performance, social class and government policy were all central. There is abundant evidence of a well-established working class in Cork at the dawn of the twentieth century, with rooted communities and a defined sense of identity. To call this class an *industrial* working class, however, would be a mistake. The region, characterised by the primacy of agriculture, and by industrial under-development, provided little in the way of modern factory employment. The arrival of Ford in 1917 was remarkable, primarily because the modern production methods and employment conditions in the firm were so utterly unlike those in the rest of the southern Irish economy. As discussed in Chapter Seven, most workers in this period had few opportunities, being forced to choose between poorly paid and insecure employment or the emigrant boat.

With the introduction of protectionism and the consequent founding of manufacturing establishments sheltered from the vagaries of competition, the situation for Cork workers improved. Although unemployment and emigration remained a constant for decades, at least some sections of the working class were able to secure stable work within the newly protected industries, of which Irish Steel, Sunbeam Wolsey and the (post-1932) Ford plant were prime examples. The new protectionist dispensation also allowed workers more scope to organise their workplaces, resulting in massive increases in trade union membership. For example, in June 1932, there were just 2,492 ITGWU members in Cork city and county.[1] By 1940, the ITGWU's growth in Cork had necessitated the creation of a second branch. In July of that year, membership figures for Cork No. 1 and No. 2 were recorded at 3,627 and 2,977 respectively.[2] The Marina plant was unusual in its resistance to trade union organisation, but even then the precedent set by the organisation of other Ford facilities, in addition to post-war legislation that strengthened the hand of trade unions, meant that the company was forced to capitulate after a relatively brief recognition strike.[3] Irish Steel and Sunbeam Wolsey unionised early and with little or no resistance from management, a reflection of the improved bargaining position won by trade unions in the 1930s. Trade unions continued to grow after the Second World War. Later, in the 1970s, a combination of full employment and the dislocations wrought by free trade brought workers in protected industries into conflict with management (see Chapters Five and Six). When recession returned in the 1980s, the power of labour receded and mass emigration returned.

How did class and gender affect working lives? As discussed in Chapter Seven, a rigid class system usually limited the career paths of the narrators, although at least some working-class men were able to acquire trades or move up the career ladder through internal promotion. The expansion of educational opportunities in the 1960s and '70s precipitated increased social mobility, though few of the narrators in this study were able to reap the benefits of these changes.

Women and men experienced paid labour differently. On the one hand, the expansion of industry in the import-substitution era meant that figures for women as a percentage of the industrial labour force rose from 20 per cent to 22.4 per cent between 1926 and 1936. This increase reflected the fact that many of the protected industries, such as textiles, footwear and clothing, were traditionally employers of female labour. However, while women's opportunities for industrial employment increased slightly, the 1930s also saw the formalisation of a Catholic, familial ideology that championed motherhood and domesticity over all else.[4] This ideology is reflected in the oral testimony of both the male and female narrators, the former defining themselves by their labour, skills and success as financially responsible breadwinners (see Chapter Eight). For men, secure jobs in protected industries often meant the ability to realise their goal of being a reliable earner who could support a family, and to actualise themselves through career advancement.

Men experienced work differently to their female counterparts. They enjoyed better wages, longer careers and the chance of promotion. Central to their self-identity were their skills, their capacity to provide for their family and their ability to embody masculinity. Men could manifest this masculinity in a number of ways: as diligent workers whose self-sacrifice supported a family; as 'men of steel' who braved dangerous and demanding working conditions; or as trade unionists who fought bravely on behalf of their colleagues and class against the Goliath of management. Women worked, and took pride in their labour, but did so knowing that their working lives were to be short. Most female workers were young and single. It was taken for granted that they would leave the labour market upon marriage. A distinctive familial ideology was reflected internally in the factories through the gender stereotyping of jobs and in the trade unions, in which women's roles were highly limited for much of the twentieth century.[5] Only in the 1970s did this situation begin to change: 'It just started to happen ... Married women were allowed to keep working, along with some other changes. There wasn't the same kind of religious atmosphere ... And the women were coming into work wearing slacks.'[6]

How do we account for the differences in strike patterns at each firm? The guaranteed profitability in protected industries had, by the 1960s, seen trade unions established at Irish Steel, Sunbeam Wolsey and Ford, and brief, insignificant and (generally unofficial) strikes or walkouts became the most common form of industrial action. Even the trade-union-averse Henry Ford and Sons was forced to accept union recognition in 1949 due to solid plant-level organisation and a successful recognition strike. In the 1970s, the norm of relative industrial quietude was replaced by more dramatic and intense strike activity at both Irish Steel and Sunbeam Wolsey (though not at the Ford Marina plant). This sea change can best be explained by the transition from protectionism to free trade. As we saw in the first six chapters, the nature of each firm's ownership had a significant effect on how they responded to the threat of free trade. Fords, as a minor branch of a major multinational, simply ceased production, ending Irish manufacturing operations on a positive note through generous severance packages. Irish Steel and Sunbeam fought on under increasingly difficult circumstances, with the former doing so only with massive injections of state aid. The adjustment from the 'good times' before free trade to the difficult new dispensation saw significant and drawn-out strikes at both Sunbeam and Irish Steel as management went on the offensive in an attempt to change working conditions in the face of powerful trade union resistance. Fords never implemented such unpopular measures and the company was spared the damaging industrial disputes that took place in domestic firms.

The period of worker-militancy ended in the 1980s. The mass unemployment of that decade greatly weakened the power of workers and trade unions. In particular, the threat of closure was wielded effectively by management when negotiating with workers at Sunbeam and Irish Steel. In the case of Sunbeam, workers were forced to accept management proposals that would have been resisted fiercely in the previous decade. Given the choice of making concessions or joining the thousands on the dole queue, workers repeatedly chose the former.[7] At Irish Steel, the spectre of closure chastened the once-militant craftsmen who had brought the factory to a standstill in a six-month strike in 1977. Repeated and expensive rescue packages by the state came at the cost of yet more concessions from the militants. When these disputes led to brinkmanship in 1985 and 1994, the craft unions blinked first.[8]

By 1990, the last of the protected industries had died out or were in the process of expiring. Industries such as car assembly had ceased to exist. Other staple industries, such as textiles and clothing, were a shadow of their former selves. The transition from an import-substitution to an export-led economic policy by the state had both winners and losers. Women, who were disproportionately likely to work in the now-expanding services sector, made considerable gains, which (combined with other victories for women from the 1960s onwards) gave them greater control over their careers, bodies and lives.[9] Similarly, many narrators were positive about the increases in social mobility that had coincided with the phasing out of protectionism, speaking with pride of the educational and career achievements of their children or grandchildren. Geography affected the experience of these changes. Cork city, from being an unemployment black spot in the 1980s, benefited from the location of new industries in the vicinity of the city, recovering its prosperity during the 'Celtic Tiger' boom that began in the 1990s. Cobh did not fare so well.

The town's location (on an island connected to the mainland by a single bridge) was not an enticing one. The industries that had located there had only done so with considerable government support. By the time Irish Steel closed its doors in 2001, the town's once considerable industrial base was gone. It was only among those interviewees from, or with a close connection to, Cobh that narratives of de-industrialisation were observed.[10] Such narratives, common in former industrial areas of the United States or Britain, stand in sharp contrast to those recounted by narrators from Cork city and other localities that had fared better in subsequent years.

The insights garnered in the preceding chapters would have been diluted had we relied entirely on traditional sources. The extensive use of oral history was crucial in examining subjective aspects of working-class life and shed light on those areas that traditional and archival sources could scarcely expect to reach. In particular, the importance of the subjective experience of work could scarcely have been understood using only documentary material; neither could the complex and varied attitudes of men and women towards their supposed roles in society – their expectations, values and beliefs – be gleaned from anything but their own recollections.

The testimony of workers was especially vital to our examination of work and industrial relations in Chapters Four, Five and Six. Without it, we would have struggled to understand the subjective effects of the labour process, the complicated mechanisms by which management regimes operated, and the day-to-day struggle for control in the workplace. It is those areas in which oral testimony was absent that reveal its importance. Much of Chapter Four sought to examine the impact of 'Americanisation' and modernisation on a labour force comprised primarily of agricultural and semi-industrial labourers. However, since those who entered employment in Fords between 1917 and 1932 are now deceased, their testimony was unavailable. While it proved possible to reach some conclusions – through careful analysis of the social memory of the plant and by reading 'against the grain' of company materials – it is clear how much has been lost with the demise of the first generation of Ford workers and their invaluable memories and experiences.

What were the meanings of work as reflected in the autobiographies of the narrators? Work was (and is) the central pivot around which our lives revolve. The continued significance of Irish Steel, Sunbeam Wolsey and the Ford Marina plant in the collective memory of Cork testifies to this fact. Work, as demonstrated in Chapter Eight, was a means to advancement, a source of comradeship and the site of conflict. The complex inter-relationship between labour and identity was highlighted by Gus McLoughlin, who, in Chapter Eight, described how decades of Ford employment had led to a situation in which his own identity and that of his industry had merged physically: 'There's a drop of petrol and a drop of oil mixed in with my blood somewhere.'[11] For Gus, the workplace was the site where he was able to provide for his family, as well as develop his skills, discipline and ability. It provided him with the opportunity to exercise his agency as a member of the working class through his involvement in trade unionism, as well as the means by which he expressed his commitment to Catholicism by putting into concrete practice the Catholic-Labour principles of the Young Christian Workers movement to which he was affiliated. However, the workplace could also be a source of monotony and boredom, to the extent that there were times when he woke up in the morning hoping that the factory had been burnt to the ground.

The workplace was also an arena characterised by an unequal power relationship, that between capital and labour, which subordinated the latter to the goals of the former. Gus felt that his career advancement had been permanently hindered by challenging this relationship (in his roles as a trade union organiser in Dagenham and Cork), leading management to block his opportunities to rise through the ranks of the Marina plant's internal promotion system. Work, for Gus, could also be a place where the body was subject to threat (as his account of the Dagenham foundry makes clear), and the existence of risk to the body was particularly characteristic of Irish Steel. If work could be the means for self-expression and fulfilment, it could also be how employees experienced pain, injury, disability or death (see Chapter Six).[12] Oral history is one of the few effective ways to understand such deep, complicated and subjective experiences.

This book has taken the scope of labour history beyond the icy peaks of national politics and avoided the top-down approach bemoaned by prominent Irish labour historians such as Emmet O'Connor and Fintan Lane, and has begun to examine the rest of the labour history 'iceberg' (to coin Peter Winn's term). Further local studies can expand and deepen our knowledge of the history of the Irish working class, and the use of oral history can shed light on the subjective and intangible experiences of working-class people that are hidden or obscured by traditional documentary sources. Such studies – taking individual areas, communities and workplaces as their focus – can enrich our understanding of labour and working-class history in Ireland, while the use of oral testimony can ensure that working-class people themselves, in their own words, can take their rightful place as the protagonists of Irish labour history – not as mere abstractions, but as living people in all their individual complexity.

Endnotes

Introduction

1. David Convery, 'Introduction', in David Convery (ed.), *Locked Out: A Century of Irish Working-Class Life* (Sallins: Irish Academic Press, 2013), p. 2. My italics.
2. David Convery, 'Uniting the Working Class: History, Memory and 1913', in Convery (ed.), *Locked Out*, p. 38.
3. Fintan Lane, 'Envisaging Labour History: Some Reflections on Irish Historiography and the Working Class', in Francis Devine, Fintan Lane and Niamh Puirséil (eds), *Essays in Irish Labour History: A Festschrift for Elizabeth and John W. Boyle* (Sallins: Irish Academic Press, 2008), pp. 21–2.
4. Ibid.
5. Emmet O'Connor and Conor McCabe, 'Ireland', in Joan Allen, Alan Campbell and John McIlroy (eds), *Histories of Labour: National and International Perspectives* (Pontypool: Merlin Press, 2010), pp. 147–8.
6. Peter Winn, 'Oral History and the Factory Study: New Approaches to Labor History', *Latin American Research Review*, vol. 14, no. 2 (1979), p. 131.
7. Ibid.
8. See, for example, Peter Winn, *Weavers of Revolution: The Yarur Workers and Chile's Road to Socialism* (New York: Oxford University Press, 1986) and Sheila Cohen, *Notoriously Militant: The Story of a Union Branch at Ford Dagenham* (London: Merlin Press, 2013).
9. Winn, 'Oral History and the Factory Study', p. 132.
10. See, for example, Edward Whelan, *Ranks Mill: The Industrial Heart of Limerick City* (Limerick: Limerick Corporation, 2012), Ruth Guiry, *Pigtown: A History of Limerick's Bacon Industry* (Limerick: Limerick City and County Council, 2016) and Miriam Nyhan, 'Narration and Memory: The Experiences of the Workforce of a Ford Plant', *Irish Economic and Social History*, vol. 33, no. 6 (2006), pp. 18–34.
11. The CFP is a non-profit organisation dedicated to preserving and making available oral testimony related to Cork, http://corkfolklore.org/.
12. For documentaries see Abú Media, *Croí an Cheantair* (Cork: TG4, 2013), Ford Ex-Workers Group, *Fords: Memories of the Line* (Cork: Framework Films, 2018) and Framework Films, *Sunbeam* (Cork: Framework Films, 2005). For stage productions see Raymond Scannell, *Losing Steam* (Cork: Corcadorca, 2004), Marian Wyatt, *Sunbeam Girls* (Cork: Stage Centre, 2007) and *The Sunbeam Girls 2* (Cork: Pat Talbot Productions, 2011).
13. Penny Summerfield, 'Culture and Composure: Creating Narratives of the Gendered Self in Oral History Interviews', *Cultural and Social History*, vol. 2 (2004), p. 65.
14. Central Statistics Office, 'Census 2016 Summary Results Part 1, Chapter 2: Geographical Distribution' <https://www.cso.ie/en/media/csoie/releasespublications/documents/population/ 2017/Chapter_2_Geographical_distribution.pdf>.
15. Andy Bielenberg, *Cork's Industrial Revolution, 1780–1880: Development or Decline?* (Cork: Cork University Press, 1991), p. 116.
16. Colin Rynne, 'Industry, 1750–1930', in J.S. Crowley, R.J.N. Devoy, D. Linehan and P. O'Flanagan (eds), *Atlas of Cork City* (Cork: Cork University Press, 2005), p. 187.

17 Protectionism refers to policies which seek to shield domestic industries from international competition. Import-substitution means replacing goods previously acquired from abroad with those produced domestically through the implementation of import taxes (tariffs).
18 Emmet O'Connor, *A Labour History of Ireland, 1824–2000* (Dublin: UCD Press, 2011), p. 143.
19 *Census of Population of Ireland 1926, Volume 7: Industries* (Dublin: Stationery Office, 1932), Table 7 and *Census of Population of Ireland 1936, Volume 7: Industries* (Dublin: Stationery Office, 1940), Table 7.
20 See Chapter Two.
21 Barry Brunt, 'Industrialisation within the Greater Cork Area', in Barry Brunt and Kevin Hourihan (eds), *Perspectives on Cork* (Cork: Geographical Society of Ireland, 1998), p. 21.
22 Ibid.
23 Ibid., p. 22.
24 The General Agreement on Tariffs and Trade (GATT) was an agreement initially signed by twenty-three countries in 1947 in which signatories agreed to a reduction in tariffs, subsidies and other protectionist measures in order to facilitate international trade. The initial signatories were later joined by many others. Ireland overwhelmingly voted in favour of EEC membership in 1972. In doing so, they were compelled by the terms of EEC membership to further dismantle protectionist measures – a process that was already well underway.
25 Barry Brunt, 'Industry and Employment', in Crowley et al., *Atlas of Cork City*, p. 372.

1. The Ford Marina plant, 1917–84

1 Joellen Vinyard, *The Irish on the Urban Frontier: Nineteenth Century Detroit, 1850–1880* (New York: Arno Press, 1976), p. 40.
2 Miriam Nyhan, *Are You Still Below? The Ford Marina Plant, 1917–1984* (Cork: Collins Press, 2007), p. 11.
3 The 1950s' automobile and Ford's mansion in Dearborn were both derived from the name of this street.
4 Henry Ford, *Today and Tomorrow* (London: William Heinemann, 1926), pp. 257–8.
5 Benson Ford Research Centre (hereafter BFRC): Myra Wilkins interview with John O'Neill, September 1960. Wilkins, Acc. 880, Box 7.
6 Myra Wilkins and Frank Earnest Hill, *American Business Abroad: Ford on Six Continents*, 2nd edition (New York: Cambridge University Press, 2011), p. 70.
7 Nyhan, *Are You Still Below?*, pp. 17–28.
8 Thomas Grimes, 'Starting Ireland on the Road to Industry: Henry Ford in Cork' (Unpublished PhD Dissertation: NUI Maynooth, 2008), pp. 61–2.
9 BFRC: Percival Perry to Henry Ford, Report on Establishing a Cork Plant, 25 February 1913, Henry Ford Office, Acc. 62, Box 59.
10 Ibid.
11 Ibid.
12 Ibid.
13 Ibid.
14 Ibid.
15 Ibid.
16 BFRC: Perry to Sorensen, 9 December 1918, Acc. 38, Box 42.
17 Ford, *Today and Tomorrow*, p. 257.

18 Throughout the text, I use 'Fords' as a shorthand for 'Henry Ford and Sons' (the Irish subsidiary) and 'Ford' for the international Ford Motor Company, in line with local usage in Cork city.
19 Nyhan, *Are You Still Below?*, p. 31.
20 Ibid., p. 37.
21 In December 1920 British forces stationed in Cork set fire to the city as a reprisal for an IRA ambush.
22 BFRC: Grace to Sorensen, 17 December 1920, Sorensen, Acc. 38, Box 46.
23 Grimes, 'Henry Ford in Cork', p. 203.
24 Ibid., pp. 210–11.
25 BFRC: Sorensen to Grace, 4 March 1922, Sorensen, Acc. 38, Box 45.
26 *The Cork Examiner*, 7 March 1922.
27 BFRC: Sorensen to Grace, 11 November 1920. Sorensen, Acc. 38, Box 43.
28 Ibid.
29 BFRC: Grace to Sorensen, 10 January 1921, Nevins and Hill, Acc. 572, Box 17.
30 BFRC: Myra Wilkins, Interview with John O'Neill, 1960, Wilkins, Acc. 880, Box 17.
31 Ibid.
32 Grimes, 'Henry Ford in Cork', p. 61.
33 A Sligo man originally, Clarke joined the Ford company in 1917 and quickly rose to become Grace's second-in-command in the Marina plant. He took over as managing director in 1926 when Grace left the company.
34 BFRC: Clarke to Sorensen, 24 December 1926, Wilkins, Acc 880, Box 7.
35 Grimes, 'Henry Ford in Cork', p. 58.
36 Wilkins and Hill, *American Business Abroad*, p. 107.
37 Ibid., p. 194.
38 Ibid., p. 197.
39 BFRC: L. Pearce to G.S. Hibberson, 28 Feb 1930, Wilkins, Acc. 880, Box 7.
40 See Chapter Four.
41 Wilkins and Hill, *American Business Abroad*, pp. 203–4.
42 Ibid., p. 228.
43 BFRC: Minutes of Meeting of Director of Henry Ford and Sons Limited, 27 April 1932, Sorensen, Acc. 38, Box 10.
44 Nyhan, *Are You Still Below?*, p. 67.
45 Wilkins and Hill, *American Business Abroad*, p. 237.
46 BFRC: Perry to Edsel Ford, 15 April 1932, Nevins and Hill, Acc. 572, Box 18.
47 Steven Tolliday and Jonathan Zeitlin 'Introduction', in Steven Tolliday and Jonathan Zeitlin (eds), *Between Fordism and Flexibility: The Automobile Industry and Its Workers* (Oxford: Berg Publishers, 1992), p. 4.
48 BFRC: Perry to Edsel Ford, 15 April 1932, Nevins and Hill, Acc. 572, Box 18.
49 Ibid.
50 BFRC: Perry to Sorensen, 3 June 1932, Nevins and Hill, Acc. 572, Box 18.
51 Ibid.
52 Ibid.
53 Ibid.
54 Ibid.
55 Ibid.
56 BFRC: Minutes of Meeting of Directors of Henry Ford and Sons Limited, 6 June 1933, Sorensen, Acc. 38, Box 16.

57 National Archives of Ireland (hereafter NAI): Dept. of Industry and Commerce – Memorandum on the Position of the Motor Car Assembly Industry in Ireland at the end of 1940, December 1940. Department of the Taoiseach (hereafter TAOIS), S 12412 A.
58 *The Irish Times*, 1 January 1936.
59 Ibid.
60 Ibid.
61 Ibid. Figure refers to sales in the twelve months before and after the declaration of war on Germany by Britain.
62 BFRC: Myra Wilkins interview with John O'Neill, September 1960, Wilkins, Acc. 880, Box 7.
63 *The Cork Examiner*, 30 December 1940.
64 For Ford employees in Britain see Chapter Four. For working-class emigration see Chapter Seven.
65 CIOs were industry-level organisations involving the state, trade unions and employers founded in 1961 which sought to prepare different industrial sectors for European integration.
66 NAI: Committee on Industrial Organisation – Report on Survey of the Motor Vehicle Assembly Industry, 17 October 1962, Department of Industry and Commerce (hereafter IND) 19/58.
67 Ibid.
68 NAI: Note on the Position of the Motor Assembly Industry as at September 1956, IND 4/225.
69 NAI: Ronan Ó Foghlú to Seán Lemass, 22 May 1962, TAOIS/97/9/1597.
70 NAI: Committee on Industrial Organisation – Report on Survey of the Motor Vehicle Assembly Industry, 17 October 1962, IND/19/58.
71 Ibid.
72 NAI: Speech by Mr Seán Lemass, Taoiseach, at banquet to celebrate the forty-fifth anniversary of Messrs. Henry Ford and Son, Ltd, at City Hall, Cork. Wednesday 23 May 1962, TAOIS/97/9/1597.
73 *Business and Finance*, 24 May 1968.
74 NAI: Committee on Industrial Organisation – Report on Survey of the Motor Vehicle Assembly Industry, 17 October 1962.
75 *The Irish Times*, 24 May 1969.
76 *Dáil Éireann Debates*, vol. 240, no. 7, col. 1013. The latter number was 38,007. See *Dáil Éireann Debates*, vol. 16, no. 15, col. 2111.
77 *The Irish Times*, 24 May 1969.
78 David Burgess-Wise, *Ford at Dagenham: The Rise and Fall of Detroit in Europe* (Derby: Derby Books, 2012), p. 154.
79 The Anglo-Irish Free Trade Agreement was signed in December 1965. It committed the United Kingdom to abolishing import duties on all Irish goods by July 1966 with Ireland reciprocating by gradually reducing import duties on British goods until these duties reached 0 per cent in 1975. The agreement marked a major step in the ending of protectionism in the Irish economy.
80 Patrick Lalor, 16 February 1971; *Dáil Éireann Debates*, vol. 251, no. 9, col. 1335.
81 *The Irish Times*, 14 March 1979; *The Cork Examiner*, 7 October 1983.
82 Ibid.
83 *The Irish Times*, 10 October 1983.
84 Ibid.
85 Ibid.

86 This figure includes those involved in distribution and other activities outside of assembly. *The Irish Times*, 18 January 1984.
87 *The Irish Times*, 7 July 1984; *The Cork Examiner*, 18 January 1984.
88 *The Irish Times*, 19 January 1984.
89 Grimes, 'Henry Ford in Cork', p. 238.
90 BFRC: Myra Wilkins interview with John O'Neill, September 1960, Wilkins, Acc. 880, Box 7.
91 NAI: 'Committee on Industrial Organisation – Report on Survey of the Motor Vehicle Assembly Industry, 17 October 1962; IND/19/58; *The Irish Press*, 30 December 1971.

2. Sunbeam Wolsey, 1927–90
1 A description from 1944 of the Sunbeam Wolsey factory complex, Millfield, Cork; Sunbeam Wolsey Limited, *Sunbeam Wolsey* (Cork: Sunbeam, 1944), p. x.
2 D.J. Coakley, *Cork: Its Trade and Commerce* (Cork: Guy & Co, 1919), p. 173.
3 Edward Lahiff, 'Industry and Labour in Cork, 1890–1921' (Unpublished MA Thesis: University College Cork, 1988), p. 87.
4 Ibid.
5 Andy Bielenberg, *Cork's Industrial Revolution, 1780–1880: Development or Decline?* (Cork: Cork University Press, 1991), p. 20.
6 Ibid.
7 Colin Rynne, *The Archaeology of Cork City and Harbour from the Earliest Times to Industrialisation* (Cork: Collins Press, 1993), p. 91.
8 *The Irish Times*, 4 February 1928.
9 Mary Leland, *Dwyers of Cork: A Family Business and a Business Family* (Cork: Ted Dwyer, 2008), p. 60.
10 Cork City and County Archives (hereafter CCCA): Committee on Industrial Progress – Questionnaire on the Hosiery Manufacturing Industry – October 1968, Sunbeam B505/BND 13 Temp 127.
11 David O'Mahony, *The Irish Economy: An Introductory Description* (Cork: Cork University Press, 1967), p. 31. Only thirty-one manufacturing establishments in Ireland in 1958 employed more than 500 workers.
12 Cork Folklore Project (hereafter CFP): SR (Sound Recording) Number Unavailable, Nancy Byrne, 13 November 2002.
13 D.J. Dwyer and L.J. Symons, 'The Development and Location of the Textiles Industries in the Irish Republic', *Irish Geography*, vol. 4, no. 6 (1963), p. 417.
14 Ibid., p. 419.
15 Ibid.
16 *Anglo-Celt*, 16 July 1927.
17 Ibid.
18 Dwyer and Symons, 'Textile Industries', p. 420.
19 Mark Frankland and Gordon Bussey (consultant), *Radio Man: The Remarkable Rise and Fall of C.O. Stanley* (London: The Institution of Electrical Engineers, 2002), p. 242.
20 Ibid.
21 Ibid.
22 CCCA: Cork Council of Trade Unions Minutes, 27 October 1932, U216 1/4.
23 *The Irish Times*, 3 March 1933.
24 *Weekly Irish Times*, 11 March 1933.
25 T.A. Linehan, 'The Development of Cork's Economy and Business Attitudes, 1910–1939' (Unpublished MA Thesis, University College Cork, 1985), p. 121.

26 Ibid.; CCCA: Report of the Eighth Ordinary General Meeting of Sunbeam Wolsey Limited, Monday 24th August 1936, Sunbeam B505/ BND 28/1 Temp 76.
27 Ibid.
28 *The Cork Examiner*, 13 January 1939.
29 Sunbeam Wolsey, *Sunbeam Wolsey*, pp. 1–2.
30 Frankland, *Radio Man*, p. 242; *Irish Independent*, 15 June 1943.
31 The numbers employed by Sunbeam Wolsey increased from 701 in 1939 to 1,049 in 1945, CCCA: Sunbeam Wolsey Limited 22nd Annual Report 1950, Sunbeam, B505/ Bundle 63/1.
32 CCCA: Sunbeam Wolsey Ltd Fifty Years of Development, 1978, Sunbeam Small Collection SM631/9/ Bnd. 1.
33 *The Irish Times*, 30 June 1951.
34 Ibid.
35 Ibid.
36 *The Irish Times*, 28 September 1957.
37 Following the signing of the AIFTA.
38 CCCA: Managing Director's Report for the Year Ended 31 December 1968, Sunbeam B505/ Box 42 Temp 20.
39 CCCA: Sunbeam Wolsey Limited – Report and Statement of Accounts December 1963, Sunbeam B505 BND28/1 Temp 76.
40 Interview with Tom Scott, Kilbrittain, 18 December 2012.
41 Roderick R. O'Mahony, 'Employment in the Textiles and Clothing Industries in Ireland, 1963–87' (Unpublished MA Thesis: University College Cork, 1990), p. 76.
42 *The Irish Times*, 3 December 1971 and 4 November 1972.
43 *The Irish Times*, 1 May 1971.
44 Ibid.
45 CCCA: Sunbeam Group of Companies – Minutes of Meeting of the Raw Material Group, 30 June 1971, Sunbeam B505/ Box 23/3.
46 Interview with Kevin Dwyer, Cloyne, 27 October 2012.
47 See Chapter Five.
48 European Commission, *European File: The European Community Textile Industry April 1982* (Brussels: European Communities Directorate-General for Information, 1982), p. 1.
49 Ibid.
50 Ibid.
51 *The Irish Times*, 23 March 1976.
52 *The Irish Times*, 16 April 1965.
53 CCCA: Sunbeam Wolsey Limited, Fifty Years of Development, 1978, Sunbeam Small Collection, SM631/9/ Bnd. 1.
54 Ibid.
55 Tom Scott, 18 December 2012.
56 See Committee on Industrial Organisation, *Report on the Hosiery and Knitwear Industry* (Dublin: Stationery Office, 1963).
57 *The Irish Times*, 26 October 1978.
58 Ibid.
59 CCCA: Sunbeam Group of Companies – Minutes of Meeting of the Raw Material Group, 30 June 1971, Sunbeam B505 / Box 23/3.
60 Tom Scott, 18 December 2012. My italics.
61 Ibid.
62 *The Cork Examiner*, 3 April 1975 and *Irish Times*, 11 May 1977.

63 *The Irish Times*, 11 May 1977.
64 *The Irish Times*, 24 August 1979.
65 CCCA: Sunbeam Wolsey Ltd Fifty Years of Development, 1978, Sunbeam Small Collection, SM631/9/ Bnd. 1.
66 Sectoral Development Committee, *Report and Recommendations on the Clothing and Textiles Industries* (Dublin: Sectoral Development Committee, 1983), pp. 2–12.
67 Ibid., p. 8.
68 *The Irish Press*, 20 November 1980.
69 Ibid.
70 *The Cork Examiner*, 23 May 1980.
71 *The Irish Press*, 4 November 1982.
72 *The Irish Press*, 1 August 1980.
73 *The Irish Press*, 3 April 1982.
74 Ibid.
75 Ibid.
76 Ibid.
77 *The Irish Press*, 7 May 1982.
78 *Irish Independent*, 31 March 1984.
79 Ibid.
80 *Irish Independent*, 3 March 1988.
81 *The Irish Press*, 7 May 1988.
82 *The Irish Times*, 9 July 1988.
83 *Irish Independent*, 30 January 1990.
84 *The Irish Press*, 7 February 1990.
85 *The Irish Times*, 23 July 1985.
86 *The Cork Examiner*, 7 March 1989.
87 *The Irish Times*, 31 January 1990.
88 *The Irish Times*, 31 January 1990.
89 *The Cork Examiner*, 2 February 1990.

3. Irish Steel, 1939–2001
1 Sarsfield Hogan, *A History of Irish Steel* (Dublin: Gill & Macmillan, 1980), p. 1.
2 Nippon Denro Ispat Limited, an Indian Steel multinational, now JSW Ispat Limited.
3 Garret FitzGerald, *State-Sponsored Bodies* (Dublin: Institute of Public Administration, 1961), p. 19.
4 Frank Barry and Joe Durkan, *TEAM and Irish Steel: An Application of the Declining High-Wages Industries Literature* (Dublin: Centre for Economic Research, 1995), p. 7.
5 *The Irish Times*, 27 June 1938.
6 Hogan, *Irish Steel*, pp. 27–8.
7 NAI: Report by the Directors on the Steel Industry at Haulbowline, 17 February 1949, IND 10/28.
8 NAI: Memorandum concerning the present position of Irish Steel, Limited, 10 October 1940, TAOIS S/11603 A.
9 The disadvantages of boat transport were apparent from an early stage. In 1946 a winter storm swamped the engine of a ferry shuttling steelmen to Haulbowline, forcing it to anchor near Monkstown. Several hours later fourteen employees and one stowaway were rescued by the coast guard. *The Cork Examiner*, 12 December 1946.
10 Susan Milner, 'The Effect of Protection on Irish Steel and the EC Steel Industry' (Unpublished MA Thesis: University College Cork, 1995), p. 4.

11 Hogan, *Irish Steel*, p. 26 and NAI: Seán Lemass, Minutes of special points for which the Minister for Supplies wishes to stress in relation to Irish Steel, Ltd, 1940, TAOIS S/11603 A.
12 Mary E. Daly, *Industrial Development and Irish National Identity, 1922–1939* (New York: Syracuse Press, 1992), p. 109.
13 Hogan, *Irish Steel*, p. 26.
14 Saorstát Éireann, *Census of Population 1926* (Dublin, 1928), Volume 1, Table 7.
15 Saorstát Éireann, *Census of Population 1936* (Dublin, 1938), Volume 1, Table 7. Population recorded as 6,178.
16 *The Southern Star*, 5 September 1936.
17 Hogan, *Irish Steel*, p. 38.
18 Daly, *Industrial Development*, pp. 106, 178.
19 *The Irish Times*, 25 August 1939. My italics.
20 *The Irish Press*, 27 July 1939.
21 NAI: Seán Lemass, Speech following opening of Haulbowline Bridge, 24 October 1966, TAOIS/98/6/127.
22 CCCA: Séamus Fitzgerald (Chairman), Speech at the 1940 annual meeting of Irish Steel, Limited, 30 September 1940, Fitzgerald PR/6/1294.
23 CCCA: J.J. Walsh to Séamus Fitzgerald, 20 June 1941, Fitzgerald PR/6/1297.
24 CCCA: Jacob Beckett to Séamus Fitzgerald, 27 June 1941, Fitzgerald PR/6/1298.
25 CCCA: *Cobh Urban District Council Minutes*, 13 June 1941.
26 Milner, 'Protection', p. 6.
27 NAI: Department of Industry and Commerce – Memorandum concerning the present position of Irish Steel, Limited, 16 October 1940, TAOIS S/11603 A.
28 Ibid.
29 Ibid.
30 Ibid.
31 Ibid.
32 Ibid.
33 Ibid.
34 Ibid.
35 Ibid.
36 Ibid.
37 NAI: J.J. McElligott to Secretary, Department of Industry and Commerce, 7 November 1940, TAOIS/S 11603 A.
38 NAI: Supplemental memorandum regarding Irish Steel, 16 October 1940, TAOIS S/11603 A.
39 Mary E. Daly writes that 'Lemass possessed an authority in industrial matters equalled only by de Valera's in foreign affairs'. Daly, *Industrial Development*, p. 64.
40 Hogan, *Irish Steel*, p, 47.
41 Seán Lemass, *Dáil Éireann Debates*, vol. 105, col. 815 (17 April 1947).
42 *The Irish Times*, 6 February 1947.
43 Seán Lemass, *Dáil Éireann Debates*, vol. 105, col. 815 (17 April 1947).
44 See, for example, Martin Corry, *Dáil Éireann Debates*, vol. 106, col. 1379 (10 June 1947).
45 Córas Iompar Éireann, the semi-state transport company. *The Cork Examiner*, 11 February 1947.
46 Hogan, *Irish Steel*, p. 64.
47 'It seems to me rather illogical that the State should go into a business which private enterprise failed to make pay, failed even to keep as a going concern. It seems to me illogical that the State should embark on steel enterprise here because, as far as I know

anything about steel, we have to depend on scrap metal for raw materials or import the iron ore from abroad and I do not know that we can attempt the manufacture of steel on anything like an economic basis here.' *Dáil Éireann Debates*, vol. 105, col. 1032 (22 April 1947).
48 Hogan, *Irish Steel*, p. 66.
49 Ibid., p. 69.
50 NAI: Observations of the Minister for Finance on the memorandum submitted to the government by the Minister for Industry and Commerce on the 31st December 1946, and Observations of the Minister for Finance on the proposals of the Minister for Industry and Commerce, 20 February 1947, TAOIS, 3/S11603 C.
51 Hogan, *Irish Steel*, p. 1.
52 Ibid., p. 69.
53 NAI: Report by the Directors on the Steel Industry at Haulbowline, 17 February 1949, TAOIS 3/S11603 D/1.
54 NAI: Irish Steel Holdings Limited – Financial Accounts, 30 June 1956, IND 4/107 and *The Irish Press*, 19 April 1951.
55 NAI: Observations of the Minister for Finance, 27 July 1953, TAOIS 11603 D/2.
56 NAI: James O'Riordan (Amalgamated Engineering Union), Memorandum on Steel Production, enclosed with letter from James Collins, Treasurer for Dublin Trades Union Council to Seán Lemass, 5 September 1957, IND 4/107.
57 NAI: Sarsfield Hogan, Note of interview with Mr E.D. Timmerman, 31 July 1957, IND 4/107.
58 NAI: Sarsfield Hogan, Notes of discussion with Sir Ernest Lever, 11 July 1957, IND 4/107.
59 Ibid.
60 NAI: Cabinet minutes regarding Irish Steel Holdings Limited – expansion of activities, 8 August 1958, TAOIS, 3/S11603 D/3.
61 *The Irish Press*, 31 August 1960.
62 NAI: 'Irish Steel Holdings Limited – Chairman's Review – Financial Year Ended 30th June 1969', TAOIS/ 2000/6 261 and 'Speech by Mr Seán F. Lemass at luncheon in Imperial Hotel, Cork, following opening of Haulbowline Bridge, Monday, 24 October 1966', TAOIS/98/6/127.
63 NAI: Industry and Commerce memorandum for the government, 15 October 1971, TAOIS 2002/8/124.
64 NAI: Irish Steel Chairman's Review, 14 October 1972, TAOIS 2003/16/168.
65 *The Cork Examiner*, 31 August 1960.
66 Daly, *Industrial Development*, pp. 67–8.
67 Eoin O'Malley, *Industry and Economic Development: The Challenges for the Latecomer* (Dublin: Gill & Macmillan, 1989), p. 105.
68 *The Irish Times*, 26 September 1968 and 19 December 1974.
69 NAI: Department of Industry and Commerce memorandum for the government – Proposal by Irish Steel Holdings Ltd to re-equip its plant and expand steel production, 23 October 1976, TAOIS 2007/116/80.
70 Ibid.
71 NAI: Department of Industry and Commerce memorandum for the government – Irish Steel, 20 April 1950, TAOIS 3/S11603.
72 NAI: Irish Steel Holdings Limited, Year Ended 30 June 1969, TAOIS 2000/6/621.
73 NAI: Department of Industry and Commerce memorandum for the government – Proposal by Irish Steel Holdings Ltd to re-equip its plant and expand steel production, 23 October 1976, TAOIS 2007/116/80.

74 International Iron and Steel Institute, *A Handbook of World Steel Statistics* (Brussels: International Iron and Steel Institute, 1974), p. 2.
75 Kenneth Warren, 'World Steel: Change and Crisis', *Geography*, vol. 70, no. 2 (April 1985), p. 111.
76 Anthony Cockerill and Aubrey Silberston, *The Steel Industry: International Comparisons of Industrial Structure and Performance* (London: Cambridge University Press, 1974), p. 108.
77 Warren, 'World Steel', p. 111.
78 International Iron and Steel Institute, *Handbook*, p. 2.
79 NAI: Memorandum for the government – Irish Steel Holdings Ltd interim expansion proposals, 12 October 1970, TAOIS 2001/6/63.
80 NAI: Department of Finance memorandum for the government – Proposal by Irish Steel Holdings Ltd to re-equip its plant and expand steel production, 26 October 1976, TAOIS 2007/116/80.
81 The 1973 oil crisis was a surge in the cost of fuel resulting from an embargo imposed by a group of oil-producing nations. Between October 1973 and March 1974 the price of oil increased fourfold, causing shortages and inflation across much of the developed world.
82 *The Economist*, 25 December 1976.
83 Warren, 'World Steel', p. 111.
84 Lydia Schulman, 'The Davignon Plan for Europe's Steel', *Economic Intelligence Review*, vol. 6, no. 13 (April 1979), p. 51.
85 One of Ireland's most prominent businessmen, Kevin McCourt had previously held the positions of director-general of Radio Teilifís Éireann (RTÉ) and managing-director of Irish Distillers Ltd. He served as chairman of Irish Steel from 1975 until 1986.
86 NAI: Presentation of accounts and report of the directors for year ended 30th June 1979 to both houses of the Oireachtas, 15 October 1979 and Kevin McCourt, speech at annual meeting, 27 September 1979, TAOIS 2009/135/75.
87 NAI: Department of Finance memorandum for the government – Proposal by Irish Steel Holdings Ltd to re-equip its plant and expand steel production, 26 October 1976, TAOIS 2007/116/80.
88 See Chapter Six.
89 Ibid.
90 NAI, Presentation of accounts and report of the directors for the year ended 30 June 1981, 2 November 1981, TAOIS 2011/127/106.
91 Ibid.
92 Barry and Durkan, *TEAM and Irish Steel*, p. 9.
93 *Steel Times*, vol. 210, no. 4 (April 1982).
94 Fifth Joint Committee on Commercial State Bodies, *Fourth Report – Irish Steel Limited* (Dublin: Stationery Office, 1988), p. 8.
95 Ibid., p. 14.
96 NAI: Department of Industry and Commerce memorandum for government – Presentation of accounts and report of the directors of Irish Steel for the year ended 30 June 1981 to both houses of the Oireachtas, 2 November 1981, TAOIS 2011/127/106.
97 Company annual reports as reported in local and national media.
98 Barry and Durkan, *TEAM and Irish Steel*, pp. 8–9.
99 *Business and Finance*, 24 March 1994.
100 David G. Tarr, 'The Steel Crisis in the United States and European Community: Causes and Adjustments', in Robert E. Baldwin, Carl B. Hamilton and Andre Sapir (eds), *Issues in US–EC Trade Relations* (Chicago: University of Chicago Press, 1988), p. 176.

101 The Davignon plan was a continent-wide rescue plan for the European steel industry that was introduced in 1978. The goal of the plan was to salvage the industry through restructuring and rationalisation. One of its centrepieces was caps on steel production by individual countries as it was feared that a glut of steel products would further exacerbate the problems of European steel producers.
102 Desmond O'Malley, *Dáil Éireann Debates*, vol. 395, col. 692 (6 February 1990).
103 *Dáil Éireann Debates*, vol. 455, col. 1958 (20 September 1995).
104 The terms of the contract between Ispat and the government stipulated that the company would have to maintain employment in the factory for a minimum of five years.

4. Working for Fords, 1917-84

1 Edward Lahiff, 'Industry and Labour in Cork, 1890–1921' (Unpublished MA Thesis: University College Cork, 1988), p. 38. Cork Town Planning Association, *Cork: A Civic Survey* (Liverpool: Liverpool University Press, 1926), p. 7.
2 Miriam Nyhan, *Are You Still Below? The Ford Marina Plant, 1917–84* (Cork: Collins Press, 2007), p. 57.
3 J.C.P., *A Visit to Henry Ford and Son, Ltd Marina, Cork* (Dublin: Sackville Press, 1926), p. 3.
4 For our purposes, the main salient features of Fordism are as follows: (i) Scientific, generalised and rationalised production methods with a significant division of labour in which individual workers perform a minimal number of tasks which are repeated throughout a shift on an industrial scale. This system is best embodied by the assembly line. (ii) Standardisation of product. Large industrial concerns producing a small number of products to maximise gains from economies of scale. (iii) High wages deriving from the efficiency and high profit margins generated by the Fordist system such that employees of Fordist concerns could expect to purchase the commodities they produced. (iv) Hostility to trade unionism. This latter aspect of Fordism gradually ceased to be a defining feature of the system after the company was forced to accept the presence of labour organisation.
5 Nyhan focuses mainly on the business history of the plant in the pre-1932 period. The experiences of the workforce in the post-1932 era, based on extensive oral histories, are examined, though there is relatively little on the earlier period. Grimes' thesis is focused almost entirely on the pre-1932 business history of the firm though his research is extensive and does include material on Marina employment policy and other labour history-related topics in a highly detailed and well-researched thesis.
6 *The Cork Examiner*, 19 March 1917.
7 CCCA: 'Monthly Bulletin of the Cork Industrial Development Association, March 1918', Cork Industrial Development Association Files, U141/1.
8 Henry Ford announced in January 1914 that he was doubling the wages of all his employees to five dollars per day which, by the standards of the time, was an almost inconceivably high wage for a manual operative. The 'five-dollar day' also became associated with a more general turn to welfare capitalism within the company.
9 Stephen Meyer III, *The Five Dollar Day: Labor Management and Social Control in the Ford Motor Company, 1908–1921* (Albany: State University of New York Press, 1981), p. 98.
10 Ibid., p. 97.
11 Robert Fitzgerald, *British Labour Management and Industrial Welfare, 1846–1939* (London: Croom Helm, 1988), p. 3.
12 Ibid.

13 BFRC: Percival Perry, 'Report on the Establishment of a Plant at Cork, 25 February 1913', Henry Ford Office, Acc. 62, Box 59.
14 Ibid.
15 BFRC: Percival Perry to C.E. Sorensen, 9 December 1918, Sorensen, Acc. 38, Box 42.
16 Meyer, *The Five Dollar Day*, p. 169. The 'American Plan' describes the intense anti-union stance of American employers in the 1920s which dismissed labour organisation as 'un-American' and even seditious.
17 Henry Ford, *My Life and Work: An Autobiography of Henry Ford* (London: Heineman, 1922), p. 176.
18 BFRC: Letter from Percival Perry to Charles Sorensen, 9 December 1918, Sorensen, Acc. 38, Box 42.
19 Grimes, 'Henry Ford in Cork', pp. 116–24.
20 Cork Town Planning Association, *Cork: A Civic Survey* (Liverpool: Liverpool University Press, 1926), p. 14.
21 Grimes, 'Henry Ford in Cork', p. 121.
22 BFRC: Edward Grace to Charles Sorensen, 4 October 1921, Sorensen, Acc. 38, Box 45.
23 The Guinness family in the late nineteenth and early twentieth century introduced 'a non-contributory pension scheme, free health care for employees and their families in the company's dispensary, and founded the Guinness Trust which provided low-cost housing' for employees and their families. See Mary Muldowney, '"A world of its own": Recollections of Women Workers in Guinness' Brewery in the 1940s', *Saothar*, vol. 23 (1998), pp. 103–17.
24 See David Toms, '"Notwithstanding the discomfort involved": Fordson's Cup Win in 1926 and How "The Old Contemptible" were Represented in Ireland's Public Sphere during the 1920s', *Sport in History* (2013), pp. 1–22.
25 For grassroots recreational culture, see David Toms, *Soccer in Munster: A Social History, 1877–1937* (Cork: Cork University Press, 2015), p. 119.
26 BFRC: *Fordson Worker*, 15 November 1920, Sorensen, Acc. 38, Box 43.
27 Henry Ford, *My Life and Work*, p. 207.
28 Ibid., pp. 209–10.
29 BFRC: Percival Perry to Charles Sorensen, 9 December 1918. Sorensen, Acc. 38, Box 42.
30 Ford abhorred tobacco and alcohol.
31 *Fordson Worker*, 15 November 1920.
32 BFRC: Edward Grace to Charles Sorensen, 24th July 1920, Nevins and Hill, Acc. 572, Box 17.
33 *Fordson Worker*, 15 November 1920.
34 J.C.P., *A Visit to Henry Ford and Son Ltd, Marina, Cork* (Dublin: Sackville Press, c.1926), p. 25.
35 BFRC: Cork Salary and Wage Schedule, 1 September 1922, Auditing Department Files, Acc. 33, Box 23.
36 BFRC: Cork Salary and Wage Schedule, 1 January 1925, Auditing Department Files, Acc. 33, Box 23.
37 Grimes, 'Henry Ford in Cork', p. 127.
38 J.C.P., *A Visit to Henry Ford and Sons*, p. 4.
39 Ibid., p. 28.
40 See Chapter Six.
41 Andrea Tone, *The Business of Benevolence: Industrial Paternalism in Progressive America* (Ithaca: Cornell University Press, 1997), pp. 102–3.
42 Meyer, *The Five Dollar Day*, pp. 1–7.

43 Fitzgerald, *British Labour Management*, pp. 10–13.
44 Gus McLoughlin, 2 August 2003.
45 Miriam Nyhan Interviews (hereafter MNI): Bob Elliott, 22 January 2003.
46 Bureau of Military History (hereafter BMH): Michael V. O'Donoghue Witness Statement, WS 1,741, File S 2676.
47 MNI: Dominic Carey, 20 January 2003.
48 Nyhan, *Are You Still Below?*, p. 79.
49 In the week of 16 December, for example, forty-four men were discharged or left. The week before that, seventy employees had exited employment in the factory. At other times, there were rapid influxes into the factory. During the week ending 29 July 1922, twenty-nine men were taken on while on the week ending 27 May 1922, seventy-six men joined the ranks of the Ford workforce. BFRC: Employment and Wages Reports, 1922, Sorensen, Acc. 38, Box 46.
50 BFRC: Cork Factory: Number of Inspectors in Relation to Labour Employed, 31 March 1930, Nevins and Hill, Acc. 572, Box 17.
51 *The Cork Examiner*, 17 February 1923.
52 'Slackage', in the common parlance of the time, meant periods when low production demands led to reductions in the number of employees within individual firms and industries. See Chapter Seven.
53 Huw Beynon, *Working for Ford* (Wakefield: EP Publishing, 1973), p. 19.
54 BFRC: Clarke to H.S. Cooper, 5th June 1930, Wilkins, Acc. 880, Box 7.
55 Meyer, *The Five Dollar Day*, p. 5.
56 *The Irish Times*, 24 December 1932.
57 Maura Murphy, 'The Working Classes of Nineteenth-Century Cork', *Journal of the Cork Historical and Archaeological Society*, vol. lxxxv, no. 241 (1980), p. 33.
58 The exact figure is 6,924. 'Pearce to G.S. Hibberson, 26 February 1930', Wilkins, Acc. 880, Box 7.
59 BFRC: E.L. Clarke to Percival Perry, 25 March 1930, Nevins and Hill, Acc. 572, Box 17.
60 *The Cork Examiner*, 14 June 1929.
61 Ibid.
62 BFRC: Harry Scott to Charles Sorensen, 27 April 1929, Nevins and Hill, Acc. 572, Box 17. My italics.
63 BFRC: William Squire to C.E. Sorensen, 12 March 1929, Nevins and Hill, Acc. 572, Box 17.
64 BFRC: E.L. Clarke to C.E. Sorensen, 2 April 1930, Nevins and Hill, Acc. 572, Box 17.
65 Beynon, *Working for Ford*, p. 32.
66 Nyhan, *Are You Still Below?*, p. 75.
67 Domhnall Mac an tSíthigh, *An Baile i bhFad Siar* (Baile Átha Cliath: Coiscéim, 2000), p. 62. My translation.
68 BFRC: E.L. Clarke to Percival Perry, 25 March 1930, Nevins and Hill, Acc. 572, Box 17.
69 Interview with Tim Murphy, Glasheen, 30 January 2013.
70 Ford, *My Life and Work*, p. 176.
71 Beynon, *Working for Ford*, p. 29.
72 Ibid.
73 Interview with Gus McLoughlin, Dunmore East, 29 July 2013.
74 MNI: Bob Elliott, 22 January 2003.
75 BFRC: Edward Grace to Charles Sorensen, 20 January 1923, Sorensen, Acc. 38, Box 108.
76 Ibid.
77 Ibid.
78 *The Cork Examiner*, 19 January 1923.

79 Ibid.
80 BFRC: Edward Grace to C.E. Sorensen, 20 January 1923, Sorensen, Acc. 38, Box 108.
81 *The Cork Examiner*, 19 January 1923.
82 Ibid. The dispute occurred at the height of the Irish Civil War and there was a large military presence in the city.
83 *Fordson Worker*, 15 November 1920.
84 Ibid.
85 Ibid.
86 Emmet O'Connor, *A Labour History of Ireland, 1824–2000* (Dublin: UCD Press, 2011), p. 102.
87 Steven Tolliday, 'Management and Labour in Britain, 1896–1939', in Steven Tolliday and Jonathan Zeitlin (eds), *Between Fordism and Flexibility: The Automobile Industry and Its Workers* (Oxford: Berg, 1992), p. 46.
88 Joan Sangster, *Earning Respect: The Lives of Working Women in Small-Town Ontario* (Toronto: University of Toronto Press, 1995), p. 140.
89 BFRC: Dan Fitzgibbon to Henry Ford, 2 March 1922, Sorensen, Acc. 38, Box 45.
90 Peter Hart, *The IRA and Its Enemies: Violence and Community in Cork, 1916–1923* (Oxford: Clarendon Press, 1998), p. 157.
91 *The Cork Examiner*, 25 August 1920.
92 BMH: Michael V. O'Donoghue Witness Statement, WS 1,741, File S 2676.
93 *The Cork Examiner*, 16 October 1920.
94 Ibid.
95 Grimes, 'Henry Ford in Cork', pp. 178–9.
96 BFRC: Edward Grace to Charles Sorensen, 20 October 1920, Nevins and Hill, Acc. 572, Box 17.
97 Ibid.
98 Ibid.
99 Ibid. My italics.
100 *The Cork Examiner*, 8 April 1932.
101 Ibid.
102 *The Cork Examiner*, 9 April 1932.
103 Ibid.
104 Ibid.
105 See Chapter One.
106 NAI: Dept. of Industry and Commerce – Memorandum on the position of the motor car assembly industry in Ireland at the end of 1940, December 1940, TAOIS/S 12412 A.
107 Ibid.
108 Ibid.
109 David Burgess-Wise, *Ford at Dagenham: The Rise and Fall of Detroit in Europe* (Derby: Derby Books, 2012), pp. 66–7.
110 Burgess-Wise, *Ford at Dagenham*, p. 72.
111 NAI: John O'Neill to A.S. McCanna, Office of the Minister for Industry and Commerce, 7 July 1941, TAOIS/3/S578 B.
112 NAI: 'Letter from Mr Murphy, Customs Dept. Head, Henry Ford and Sons to T.J. Horan, Passport Office, 3 July 1941 and 4 July 1941', Department of Foreign Affairs (hereafter DFA) 4/202/1517.
113 NAI: 'Letters from M. Muldowney, Employment Dept., Henry Ford and Sons to M. O'Flaherty, Department of External Affairs', 1 December 1943, 22 November 1943, 12 November 1943, 20 October 1943, 20 July 1943, DFA/4/202/1517.

114 MNI: Vaunie Downey, 11 June 2003.
115 Burgess-Wise, *Ford at Dagenham*, p. 38.
116 Sheila Cohen, *Notoriously Militant: The Story of a Union Branch* (London: Merlin, 2013), p. 25.
117 See Chapter Seven.
118 Gus McLoughlin, 29 July 2013.
119 Steven Tolliday, 'Ford and "Fordism" in Postwar Britain', in Steven Tolliday and Jonathan Zeitlin (eds), *The Power to Manage? Employers and Industrial Relations in Comparative-Historical Perspective* (London: Routledge, 1991), p. 83.
120 Cohen, *Militant*, p. 35.
121 Gus McLoughlin, 29 July 2013.
122 MNI: Dominic Carey, 20 January 2003.
123 Mac an tSíthigh, *An Baile i bhFad Siar*, p. 62. My translation.
124 *The Cork Examiner*, 16 April 1965.
125 *Irish Independent*, 30 November 1945.
126 Emmet O'Connor, *A Labour History of Ireland* (Dublin: UCD Press, 2011), p. 170.
127 Christopher Coleman Doyle, 'Industrial Relations in Post-World War Two Ireland, 1946–1950' (Unpublished MPhil Thesis: University College Cork, 1999), p. 11.
128 *Liberty*, August 1949.
129 *The Irish Times*, 23 September 1949.
130 *The Irish Times*, 28 September 1949.
131 MNI: Max Hayes, 5 December 2002.
132 MNI: Arthur Owens, 27 November 2002.
133 MNI: Eddie Cleary, 6 December 2002.
134 *Liberty*, December 1949.
135 MNI: Eddie Cleary, 6 December 2002.
136 *Liberty*, December 1949.
137 MNI: Eddie Mullins, 28 November 2002.
138 *The Cork Examiner*, 1 June 1954 – 30 September 1954.
139 NAI: Committee on Industrial Organisation – Report on survey of the motor vehicle assembly industry, 17 October 1962, IND 19/58.
140 NAI: Report of Meetings – Subject: level of activity in motor assembly industry, undated, IND 4/225.
141 See Chapter Eight.
142 Interview with Denis Forde, Gurranabraher, 12 September 2013.
143 Nyhan, *Are You Still Below?*, p. 101.
144 Interview with Michael Lenihan, Grange, 31 January 2013.
145 Interview with Michael Costelloe, Blackrock, 28 February 2013.
146 Nyhan, *Are You Still Below?*, p. 100.
147 Beynon, *Working for Ford*, p. 109.
148 Paul Thompson, 'Playing at Being Skilled Men: Factory Culture and Pride in Work Skills Among Coventry Car Workers', *Social History*, vol. 31, no. 1 (January 1988), p. 57.
149 Pat Dunlea, 10 December 2013.
150 Gus McLoughlin, 29 July 2013.
151 Michael Lenihan, 31 January 2013.
152 Nyhan, *Are You Still Below?*, p. 82.
153 Michael Lenihan, 31 January 2013.
154 Ibid.
155 Tim Murphy, 30 January 2013.

156 Ibid.
157 See Chapter Eight.
158 Michael Lenihan, 31 January 2013.
159 Tim Murphy, 30 January 2013.
160 Robert Bruno, *Steelworker Alley: How Class Works in Youngstown* (London: Cornell University Press, 1999), p. 106.
161 *The Irish Times*, 25 August 1977. The claims were made by the magazine *Business and Finance*.
162 *The Irish Times*, 26 August 1977.
163 Ibid.
164 'In terms of US dollars, average hourly earnings in the Irish industry came to $2.73 in 1976, compared with $3.28 in Britain.' *The Irish Times*, 26 August 1977.
165 H.A. Turner, Garfield Clack and Geoffrey Roberts, *Labour Relations in the Motor Industry* (London: George Allen & Unwin Ltd, 1967), p. 46.
166 *The Irish Times*, 10 September 1977.
167 Tim Murphy, 30 January 2013.
168 The redundancy payments of eleven and a half weeks per year of service were, after some negotiation, accepted by a three-to-one majority. Ford also took the unusual step of paying the first year of tuition fees for any children of Ford workers beginning university in the following year. See *The Cork Examiner*, 7 July and 6 September 1984.

5. Working for Sunbeam Wolsey, 1927–90

1 Mary Leland. *Dwyers of Cork: A Family Business and a Business Family* (Cork: Ted Dwyer, 2008), p. 62.
2 *The Irish Times*, 9 September 1949. The claim was not entirely true.
3 *Liberty*, December 1955.
4 Philip Scranton, 'Varieties of Paternalism: Industrial Structures and the Social Relations of Production in American Textiles', *American Quarterly*, vol. 36, no. 2 (Summer 1984), p. 236.
5 See, for example, Marilyn Cohen, 'Urbanisation and the Milieux of Factory Life: Gilford/Dunbarton, 1825–1914', in Chris Curtin, Hastings Donnan and Thomas M. Wilson (eds), *Irish Urban Cultures* (Belfast: Institute of Irish Studies, 1993), pp. 227–42.
6 Andrea Tone, *The Business of Benevolence: Industrial Paternalism in Progressive America* (London: Cornell University Press, 1997), p. 1.
7 Walter Licht, 'Fringe Benefits: A Review Essay on the American Workplace', *International Labor and Working-Class History*, no. 53 (Spring 1998), p. 168.
8 *The Irish Times*, 9 September 1949.
9 Licht, 'Fringe Benefits', p. 168.
10 CFP: SR97, Greta Kiely, 8 October 1997.
11 CFP: SR95, Madge Barry, 28 August 1997.
12 CFP: SR224, Peggy Payne, 5 August 1998.
13 Ibid.
14 CFP: SR93, Catherine O'Callaghan, 29 April 1997.
15 CFP: SR95, Madge Barry, 28 August 1997.
16 CFP: SR95, Madge Barry, 28 August 1997.
17 Interview with Rena McCarthy conducted by Clodagh O'Driscoll, 20 September 2011, Women's Oral History Project (hereafter WOHP). Transcript kindly provided by Máire Leane and Elizabeth Kiely.
18 Ibid.

19 Ibid.
20 Ibid.
21 *Liberty*, June 1957.
22 Joan Sangster, 'The Softball Solution: Female Workers, Male Managers and the Operation of Paternalism at Westclox, 1923–1960', *Labour Le Travail*, vol. 32 (Fall, 1993), p. 190.
23 CFP: Peggy Payne.
24 Ibid.
25 Bob Morris and Jim Smyth, 'Paternalism as an Employer Strategy, 1800–1960', in Jill Rubery and Frank Wilkinson (eds), *Employer Strategy and the Labour Market* (Oxford: Oxford University Press, 1994), p. 217.
26 Howard Newby, 'Paternalism and Capitalism', in Richard Scase (ed.), *Industrial Society: Class, Cleavage and Control* (London: Allen & Unwin, 1977), p. 67.
27 Ibid., p. 68.
28 Dwyer was also a patron of the arts, furthering the careers of sculptor Seamus Murphy and composer Aloys Fleischmann.
29 *The Irish Times*, 11 May 1951.
30 *Irish Independent*, 31 August 1946.
31 *Irish Independent*, 1 June 1944.
32 Joan Sangster, *Earning Respect: The Lives of Working Women in Small-Town Ontario, 1920–1960* (Toronto: University of Toronto Press, 1995), p. 57.
33 CFP: SR300, Billy Foley – Guided Tour of Sunbeam, date unknown.
34 CFP: SR224, Peggy Payne, 5 August 1998.
35 CFP: SR96, Linda McCarthy, 16 September 1997.
36 CCCA: Personnel Manager – Definition of Duties, 1966, Sunbeam, B505/Box 8/Temp 137.
37 CFP: Billy Foley.
38 Sangster, 'Softball Solution', p. 181.
39 CFP: SR96, Linda McCarthy, 16 September 1997.
40 CCA: Committee on Industrial Progress – Questionnaire on the Hosiery Manufacturing Industry 1968, Sunbeam, B505/BND13 Temp 27.
41 See Chapter Eight.
42 CFP: SR93, Catherine O'Callaghan, 29 April 1997.
43 Sunbeam Wolsey Ltd, *Sunbeam Wolsey* (Cork: Sunbeam, 1944), p. 16.
44 Tone, *Business of Benevolence*, p. 3.
45 Ibid.
46 S.R. Dennison and Oliver MacDonagh, *Guinness, 1886–1939: From Incorporation to the Second World War* (Cork: Cork University Press, 1998), pp. 116 and 224.
47 *The Irish Press*, 13 January 1939.
48 Brian Girvin, 'Industrialisation and the Irish Working Class Since 1922', *Saothar*, vol. 10 (1984), p. 33.
49 Interview with Kathleen Fitzgibbon conducted by Margaret Kearns, 21 August 2001, Women's Oral History Project (hereafter WOHP), http://www.ucc.ie/acad/appsoc/OralHistoryProject/Audio/interviews/F.K1.wma.
50 Ibid.
51 CCCA: Cork Trades Council Minutes, 10 May 1951, U216/1/11.
52 Alessandro Portelli, 'Patterns of Paternalism in Harlan County', *Appalachian Journal*, vol. 17, no. 2 (Winter 1990), p. 146.
53 The phrase 'commercial traveller' means 'travelling salesman'. The former term was more common in Ireland.

54 CCCA: *Cork Workers' Council Meeting Minutes*, 31 January 1935, U216 1/5.
55 CCCA: Letter from William Dwyer to C.O. Stanley, 11 June 1936, and Letter from P. Shanahan, Secretary Cork and District Worker's Council to William Dwyer, 7 April 1936, Sunbeam B505/BND 27 Temp 71.
56 CCCA: Unsent Press Statement, 11 June 1936, Sunbeam, B505/BND 27 Temp 71.
57 CCCA: Minutes of Board Meeting, 15th June 1936, Sunbeam, B505, Deed Box 1/1. My italics.
58 CCCA: Letter from William Dwyer to C.O. Stanley, 27 April 1936, Sunbeam B505, BND 27, Temp 71. My italics.
59 Betty Messenger, *Picking Up the Linen Threads* (Belfast: Blackstaff Press, 1980), pp. 219–23.
60 *The Irish Times*, 15 May 1963. In Cork parlance, the 'merchant princes' were the traditional bourgeoisie of the city who dominated trade and politics during the eighteenth, nineteenth and early twentieth centuries.
61 Edward Lahiff, 'Industry and Labour in Cork, 1890–1921' (Unpublished MA Thesis: University College Cork, 1988), p. 86. My italics.
62 D.J. Coakley, *Cork: Its Trade and Commerce. Official Handbook of the Cork Incorporated Chamber of Commerce and Shipping* (Cork: Guy & Co. Ltd, 1919), p. 173.
63 CCCA: Report of the Directors for the Year Ending 31st December 1891, Cork Spinning and Weaving Company Files B530/2/1. 1911 report (B530/2/5) also includes references to the building of workers' dwellings.
64 Máire Leane and Elizabeth Kiely, *Irish Women at Work, 1930–1960: An Oral History* (Sallins: Irish Academic Press, 2012), p. 197.
65 *Irish Independent*, 11 May 1951.
66 *The Cork Examiner*, 29 May 1951.
67 A general committee meeting in 1944 for example included eighteen employees and seven management representatives. CCCA: General Committee Meeting Minutes, 4th April 1944, Sunbeam B505 /Box 9.
68 CCCA: Sunbeam Wolsey Limited 22nd Annual Report 1950, Sunbeam B505/ Bundle 63/1.
69 Pius X, *Quadragesimo Anno*, 1931, http://www.vatican.va/holy_father/pius_xi/encyclicals/documents/hf_p-xi_enc_19310515_quadragesimo-anno_en.html
70 *The Cork Examiner*, 15 April 1943.
71 Ibid.
72 J.H. Whyte, *Church and State in Modern Ireland, 1923–1979* (Dublin: Gill & Macmillan, 1980), p. 69. Muintir na Tíre (translated into English as 'People of the Country') is a voluntary community development organisation that focuses particularly on rural areas.
73 *Liberty*, February 1952.
74 See, for example, features on the Limerick Clothing Factory (February 1955), Clara Mills (June 1955) and Smithwick's (May 1955).
75 CCCA: Sunbeam Wolsey Limited – Annual Meeting 7th September 1944, Sunbeam, B505/BND 28/1 Temp 76.
76 Sunbeam Wolsey Ltd, *Sunbeam Wolsey*, p. 15.
77 Ibid.
78 CCCA: Letter from William Dwyer to Alfred O'Rahilly, 22 June 1936, Sunbeam, B505/ BND27 Temp 71.
79 Morris and Smyth, 'Paternalism as an Employer Strategy', p. 223.
80 CCCA: Cork Economic Development Council, *City of Cork – Community Monograph – Facts for Industry* (First Draft, June 1966), Sunbeam B505/ BND 20/2 Temp 102.

81 *The Cork Examiner*, 24 February 1968.
82 *Evening Echo*, 19 February 1968.
83 *Evening Echo*, 3 May 1971. In 1974 there was a further unofficial strike in support of a pay increase for female linkers, which escalated into a factory-wide withdrawal of labour. See *Cork Examiner*, 25 April 1974.
84 *Evening Echo*, 6 January 1975.
85 *Evening Echo*, 11 January 1975.
86 *Evening Echo*, 13 January 1975.
87 *The Cork Examiner*, 8 February 1975; *Evening Echo*, 4 February and 7 February 1975.
88 *Evening Echo*, 5 February 1975.
89 *Evening Echo*, 29 January 1975.
90 *The Cork Examiner*, 24 February 1975.
91 Scranton, 'Varieties of Paternalism', p. 237.
92 Tom Scott, 18 December 2012.
93 CCCA: Sunbeam Annual Report 1975, Sunbeam, B505/BND 9/1 Temp 65.
94 *Evening Echo*, 1 February 1975.
95 Tom Scott, 18 December 2012.
96 *Liberty*, March 1971.
97 Francis Devine, *Organising History: A Centenary of SIPTU, 1909–2009* (Dublin: Gill & Macmillan 2009), p. 502.
98 *The Irish Times*, 7 November 1972, 21 August 1973 and 3 May 1972.
99 CCCA: Sunbeam Annual Report 1975, Sunbeam, B505/ BND 9/1 TEMP 65. See also Girvin, 'Industrialisation', p. 37.
100 Interview with Frank Wallace, Nash's Boreen, 28 August 2013.
101 Ibid.
102 Ibid.
103 Sectoral Development Committee, *Reports and Recommendations on the Clothing and Textile Industries* (Dublin: Sectoral Development Committee, 1983), p. 14.
104 *Liberty*, June 1973.
105 CCCA: Minutes of meeting of Sunbeam Ltd on 14/10/81 to discuss IIRS scheme, Sunbeam, B505 BND 10 Temp 126.
106 Ibid.
107 Interview with Marian Hickey, Midleton, 2 April 2013.
108 CFP: SR98, June Hickey, 12 January 1998.
109 Ibid.
110 CFP: SR96, Linda McCarthy, 16 September 1997.
111 *The Cork Examiner*, 23 March 1990.
112 *The Cork Examiner*, 13 March 1990.
113 SIPTU is the successor to the ITGWU. The union was renamed following a merger with the Workers' Union of Ireland in 1990.
114 *The Cork Examiner*, 21 April 1990.
115 P.K. Edwards, *Conflict at Work: A Materialist Analysis of Workplace Relations* (Oxford: Basil Blackwell, 1986), p. 46.

6. Working for Irish Steel, 1939–2001

1 *Inside Cobh*, September 2006.
2 *The Irish Press*, 15 August 1977.
3 Ibid.
4 Ibid.

5 *Evening Echo*, 1 April 1938.
6 The one exception is the Ford foundry, which was moved to Dagenham in 1932 and for which we possess little in the way of oral or documentary testimony.
7 Interview with Jim Shealy, Cobh, 23 September 2013.
8 *The Irish Times*, 20 July 1950.
9 *The Southern Star*, 9 October 1982.
10 Jim Shealy, 23 September 2013.
11 Ibid.
12 Interview with Billy McMurty, Cobh, 28 February 2015.
13 Interview with Christy Buckley, Cobh, 3 July 2013.
14 Interview with Robert Walsh, Cobh, 19 August 2013.
15 Christy Buckley, 3 July 2013.
16 Tongsmen, as their title implies, were tasked with moving hot steel bars between different channels in the rolling mills. Long tongs were used for the purpose.
17 Jim Shealy, 23 September 2013.
18 Robert Walsh, 19 August 2013.
19 Francis Devine, 'Safety, Health and Welfare at Work in the Irish Free State and the Republic of Ireland, 1922–1990: Measuring the Problem', *Saothar*, vol. 31 (2006), p. 65.
20 Donal Barrington, *Report of the Commission of Inquiry on Safety, Health and Welfare at Work* (Dublin: Stationery Office, 1983), p. 12.
21 The official body tasked with inspecting and ensuring the safety of industrial workplaces. Introduced under the 1955 factories act which replaced the previously decentralised system of factory inspectors.
22 Department of Labour, *Report of the Factory Inspectorate for the Year Ended 30 September 1968* (Dublin: Stationery Office, 1968), p. 42.
23 Department of Labour, *Report of the Factory Inspectorate for the Year Ended 20 September 1969* (Dublin: Stationery Office, 1969), p. 9.
24 'Accident' in the Industrial Inspectorate reports is defined as an incident which 'causes an employee to be killed, or to be disabled for more than three days from earning full wages'. Department of Labour, *Report of the Industrial Inspectorate, for the Year 1976* (Dublin: Stationery Office, 1977), p. 9.
25 The construction industry had a low accident rate but was consistently the industry with the highest number of fatalities, frequently accounting for a plurality, often a majority, of fatal accidents in any given year. The 1975 report, for example, records that of twenty-one fatal accidents in total, ten of these occurred in construction. That year was far from atypical.
26 *Census of Population of Ireland, 1966, Vol.3: Industries* (Dublin: Stationery Office, 1968), Table 2. Department of Labour, *Report of the Factory Inspectorate for the Year Ended 30 September 1966* (Dublin: Stationery Office, 1966). These rates refer to accidents or fatalities per 100,000 workers.
27 Percentage figure worked out from Devine's figure of 964.28 accidents per 100,000 employed. Devine, 'Safety, Health and Welfare at Work', p. 68.
28 *Census of Population of Ireland, 1966, Vol. 3: Industries* (Dublin: Stationery Office, 1968), Table 2 and Department of Labour, *Report of the Factory Inspectorate for the Year Ended 30 September 1969* (Dublin: Stationery Office, 1969).
29 Devine, 'Safety, Health and Welfare', p. 68.
30 Department of Labour, *Reports of the Industrial Inspectorate for 1973 and 1974* (Dublin: Stationery Office, 1974 and 1975).
31 Ibid.

32 Jim Shealy, 23 September 2013.
33 Interview with Fionnán Kerrigan, Midleton, 18 December 2014.
34 Upham, Martin, *Tempered – Not Quenched: The History of the ISTC, 1951–1997* (London: Lawrence & Wishart, 1997), p. 29.
35 David Hall, *Working Lives: The Forgotten Voices of Britain's Post-War Working Class* (London: Bantam Press, 2012), p. 5.
36 Robert Bruno, *Steelworker Alley: How Class Works in Youngstown* (London: Cornell University Press, 1999) pp. 63–79.
37 Billy McMurty, 28 February 2015.
38 Interview with Tony Cummins, Bishopstown, 17 February 2014.
39 Robert Walsh, 19 August 2013.
40 Arthur McIvor, *Working Lives: Work in Britain Since 1945* (Basingstoke: Palgrave Macmillan, 2013), p. 163.
41 Ibid., p. 5.
42 Fionnán Kerrigan, 18 December 2014.
43 Billy McMurty, 28 February 2015.
44 Jim Shealy, 23 September 2013.
45 Billy McMurty, 28 February 2015.
46 *The Irish Times*, 16 January 2001.
47 Ibid.
48 Department of Labour, *Report of the Factory Inspectorate for the Year Ended 30 September 1968* (Dublin: Stationery Office, 1968), pp. 8–9.
49 Department of Labour, *Report of the Factory Inspectorate for the Year Ended 30 September 1967* (Dublin: Stationery Office, 1967), p. 8.
50 Devine, 'Safety, Health and Welfare', p. 69.
51 Ibid.
52 Ronald Johnston and Arthur McIvor, *Lethal Work: A History of the Asbestos Tragedy in Scotland* (East Lothian: Tuckwell Press, 2000), p. 212.
53 Ibid., p. 220.
54 Ibid., pp. 220–1.
55 The 1980 Safety in Industry Act greatly improved upon the provisions of the 1955 Factories Act. The 1989 Safety, Health and Welfare at Work Act made further improvements.
56 NAI: Department of Industry and Commerce (IND) Irish Steel Holdings Limited – Report by the Directors on the Steel Industry at Haulbowline, 17 February 1949, IND 10/28.
57 Ibid.
58 Ibid.
59 Sarsfield Hogan, *A History of Irish Steel* (Dublin: Gill & Macmillan, 1980), p. 89.
60 Ibid.
61 Ibid., p. 96. A closed shop refers to workplaces where membership of a trade union is a condition of employment.
62 Ibid.
63 Ibid.
64 Frank Barry and Joe Durkan, *TEAM and Irish Steel: An Application of the Declining High-Wages Industries Literature* (Dublin: Centre for Economic Research Working Paper Series, 1995), p. 10.
65 Ibid.
66 Interview with Donal Brady, Shanbally, 26 November 2013.
67 Robert Walsh, 19 August 2013.

68 Jim Shealy, 23 September 2013.
69 Hogan, *Irish Steel*, p. 208.
70 Ibid.
71 Patrick Gunnigle, Joseph Wallace and Gerard McMahon, *Industrial Relations in Ireland*: 3rd edition (Dublin: Gill & Macmillan, 2004), p. 11.
72 The National Wage Agreements were centrally negotiated pay agreements between employer organisations and trade unions at the national level introduced in 1970. They came to an end in 1981 and were replaced by the more explicitly corporatist system of 'social partnership' in 1987 which saw wage agreements determined by employers, unions and the government at the national level.
73 *The Irish Times*, March 11 to 27 April 1974.
74 *The Irish Times*, 23 July 1976.
75 *The Irish Times*, 5 January 1982, 3 February 1982 and 11 April 1974.
76 *The Irish Times*, 1 January 1970.
77 *The Irish Times*, 17 September 1969.
78 Ibid.
79 *The Irish Times*, 11 March 1974 and 3 February 1982.
80 The Amalgamated Union of Engineering Workers, the Electrical Trade Union, the Union of Construction Allied Trades and Technicians, the Amalgamated Society of Boilermakers, Shipwrights, Blacksmiths and Structural Workers and the Ancient Guild of Incorporated Brick and Stonelayers.
81 *The Irish Press*, 15 August 1977 and *Sunday Independent*, 21 August 1977.
82 Andrew Pendleton, 'The Evolution of Industrial Relations in UK Nationalised Industries', *British Journal of Industrial Relations*, vol. 35, no. 2 (June 1997), p. 153.
83 *The Cork Examiner*, 20 October 1977; *Irish Independent*, 12 September 1977.
84 *Evening Echo*, 12 September 1977.
85 Ibid.
86 Ibid.
87 *The Irish Press*, 15 August 1977.
88 Ibid.
89 Ibid.
90 *Business and Finance*, 18 August 1977.
91 Donal Brady, 26 November 2013.
92 *The Cork Examiner*, 21 June 1977.
93 *Evening Echo*, 20 June 1977.
94 Ibid.
95 Ibid.
96 Donal Brady, 26 November 2013.
97 NAI: Letter to Taoiseach Jack Lynch, 5 July 1977, TAOIS 2007/116/80.
98 Interview with James Cronin, Cobh, 25 June 2013.
99 *The Irish Press*, 15 August 1977.
100 Robert Walsh, 19 August 2013.
101 Billy McMurty, 28 February 2015.
102 Robert Walsh, 19 August 2013.
103 Alessandro Portelli, 'Introduction', in *The Death of Luigi Trastulli and Other Stories: Form and Meaning in Oral History* (New York: State University of New York Press, 2001), p. xii.
104 NAI: Memorandum for the Government – Proposal by Irish Steel Holdings Ltd to re-equip its plant and expand steel production, 23 October 1976, TAOIS 2007/116/80.

105 Tony Cummins, 17 February 2014.
106 Emmet O'Connor, *A Labour History of Ireland, 1824–2000* (Dublin: UCD Press, 2001), pp. 250–1.
107 Gunnigle et al., *Industrial Relations*, p. 12.
108 *Sunday Independent*, 25 August 1985. My italics.
109 *The Southern Star*, 27 July 1985.
110 *Irish Independent*, 14 June 1985.
111 *The Cork Examiner*, 30 August 1985.
112 Ibid.
113 Billy McMurty, 28 February 2015.
114 *The Irish Press*, 25 August 1987.
115 *Irish Independent*, 12 April 1991.
116 *The Cork Examiner*, 11 November 1993; *Irish Independent*, 16 October 1993.
117 Ibid. The use of outside contractors had long been a bugbear within the plant.
118 *The Southern Star*, 30 July 1994.
119 *The Irish Press*, 16 September 1994.
120 Ibid.
121 *The Irish Press*, 22 September 1994.
122 Ibid.
123 Clergy often played such a mediating role in industrial disputes in twentieth-century Ireland.
124 *Irish Independent*, 23 September 1994.
125 *The Cork Examiner*, 26 September 1994.
126 *Irish Independent*, 21 January 1995.
127 *The Southern Star*, 30 November 1996.
128 Fionnán Kerrigan, 18 December 2014.
129 Donal Brady, 26 November 2013.
130 *Inside Cobh*, September 2006.
131 *Sunday Independent*, 3 March 2002.
132 Ibid.
133 *Sunday Independent*, 3 March 2002 and 31 March 2002.
134 Ibid.
135 *Sunday Independent*, 3 March 2002.
136 Fionnán Kerrigan, 18 December 2014.
137 Ibid.
138 Christy Buckley, 3 July 2013.
139 Jim Shealy, 23 September 2013.
140 James Cronin, 25 June 2013.

7. Employment, Inequality and Emigration

1 Perry Share, Hilary Tovey and Mary P. Corcoran, *A Sociology of Ireland*: 3rd edition (Dublin: Gill & Macmillan, 2007), p. 172.
2 Richard Breen and Christopher T. Whelan, *Social Mobility and Social Class in Ireland* (Dublin: Gill & Macmillan, 1996), p. 1.
3 David B. Rottman, Damian F. Hannan, Niamh Hardiman and Miriam M. Wiley, *The Distribution of Income in the Republic of Ireland: A Study in Social Class and Social Cycle Inequalities* (Dublin: Economic and Social Research Institute, 1982), p. 51.
4 Ibid., p. 181.
5 Enda Delaney, *Irish Emigration Since 1921* (Dublin: Dundalgan Press, 2002), p. 14.

6 Enda Delaney, 'The Churches and Irish Emigration to Britain, 1921–60', *Archivum Hibernicum*, vol. 52 (1998), p. 98.
7 John A. Jackson, *Report on the Skibbereen Social Survey* (Dublin: Human Sciences Committee, 1967), p. 13.
8 Conor K. Ward, *Manpower in a Developing Community: A Pilot Survey of Drogheda* (Drogheda: University College Dublin Department of Social Sciences, 1967), 16.5.
9 *Report on the Census of Ireland 1936, Volume 2: Industrial Status* (Dublin: Stationery Office, 1941), p. 92.
10 *Report on the Census of Ireland, 1951, Volume 3: Occupations, Industries and Industrial Status* (Dublin: Stationery Office, 1954), Table 7a.
11 Interview with John O'Shea, Parklands, 12 October 2012.
12 Christy Buckley, 3 July 2013. Even among workers in Cork city, agricultural employment was typical in the period immediately before and after the Second World War.
13 Michael Costelloe, 28 February 2013.
14 Ibid.
15 John O'Shea, 12 October 2012.
16 Ibid.
17 Ibid.
18 Christy Buckley, 3 July 2013.
19 Gus McLoughlin, 29 July 2013.
20 Tim Murphy, 30 January 2013. My italics.
21 Gene Kerrigan, *Another Country: Growing Up in 50s Ireland* (Dublin: Gill & Macmillan, 1998), p. 11. My italics.
22 *The Irish Press*, 9 December 1949 and 23 February 1950.
23 *The Irish Press*, 17 October 1949.
24 *The Irish Press*, 25 October 1949.
25 *The Irish Press*, 21 November and 26 December 1949.
26 Tom Garvin, *News from a New Republic* (Dublin: Gill & Macmillan, 2010), p. 149.
27 *The Irish Press*, 27 October 1949.
28 Donal Brady, 26 November 2013.
29 Ibid.
30 Hence the old joke from the butchering trade: 'What's the difference between the pope and a pork butcher? A pork butcher can become pope but the pope can never become a pork butcher', Ruth Guiry, *Pigtown: A History of Limerick's Bacon Industry* (Limerick: Limerick City and County Council, 2016), p. 85.
31 James Cronin, 25 June 2013.
32 Michael Costelloe, 28 February 2013.
33 Gus McLoughlin, 29 July 2013.
34 Jim Shealy, 23 September 2013.
35 Billy McMurty, 28 February 2015.
36 Michael Costelloe, 28 February 2013.
37 Ibid.
38 Billy McMurty, 28 February 2015.
39 Tony Cummins, 17 February 2014.
40 Ibid.
41 Emmet O'Connor, *A Labour History of Ireland, 1824–2000* (Dublin: UCD Press, 2011), p. 218.
42 Jane Gray, *Poverty and the Life Cycle in Twentieth Century Ireland: Changing Experiences of Childhood, Education and the Transition to Adulthood* (Dublin: Combat Poverty Agency, 2010), p. 45.

43 Rottman et al., *The Distribution of Income in the Republic of Ireland*, p. 3.
44 Ibid., p. 51.
45 Bertram Hutchinson, *Social Status in Dublin: Marriage, Mobility and First Employment* (Dublin: Economic and Social Research Institute, 1973), p. 10.
46 Arthur McIvor, *Working Lives: Work in Britain Since 1945* (Basingstoke: Palgrave Macmillan, 2013), p. 16.
47 Delaney, *Irish Emigration*, p. 1.
48 Mary Cronin, Tim Murphy, Jim Shealy, Billy McMurty, Michael Costelloe, Eleanor Ford, Gus McLoughlin and Denis Forde.
49 Delaney, *Irish Emigration*, p. 41.
50 Michael Costelloe, 28 February 2013.
51 John O'Shea, 12 October 2012.
52 Michael Costelloe, 28 February 2013.
53 Sara Goek, '"I never would return again to plough the rocks of bawn": Irishmen in Post-War Britain', in David Convery (ed.), *Locked Out: A Century of Irish Working-Class Life* (Sallins: Irish Academic Press, 2013), p. 160.
54 Frank Wallace, 28 August 2013.
55 Donal Brady, 26 November 2013.
56 Jim Shealy, 23 September 2013.
57 Fionnán Kerrigan, 18 December 2014.
58 Delaney, *Irish Emigration*, p. 31.
59 Interview with Mary Cronin, Farranree, 22 October 2012.
60 Jim Shealy, 23 September 2013.
61 Ibid.
62 Michael Costelloe, 28 February 2013.
63 With the exception of Billy McMurty, who worked in the less typical destination of Holland.
64 Michael Costelloe, 28 February 2013.
65 Interview with Eleanor Ford and Rita Sisk, Sunday's Well, 11 September 2013.
66 Mary Cronin, 22 October 2012.
67 Eleanor Ford and Rita Sisk, 11 September 2013.
68 Ibid.
69 Ibid.
70 Gus McLoughlin, 29 July 2013.
71 Delaney, *Demography, State and Society*, p. 112.
72 MNI: Vaunie Downey, 11 June 2003.
73 Closely related to the ideology of the family unit examined in Chapter Eight.
74 MNI: Vaunie Downey, 11 June 2003.

8. Gender, Status and Resistance

1 Gus McLoughlin, 29 July 2013.
2 Ibid.
3 Arthur McIvor, *Working Lives: Work in Britain Since 1945* (Basingstoke: Palgrave Macmillan, 2013), p. 238.
4 Máire Leane and Elizabeth Kiely, *Irish Women at Work, 1930–1960: An Oral History* (Sallins: Irish Academic Press, 2012), p. 13.
5 Ibid.; Maryann Valiulis, 'Neither Feminist nor Flapper: The Ecclesiastical Construction of the Ideal Irish Woman', in Alan Hayes and Diane Urquhart (eds), *The Irish Women's History Reader* (London: Routledge, 2001), p. 152.

6 *Bunreacht na hÉireann,* Article 41, https://www.constitution.ie/Documents/Bhunreacht_na_hEireann_web.pdf. My italics.
7 Tony Cummins, 17 February 2014.
8 Marian Hickey, 2 April 2013.
9 WOHP: Kathleen Fitzgibbon.
10 Eleanor Ford and Rita Sisk, 11 September 2013.
11 Ibid.
12 Brendan M. Walsh and Annette O'Toole, *Women and Employment in Ireland: Results of a National Survey* (Dublin: Economic and Social Research Institute, 1973), p. 22.
13 Leane and Kiely, *Irish Women at Work,* pp. 185–6.
14 Interview with John O'Shea, Parklands, 18 October 2012.
15 Christy Buckley, 3 July 2013.
16 Michael Lenihan, 31 January 2013.
17 Tim Murphy, 30 January 2013.
18 Fionnán Kerrigan, 18 December 2014.
19 Eibhlís de Barra, *Bless 'em All: The Lanes of Cork* (Cork: Mercier, 1997), p. 139.
20 Marian Hickey, 2 April 2013.
21 Leane and Kiely, *Irish Women at Work,* p. 12.
22 Ibid.
23 Ibid.
24 Eleanor Ford and Rita Sisk, 11 September 2013.
25 WOHP: Rena McCarthy.
26 Interview with Pat Dunlea, University College Cork, 10 December 2013; McIvor, *Working Lives,* p. 90.
27 *The Irish Press,* 20 October 1949 and 26 December 1949.
28 *The Irish Press,* 8 November 1949.
29 Ethel Crowley, 'Making a Difference? Female Employment and Multinationals in the Republic of Ireland', in Anne Byrne and Madeline Leonard (eds), *Women in Irish Society: A Sociological Reader* (Belfast: Beyond the Pale, 1997), pp. 89–90.
30 Leane and Kiely, *Irish Women at Work,* p. 146.
31 CCCA: Memo from P.J. O'Donoghue, Personnel Manager, 12 November 1968, Sunbeam B505/BND 34 Temp 67.
32 Marian Hickey, 2 April 2013.
33 Leane and Kiely, *Irish Women at Work,* p. 187.
34 CCCA: T.J. Sexton (Personnel Manager) Proposed Pension Scheme Report, 5 October 1956, Sunbeam B505/BND31/1 Temp 72.
35 Ibid.
36 Conor K. Ward, *Manpower in a Developing Community: A Pilot Survey in Drogheda* (Dublin: University College Dublin Department of Social Science, 1967), 12.6 and 16.5.
37 Mary Cronin, 22 October 2012.
38 Marian Hickey, 2 April 2013.
39 Marie-Jeanne Da Col Richert, 'Irish Women's Changing Status and Role in Rural and Urban Ireland from the 1970s to the End of the Celtic Tiger Era', *Nordic Irish Studies,* vol. 12 (2013), p. 129.
40 *Liberty,* February 1950.
41 Gus McLoughlin, 29 July 2013.
42 This tendency was also noted by Ruth Guiry in her research on the Limerick pork trade. She comments that staff/white-collar employees were considered a 'different class of people' and an 'elite crowd' who 'occupied different worlds to people on the factory floor'.

Ruth Guiry, *Pigtown: A History of Limerick's Bacon Industry* (Limerick: Limerick City and County Council, 2016), p. 82.
43 Jim Shealy, 23 September 2013.
44 MNI: Arthur O'Callaghan, 22 January 2003.
45 Donal Brady, 26 November 2013.
46 Sarsfield Hogan, *A History of Irish Steel* (Dublin: Gill & Macmillan, 1980), p. 89.
47 CCCA: Letter from William Dwyer to C.O. Stanley, 11 June 1936, Sunbeam B505/BND 27 Temp 71.
48 MNI: Max Hayes, 5 December 2002.
49 Ibid.
50 Michael Costelloe, 28 February 2013.
51 Robert Walsh, 19 August 2013.
52 Mary Cronin, 22 October 2012.
53 Aidan Kelly, 'White-Collar Trade Unionism', in Donal Nevin (ed.), *Trade Unions and Change in Irish Society* (Cork: Mercier, 1980), p. 67.
54 WOHP: Rena McCarthy.
55 Ibid.
56 Ibid.
57 Mary Muldowney, 'We were conscious of the sort of people we mixed with', *The History of the Family*, vol. 13, no. 4 (2008), p. 409.
58 Ibid., p. 411.
59 Conor K. Ward, *Manpower in a Developing Community*, 16.5.
60 CFP: Billy Foley.
61 CFP: SR Number Unavailable, Nancy Byrne, 6 June 2002.
62 WOHP: Rena McCarthy.
63 CFP: Billy Foley.
64 Muldowney, 'We were conscious', p. 411.
65 Ibid., p. 410.
66 Kelly, 'White-Collar Trade Unionism', p. 68.
67 Both of these were Irish Steel employees where the context of the 1977 craft strike must be borne in mind.
68 Robert Walsh, 19 August 2013.
69 Tony Cummins, 17 February 2014.
70 Ibid.
71 Christopher T. Whelan, *Employment Conditions and Job Satisfaction: The Distribution, Perception and Evaluation of Job Rewards* (Dublin: Economic and Social Research Institute, 1980), p. 35.
72 Ibid., p. 126.
73 Ibid.
74 Michael Costelloe, 28 February 2013.
75 Frank Wallace, 28 August 2013.
76 Ibid.
77 Gus McLoughlin, 29 July 2013.
78 Robert Walsh, 19 August 2013.
79 Michael Costelloe, 28 February 2013.
80 Tim Murphy, 30 January 2013.
81 Jim Shealy, 23 September 2013.
82 Ibid.
83 John O'Shea, 12 October 2012.

84 Charles McCarthy, *The Decade of Upheaval: Irish Trade Unions in the Nineteen Sixties* (Dublin: Institute of Public Administration, 1973), p. 17.
85 Joseph Wallace, Patrick Gunnigle and Gerard McMahon, *Industrial Relations in Ireland*, 3rd edition (Dublin: Gill & Macmillan, 2004), p. 230. Although it must be remembered that the line between an 'official' and 'unofficial' strike could be very fine indeed.
86 Tony Cummins, 17 February 2014.
87 Ibid.
88 Fionnán Kerrigan, 18 December 2014.
89 Jim Shealy, 23 September 2013.
90 Frank Wallace, 28 August 2013.
91 Marian Elders, Elizabeth Kiely, Máire Leane and Clodagh O'Driscoll, 'A Union in those days was husband and wife': Women's Narratives on Trade Unions in Munster, 1936–60', *Saothar*, vol. 27 (2002), p. 123.
92 *Liberty*, August 1967.
93 See Crowley, 'Making a Difference?', p. 92.
94 Kathleen Fitzgibbon.
95 Ibid.
96 Rena McCarthy.
97 These exceptions include the unusually divisive Irish Steel craft strike of 1977, when general operatives passed pickets under instructions from the ITGWU, which the craft unions did not object to. They also include Pat Dunlea, who frequently refused to observe pickets or walkouts when he considered the dispute to be pointless or trivial.
98 Michael Lenihan, 31 January 2013.
99 Robert Walsh, 19 August 2013.
100 Marian Hickey, 2 April 2013.
101 Eleanor Ford and Rita Sisk, 11 September 2013.
102 Marian Hickey, 2 April 2013.
103 Jim Shealy, 23 September 2013.
104 Michael Lenihan, 31 January 2013.
105 Paul Thompson, 'Playing at Being Skilled Men: Factory Culture and Pride in Work Skills Among Coventry Car Workers', *Social History*, vol. 13, no. 1 (January 1988), p. 66.
106 CFP: SR96 TR93, Linda McCarthy, 16 September 1997.
107 Michael Lenihan, 31 January 2013.
108 Tim Murphy, 30 January 2013. My italics.
109 'Runners' were the youngest and newest Sunbeam workers who fetched boxes and supplies for the machinists.
110 McIvor, *Working Lives*, p. 61. John Kirk, Class, *Culture and Social Change: On the Trail of the Working Class* (New York: Palgrave Macmillan, 2007), p. 170.
111 Michael Lenihan, 31 January 2013.
112 Eleanor Ford and Rita Sisk, 11 September 2013.
113 Patsy Corcoran, 2 October 2012.
114 Robert Bruno, *Steelworker Alley: How Class Works in Youngstown* (London: Cornell University Press, 1999), p. 66.
115 Eleanor Ford and Rita Sisk, 11 September 2013.
116 Tim Murphy, 30 January 2013.
117 Michael Lenihan, 14 January 2013.
118 David Toms, '"The brightest couple of hours": Inter-Firm and Pubs Leagues of Ireland, 1922–73', in David Convery (ed.), *Locked Out: A Century of Irish Working-Class Life* (Sallins: Irish Academic Press, 2013), p. 155.

119 *The Ingot*, March/April 1975 and September 1989. Private collections.
120 Toms, '"The brightest couple of hours"', p. 155.
121 *Holly Bough*, 1 December 2003.

Conclusion
1 Francis Devine, *Organising History: A Centenary of SIPTU, 1909-2009* (Dublin: Gill & Macmillan, 2009), p. 226.
2 Ibid., p. 291.
3 See Chapter Four.
4 Maryann Valiulis, 'Neither Feminist nor Flapper: The Ecclesiastical Construction of the Ideal Irish Woman', in *The Irish Women's History Reader*, p. 152.
5 See Chapter Eight.
6 *The Irish Times*, 10 February 2007.
7 See Chapter Five.
8 See Chapter Six.
9 Among other legislative gains, women were granted the right to serve on juries in 1976, to live apart from their spouse in 1988 and to divorce in 1996.
10 See Chapter Six.
11 Gus McLoughlin, 29 July 2013.
12 Much research still needs to be done on the history of occupational health in Ireland.

Bibliography

PRIMARY SOURCES

Newspapers, Periodicals and Magazines

Archive: Magazine of the Cork Folklore Project
Business and Finance
Cork News
Evening Echo
Holly Bough
Industrial Relations News
Inside Cobh
Irish Examiner
Irish Independent
Irish Industry and Industrial News
Liberty
Liberty News
Newsline
Steel Times
Sunday Independent
The Anglo-Celt
The Cork Examiner
The Economist
The Ingot (Private Collection)
The Irish Press
The Irish Times
The Munster Express
The Southern Star
Trade Union Bulletin
Weekly Irish Times

Archival Sources

National Archives of Ireland
Department of An Taoiseach Records, TAOIS
Department of Industry and Commerce Records, IND
Department of Foreign Affairs Records, DFA

Benson Ford Research Centre
Mira Wilkins Papers – Ireland
Nevins and Hill Interview Series
Charles E. Sorensen Records Series, 1913–46
Henry Ford and Sons Collection
Foreign Corporation Records Series, 1911–55 – Ireland

Controller's Office Records Series, 1917–48 – Ireland
Ford Motor Company Ltd Collection, 1903–90 – Ireland
Housing in Cork photograph album, c.1920

Cork City and County Archives
Cobh Urban District Council Minute Books, CCCA/TC/CQ
Cork City Council Minute Books, CP/CO/M
Cork Council of Trade Unions Minute Books, U216
Cork Industrial Development Association Files, U141
Cork Spinning and Weaving Company Archives, B530
Séamus Fitzgerald Papers, PR6
Sunbeam Wolsey Business Records, B505
Sunbeam Wolsey Irish Painting and Reports (Small Collections), SM631

Cork Northside Folklore Project
Sound Recording Collection

Myriam Nyhan Interviews
Interviews with Maurice Ahern, Oliver Barriscale, Bobby Broderick, Dominic Carey, Eddie Cleary, Michael Corkery, Donal Creamers, Derry Creedon, John Curran, Frank Dillon, Vaunie Downey, Bob Elliott, Denis Forde, Ken Galvin, Pat Gillen, Max Hayes, Paddy Hayes, Tim Healy, Billy Hurley, Eddie Kehelly, Noreen Kelly, Denis Manning, Gus McLoughlin, Denis McSweeney, Tom Morrissey, Michael Mulconry, Eddie Mullins, Frank Norberg, Arthur O'Callaghan, John O'Callaghan, Bill O'Donnell, Michael V. O'Donoghue, Tom A. O'Donoghue, Jim V. O'Donovan and Michael Quinlan (private collection)

Bureau of Military History, Irish Military Archives
Michael V. O'Donoghue Witness Statement

University College Cork Women's Oral History Project
Interview with Kathleen Fitzgibbon
Interview with Rena McCarthy

Dáil Debates
http://debates.oireachtas.ie/dail/

Official Publications

Barrington, Donal, *Report of the Commission of Inquiry on Safety, Health and Welfare at Work* (Dublin: Stationery Office, 1983)

Census of Ireland Reports, 1926–91 (Dublin: Stationery Office)

Committee on Industrial Organisation, Report on the Hosiery and Knitwear Industry (Dublin: Stationery Office, 1963)

Department of Labour, *Factory Inspectorate Reports*, 1961–88 (Dublin: Stationery Office)

European Commission, *European File: The European Community Textile Industry April 1982* (Brussels: European Communities Directorate-General for Information, 1982)

Fifth Joint Committee on Commercial State Bodies, *Fourth Report – Irish Steel Limited* (Dublin: Stationery Office, 1988)

FitzGerald, Garret, *State-Sponsored Bodies* (Dublin: Institute of Public Administration, 1961)

Labour Court, *The Labour Court: What Is It? What Does It Do?* (Dublin: Labour Court, 1971)

National Prices Commission, *Motor Vehicle Assembly Study* (Dublin: Stationery Office, 1978)

Sectoral Development Committee, *Report and Recommendations on the Clothing and Textiles Industries* (Dublin: Sectoral Development Committee, 1983)

Wallace, Joseph and O'Shea, Frank, *A Study of Unofficial Strikes in Ireland: Final Report* (Dublin: Stationery Office, 1987)

Contemporary Studies, Reports and Publications

Coakley, D.J., *Cork: Its Trade and Commerce* (Cork: Guy & Co., 1919)

Cork Town Planning Association, *Cork: A Civic Survey* (Liverpool: Liverpool University Press, 1926)

Fawsitt, J.L., 'New Industries for a Greater Cork', *Studies: An Irish Quarterly Review* vol. 6, no. 23 (September 1917), pp. 462–9

Federated Union of Employers, *A Brief Guide to Industrial Relations in Ireland* (Dublin: Federated Union of Employers, 1972)

Hutchinson, Bertram, *Social Status and Inter-Generational Mobility in Dublin* (Dublin: Economic and Social Research Institute, 1969)

Hutchinson, Bertram, *Social Status in Dublin: Marriage, Mobility and First Employment* (Dublin: Economic and Social Research Institute, 1973)

International Iron and Steel Institute, *A Handbook of World Steel Statistics* (Brussels: International Iron and Steel Institute, 1974)
Jackson, John A., *Report on the Skibbereen Social Survey* (Dublin: Human Sciences Committee, 1967)
J.C.P., *A Visit to Henry Ford and Son, Ltd. Marina, Cork* (Dublin: Sackville Press, 1926)
McNabb, Patrick, 'Social Structure', in Jeremiah Newman (ed.), *The Limerick Rural Survey* (Tipperary: Muintir na Tíre Rural Publications, 1964), pp. 193–247
Ní Bhroin, Nóirín, *The Motivation and Productivity of Young Women Workers* (Dublin: Irish National Productivity Committee, 1969)
O'Rahilly, Alfred J., 'The Social Problem in Cork', *Studies: An Irish Quarterly Review*, vol. 6, no. 22 (June 1917), pp. 177–88
Riordan, E.J., *Modern Irish Trade and Industry* (London: Methuen, 1920)
Rottman, David B., Hannan, Damian F., Hardiman, Niamh and Wiley, Miriam M., *The Distribution of Income in the Republic of Ireland: A Study in Social Class and Social Cycle Inequalities* (Dublin: Economic and Social Research Institute, 1982)
Schulman, Lydia, 'The Davignon Plan for Europe's Steel', *Economic Intelligence Review*, vol. 6, no. 13 (April 1979), pp. 51–4
Sunbeam-Wolsey Limited, *Sunbeam Wolsey* (Cork: Sunbeam, 1944)
Walsh, Brendan M. and O'Toole, Annette, *Women and Employment in Ireland: Results of a National Survey* (Dublin: Economic and Social Research Institute, 1973)
Ward, Conor K., *Manpower in a Developing Community: A Pilot Survey of Drogheda* (Dublin: University College Dublin Department of Social Sciences, 1967)
Whelan, Christopher T., *Employment Conditions and Job Satisfaction: The Distribution, Perception and Evaluation of Job Rewards* (Dublin: Economic and Social Research Institute, 1980)

Memoirs and Autobiographies
De Barra, Eibhlís, *Bless 'em All: The Lanes of Cork* (Cork: Mercier, 1997)
Ford, Henry, *My Life and Work* (London: William Heinemann, 1922)
Ford, Henry, *Today and Tomorrow* (London: William Heinemann, 1926)
Kenneally, Christy, *Small Wonders* (Cork: Mercier Press, 2005)

Kerrigan, Gene, *Another Country: Growing Up in 50s Ireland* (Dublin: Gill & Macmillan, 1998)
Mac an tSíthigh, Domhnall, *An Baile i bhFad Siar* (Baile Átha Cliath: Coiscéim, 2000)
MacSweeney, A.M, *Poverty in Cork* (Cork: Purcell & Company, 1917)
Norris, David, *A Kick Against the Pricks: The Autobiography* (London: Transworld, 2012)
O'Connor, Frank, *An Only Child* (London: Macmillan, 1964)
O'Shea, John, *Cork's Red City* (Cork: Litho Press, 2005)
Rafferty, Mick, 'A Family of Dockers', in Patrick O'Dea (ed.), *A Class of Our Own: Conversations about Class in Ireland* (Dublin: New Island Books, 1994), pp. 75–93
Rashad, Ibrahim, *An Egyptian in Ireland* (Privately Printed, 1920)

Stage Productions
Scannell, Raymond, *Losing Steam* (Cork: Corcadorca, 2004)
Wyatt, Marian, *The Sunbeam Girls* (Cork: Stage Centre, 2007)
Wyatt, Marian, *The Sunbeam Girls 2* (Cork: Pat Talbot Productions, 2011)

Miscellaneous
Bunreacht na hÉireann (1937), https://www.constitution.ie/Documents/Bhunreacht_na_hEireann_web.pdf
Central Statistic Office, 'Area Profile for Cork City and Suburbs, 2011', http://census.cso.ie/areaprofiles/PDF/ST/corkcityandsuburbs.pdf
Pius X, *Quadragesimo Anno*, 1931, http://www.vatican.va/holy_father/pius_xi/encyclicals/documents/hf_p-xi_enc_19310515_quadragesimo-anno_en.html

SECONDARY SOURCES

Theses
Condon, Johanna, 'Limerick Women, 1900–40: An Oral History' (Unpublished MA Thesis: University of Limerick, 2001)
Doyle, Christopher Coleman, 'Industrial Relations in Post-World War Two Ireland, 1946–1959' (Unpublished MPhil Thesis: University College Cork, 1999)

Flynn, Charles, 'Dundalk: An Oral History, 1900–60' (Unpublished PhD Dissertation: NUI Maynooth, 2000)
Gough, Michael J., 'A History of the Physical Development of Cork City' (Unpublished MA Thesis: University College Cork, 1973)
Grimes, Thomas, 'Starting Ireland on the Road to Industry: Henry Ford in Cork' (Unpublished PhD Dissertation: NUI Maynooth, 2008)
Jacobson, David, 'A Political Economy of the Motor Industry in Ireland' (University of Dublin: Unpublished PhD Dissertation, 1981)
Lahiff, Edward, 'Industry and Labour in Cork, 1890–1921' (Unpublished MA Thesis: University College Cork, 1988)
Linehan, Thomas Anthony, 'The Development of Cork's Economy and Business Attitudes, 1910–1939' (Unpublished MA Thesis: University College Cork, 1995)
Milner, Susan, 'The Effect of Protection on Irish Steel and the EU Steel Industry' (Unpublished MA Thesis: University College Cork, 1995)
O'Connor, Catherine, 'Southern Protestantism: The Inter-Relationship Between Religious, Social and Gender Identity in the Diocese of Ferns, 1945–65' (Unpublished PhD Dissertation: University of Limerick, 2007)
O'Mahony, Roderick R., 'Employment in the Textiles and Clothing Industries in Ireland, 1963–87' (Unpublished MA Thesis: University College Cork, 1990)

Documentaries
Abú Media, *Croí an Cheantair* (Cork: TG4, 2013)
Ford Ex-Workers Group, *Fords: Memories of the Line* (Cork: Framework Films, 2018)
Framework Films, *Sunbeam* (Cork: Framework Films, 2005)

Book Chapters and Journal Articles
Beiner, Guy and Bryson, Anna, 'Listening to the Past and Talking to Each Other: Problems and Possibilities Facing Oral History in Ireland', *Irish Economic and Social History*, vol. XXX (2003), pp. 71–8
Benenati, Elisabetta, 'Americanism and Paternalism: Management and Workers in Twentieth Century Italy', *International Labour and Working-Class History*, No. 53 (Spring 1998), pp. 5–26
Bodnar, John, 'Power and Memory in Oral History: Workers and Managers at Studebaker', *The Journal of American History*, vol. 75, no. 4 (March 1989), pp. 1201–21

Brannick, Theresa, Devine, Francis and Kelly, Aidan, 'Social Statistics for Labour Historians: Strike Statistics, 1922–99', *Saothar*, vol. 25 (2000), pp. 114–20

Brunt, Barry, 'Industrialisation Within the Greater Cork Area', in Barry Brunt and Kevin Hourihan (eds), *Perspectives on Cork* (Cork: Geographical Society of Ireland, 1998), pp. 19–37

Brunt, Barry, 'Industry and Employment', in J.S. Crowley, R.J.N. Devoy, D. Linehan and P. O'Flanagan (eds), *Atlas of Cork City* (Cork: Cork University Press, 2005), pp. 369–76

Bryson, Anna, '"Whatever you say, say nothing": Researching Memory and Identity in Mid-Ulster, 1945–1969', *Oral History*, vol. 35, no. 2 (Autumn 2007), pp. 45–56

Clegg, H.A., 'Pluralism in Industrial Relations', *British Journal of Industrial Relations*, vol. 13, no. 3 (November 1975), pp. 300–16

Chubb, Basil, 'Introduction', in Donal Nevin (ed.), *Trade Unions and Change in Irish Society* (Cork: Mercier Press, 1980), pp. 5–10

Cohen, Marilyn, 'Urbanisation and the Milieux of Factory Life: Gilford/Dunbarton, 1825–1914', in Chris Curtin, Donnan Hastings and Thomas M. Wilson (eds), *Irish Urban Cultures* (Belfast: Institute of Irish Studies, 1993), pp. 227–42

Convery, David, 'Introduction', in David Convery (ed.), *Locked Out: A Century of Irish Working-Class Life* (Sallins: Irish Academic Press, 2013), pp. 1–8

Convery, David, 'Uniting the Working Class: History, Memory and 1913', in David Convery (ed.), *Locked Out: A Century of Irish Working-Class Life* (Sallins: Irish Academic Press, 2013), pp. 23–38

Cronin, Maura, 'Class and Status in Twentieth Century Ireland: The Evidence of Oral History', *Saothar*, vol. 32 (2007), pp. 33–43

Crowley, Ethel, 'Making a Difference? Female Employment and Multinationals in the Republic of Ireland', in Anne Byrne and Madeline Leonard (eds), *Women in Irish Society: A Sociological Reader* (Belfast: Beyond the Pale, 1997), pp. 81–96

Da Col Richert, Marie-Jeanne, 'Irish Women's Changing Status and Role in Rural and Urban Ireland from the 1970s to the End of the Celtic Tiger Era', *Nordic Irish Studies*, vol. 12 (2013), pp. 127–46

Daly, Mary E., 'Essay in Review. Women and Labour: Margins to Mainstream?', *Saothar*, vol. 19 (1993), pp. 70–4

Daly, Mary E., 'Women and Irish Trade Unions', in Donal Nevin (ed.), *Trade Union Century* (Cork: Mercier Press, 1994), pp. 106–16

Daly, Mary E., 'Women in the Irish Workforce from Pre-Industrial to Modern Times', *Saothar*, vol. 7 (1981), pp. 74–81

Delaney, Enda, 'The Churches and Irish Emigration to Britain, 1921-60', *Archivum Hibernicum*, vol. 52 (1998), pp. 98–114

Devine, Francis, 'Safety, Health and Welfare at Work in the Irish Free State and the Republic of Ireland, 1922–1990: Measuring the Problem', *Saothar*, vol. 31 (2006), pp. 65–74

Dwyer, D.J. and Symons, L.J., 'The Development and Location of the Textiles Industries in the Irish Republic', *Irish Geography*, vol. 4, no. 6 (1963), pp. 415–31

Dwyer, Michael, 'Housing Conditions of the Working-Classes in Cork City in the Early Twentieth Century', *Journal of the Cork Historical and Archaeological Society*, vol. 117 (2012), pp. 91–9

Elders, Marian, Kiely, Elizabeth, Leane, Máire and O'Driscoll, Clodagh, '"A union in those days was husband and wife": Women's Narratives on Trade Unions in Munster, 1936–60', *Saothar*, vol. 27 (2002), pp. 121–9

Ferriter, Diarmaid, 'Oral Archives in Ireland: A Preliminary Report, November 1997', *Irish Economic and Social History*, vol. 25 (1998), pp. 91–5

Girvin, Brian, 'Industrialisation and the Irish Working Class Since 1922', *Saothar*, vol. 10 (1984), pp. 31–42

Goek, Sara, '"I never would return again to plough the rocks of bawn": Irishmen in Post-War Britain', in David Convery (ed.), *Locked Out: A Century of Irish Working-Class Life* (Sallins: Irish Academic Press, 2013), pp. 157–72

Hillery, Brian, 'Industrial Relations: Compromise and Conflict', in Donal Nevin (ed.), *Trade Unions and Change in Irish Society* (Cork: Mercier 1980), pp. 39–52

Holden, Len, '"Think of me simply as the skipper": Industrial Relations at Vauxhalls, 1920–1950', *Oral History*, vol. 9, no. 2 (Autumn 1981), pp. 18–32

Jacobson, David, 'Theorising Irish Industrialisation: The Case of the Motor Industry', *Science and Society*, vol. 53, no. 2 (Summer 1989), pp. 165–91

Jowlitt, J.A. and McIvor, Arthur, 'Introduction', in J.A. Jowlitt and Arthur McIvor (eds), *Employers and Labour in the English Textile Industries, 1859–1939* (London: Routledge, 1988), pp. vii–xviii

Kelly, Aidan, 'White Collar Trade Unionism', in Donal Nevin (ed.), *Trade Unions and Change in Irish Society* (Cork: Mercier, 1980), pp. 65–81

Kelly, Aidan and Brannick, Theresa, 'Explaining the Strike Proneness of British Companies in Ireland', *British Journal of Industrial Relations*, vol. 26, no. 1 (March 1988), pp. 37–55

Kiely, Elizabeth and Leane, Máire, 'Female Domestic and Farm Workers in Munster, 1936-1960: Some Insights from Oral History', *Saothar*, vol. 29 (2004), pp. 57-65

Kiely, Elizabeth and Leane, Máire, 'Money Matters in the Lives of Working Women in Ireland in the 1940s and 1950s', in Francis Devine, Fintan Lane and Niamh Puirséil (eds), *Essays in Irish Labour History: A Festschrift for Elizabeth and John W. Boyle* (Dublin: Irish Academic Press, 2008), pp. 219-37

Lane, Fintan, 'Envisaging Labour History: Some Reflections on Irish Historiography and the Working Class', in Francis Devine, Fintan Lane and Niamh Puirséil (eds), *Essays in Irish Labour History: A Festschrift for Elizabeth and John W. Boyle* (Sallins: Irish Academic Press, 2008), pp. 9-25

Licht, Walter, 'Fringe Benefits: A Review Essay on the American Workplace', *International Labor and Working-Class History*, vol. 52 (Spring 1998), pp. 164-78

Lindop, Fred, 'Unofficial Militancy in the Royal Group of Docks, 1945-67', *Oral History*, vol. 11, no. 2 (Autumn 1983), pp. 21-33

Linehan, Denis, 'Urban Differentiation', in J.S. Crowley, R.J.N. Devoy, D. Linehan and P. O'Flanagan (eds), *Atlas of Cork City* (Cork: Cork University Press, 2005), pp. 403-8

Luddy, Maria, 'Working Women, Trade Unionism and Politics in Ireland, 1830-1945', in Donal Ó Drisceoil and Fintan Lane (eds), *Politics and the Irish Working-Class, 1830-1945* (Basingstoke: Palgrave Macmillan, 2005), pp. 44-61

Mac Con Iomaire, Máirtín, 'Culinary Voices: Perspectives from Dublin Restaurants', *Oral History*, vol. 39, no. 1 (Spring 2011), pp. 77-90

MacNeill, Hugh, 'Management View', in Donal Nevin (ed.), *Trade Unions and Change in Irish Society* (Cork: Mercier, 1980), pp. 53-64

McIvor, Arthur, 'The Realities and Narratives of Paid Work: The Scottish Workplace', in Lynn Abrams and Callum Brown (eds), *A History of Everyday Life in Twentieth Century Scotland* (Edinburgh: Edinburgh University Press, 2010), pp. 103-30

McKenna, Yvonne, 'Making Sense of "Mistakes" in Oral Sources', in Nessa Cronin, Seán Crosson and John Eastlake (eds), *Anáil an Bhéil Bheo: Orality and Modern Irish Culture* (Newcastle: Cambridge Scholars Publishing, 2009), pp. 149-58

Morris, Bob and Smyth, Jim, 'Paternalism as an Employer Strategy, 1800–1960', in Jill Rubery and Frank Wilson (eds), *Employer Strategy and the Labour Market* (New York: Oxford University Press, 1994), pp. 195–225

Muldowney, Mary, '"A world of its own": Recollections of Women Workers in Guinness's Brewery in the 1940s', *Saothar*, vol. 23 (1998), pp. 103–15

Muldowney, Mary, 'We were conscious of the sort of people we mixed with', *The History of the Family*, vol. 13, no. 4 (2008), pp. 402–15

Murphy, Maura, 'The Working Classes of Nineteenth-Century Cork', *Journal of the Cork Historical and Archaeological Society*, vol. lxxxv, no. 241 (1980), pp. 26–51

Newby, Howard, 'Paternalism and Capitalism', in Richard Scase (ed.), *Industrial Society: Class, Cleavage and Control* (London: Allen & Unwin, 1977), pp. 59–73

Nyhan, Miriam, 'Narration and Memory: The Experiences of the Workforce of a Ford Plant', *Irish Economic and Social History*, vol. XXXIII (2006), pp. 18–34

O'Brien, Sarah, 'Narrative Encounters with the Irish in Birmingham', in Nessa Cronin, Seán Crosson and John Eastlake (eds), *Anáil an Bhéil Bheo: Orality and Modern Irish Culture* (Newcastle: Cambridge Scholars Publishing, 2009), pp. 159–71

O'Connor, Catherine, '"The smell of her apron": Issues of Gender and Religious Identity in the Oral Testimonies of Church of Ireland Women in Ferns, 1945–1965', in Nessa Cronin, Seán Crosson and John Eastlake (eds), *Anáil an Bhéil Bheo: Orality and Modern Irish Culture* (Newcastle: Cambridge Scholars Publishing, 2009), pp. 126–36

O'Connor, Emmet and McCabe, Conor, 'Ireland', in Joan Allen, Alan Campbell and John McIlroy (eds), *Histories of Labour: National and International Perspectives* (Pontypool: Merlin Press, 2010), pp. 137–63

Owen-Jones, Sheila, 'Women in the Tinplate Industry: Llanelli, 1930–1950', *Oral History*, vol. 15, no. 1 (Spring 1987), pp. 42–9

Peillon, Michel, 'Stratification and Class', in Patrick Clancy, Sheelagh Drudy, Kathleen Lynch and Liam O'Dowd (eds), *Ireland: A Sociological Reader* (Dublin: Institute of Public Administration, 1987), pp. 97–115

Pendleton, Andrew, 'The Evolution of Industrial Relations in UK Nationalised Industries', *British Journal of Industrial Relations*, vol. 35, no. 2 (1997), pp. 145–72

Phillips, Andrew, 'Women on the Shop Floor: The Colchester Rag Trade, 1918–1950', *Oral History*, vol. 22, no. 1 (Spring 1994), pp. 56–65

Portelli, Allessandro, 'Patterns of Paternalism in Harlan County', *Appalachian Journal*, vol. 17, no. 2 (Winter 1990), pp. 140–55

Portelli, Alessandro, 'The Peculiarities of Oral History', *History Workshop*, no. 12 (August 1981), pp. 96–107

Reid, Donald, 'Industrial Paternalism: Discourse and Practice in Nineteenth-Century French Mining and Metallurgy', *Comparative Studies in Society and History*, vol. 27, no. 4 (October 1985), pp. 579–607

Roche, W.K., 'Industrial Relations', in Donal Nevin (ed.), *Trade Union Century* (Cork: Mercier Press, 1994), pp. 133–45

Rynne, Colin, 'Industry, 1750–1930', in J.S. Crowley, R.J.N. Devoy, D. Linehan and P. O'Flanagan (eds), *Atlas of Cork City* (Cork: Cork University Press, 2005), pp. 183–9

Sangster, Joan, 'The Softball Solution: Female Workers, Male Managers and the Operation of Paternalism at Westclox, 1923–60', *Labour/Le Travail*, vol. 32 (Fall 1993), pp. 167–99

Scranton, Philip, 'Varieties of Paternalism: Industrial Structures and the Social Relations of Production in American Textiles', *American Quarterly*, vol. 36, no. 2 (Summer 1984), pp. 235–57

Shields, John, 'Working Life and the Voice of Memory: An Introduction', in John Shields (ed.), *All Our Labours: Oral Histories of Working Life in Twentieth Century Sydney* (Kensington: New South Wales University Press, 1992), pp. 1–9

Summerfield, Penny, 'Culture and Composure: Creating Narratives of the Gendered Self in Oral History Interviews', *Cultural and Social History*, vol. 2 (2004), pp. 65–93.

Sutherland, John F., 'Of Mills and Memories: Labor-Management Interdependence in the Cheney Silk Mills', *Oral History Review*, vol. 11 (1983), pp. 17–41

Tarr, David G., 'The Steel Crisis in the United States and European Community: Causes and Adjustments', in Robert E. Baldwin, Carl B. Hamilton and Andre Sapir (eds), *Issues in US–EC Trade Relations* (Chicago: University of Chicago Press, 1988), pp.173–200

Tolliday, Steven, 'Ford and "Fordism" in Postwar Britain', in Steven Tolliday and Jonathan Zeitlin (eds), *The Power to Manage? Employers and Industrial Relations in Comparative-Historical Perspective* (London: Routledge, 1991), pp. 81–116

Tolliday, Steven and Zeitlin, Jonathan, 'Introduction', in Steven Tolliday and Jonathan Zeitlin (eds), *Between Fordism and Flexibility: The Automobile Industry and Its Workers* (Oxford: Berg Publishers, 1992), pp. 1–25

Toms, David, '"Notwithstanding the discomfort involved": Fordson's Cup Win in 1926 and How "The Old Contemptible" Were Represented in Ireland's Public Sphere during the 1920s', *Sport in History* (2013), pp. 1–22

Toms, David, '"The Brightest Couple of Hours": Inter-Firm and Pubs Leagues of Ireland, 1922–73', in David Convery (ed), *Locked Out: A Century of Irish Working-Class Life* (Sallins: Irish Academic Press, 2013), pp. 141–56

Thompson, Paul, 'Playing at Being Skilled Men: Factory Culture and Pride in Work Skills among Coventry Car Workers', *Social History*, vol. 13, no. 1 (January 1988), pp. 45–69

Valiulis, Maryann, 'Neither Feminist nor Flapper: The Ecclesiastical Construction of the Ideal Irish Woman', in Alan Hayes and Diane Urquhart (eds), *The Irish Women's History Reader* (Routledge: London, 2001), pp. 152–7

Warren, Kenneth, 'World Steel: Change and Crisis', *Geography*, vol. 70, no. 2 (April 1985), pp. 106–17

Winn, Peter, 'Oral History and the Factory Study: New Approaches to Labour History', *Latin American Research Review*, vol. 14, no. 2 (1979), pp. 130–40

Books

Abrams, Lynn, *Oral History Theory* (London: Routledge, 2010)

Abrams, Lynn and Brown, Callum (eds), *A History of Everyday Life in Twentieth Century Scotland* (Edinburgh: Edinburgh University Press, 2010)

Allen, Joan, Campbell, Alan and McIlroy, John (eds), *Histories of Labour: National and International Perspectives* (Pontypool: Merlin Press, 2010)

Allen, Kieran, *Fianna Fáil and Irish Labour: From 1926 to the Present* (London: Pluto Press, 1997)

Baldwin, Robert E., Hamilton, Carl B. and Sapir, Andre (eds), *Issues in US–EC Trade Relations* (Chicago: University of Chicago Press, 1988)

Barry, Frank and Durkan, Guy, *TEAM and Irish Steel: An Application of the Declining High Wages Industries Literature* (Dublin: Department of Economics, Trinity College Dublin, 1995)

Baum, Willa K., *Transcribing and Editing Oral History* (Oxford: AltaMira Press, 1991)

Bew, Paul and Patterson, Henry, *Seán Lemass and the Making of Modern Ireland* (Dublin: Gill & Macmillan, 1982)

Beynon, Huw, *Working for Ford* (Wakefield: EP Publishing, 1978)

Beynon, Huw and Blackburn, R.M., *Perceptions of Work: Variations Within a Factory* (Cambridge: Cambridge University Press, 1972)

Bielenberg, Andy, *Cork's Industrial Revolution, 1780–1880: Development or Decline?* (Cork: Cork University Press, 1991)

Bielenberg, Andy and Ryan, Raymond, *An Economic History of Ireland Since Independence* (New York: Routledge, 2013)

Blackpool Historical Society, *Blackpool: Rare and Recent Photographs* (Cork: Blackpool Historical Society, 2000)

Blackpool Historical Society, *Cork's Own Blackpool: Photographic Memories* (Cork: Blackpool Historical Society, 2003)

Boyd, Andrew, *The Rise of the Irish Trade Unions, 1729–1970* (Dublin: Anvil, 1972)

Bradley, Anthony and Valiulis, Maryann Gialanella, *Gender and Society in Modern Ireland* (Amherst: University of Massachusetts Press, 1997)

Bradley, Harriet, *Men's Work, Women's Work* (Cambridge: Polity Press, 1989)

Bradley, James F., *Industrial Development in Northern Ireland and the Republic of Ireland* (Belfast: Co-operation North, 1983)

Breen, Richard and Whelan, Christopher T., *Social Mobility and Social Class in Ireland* (Dublin: Gill & Macmillan, 1996)

Broderick, Mary, *A History of Cobh (Queenstown)* (Cork: Mary Broderick, 1989)

Brown, Terence, *Ireland: A Social and Cultural History, 1922–2002* (London: Harper Perennial, 2004)

Bruno, Robert, *Steelworker Alley: How Class Works in Youngstown* (London: Cornell University Press, 1999)

Brunt, Barry and Hourihan, Kevin (eds), *Perspectives on Cork* (Cork: Geographical Society of Ireland, 1998)

Burawoy, Michael, *The Politics of Production: Factory Regimes Under Capitalism and Socialism* (London: Verso, 1985)

Burgess-Wise, David, *Ford at Dagenham: The Rise and Fall of Detroit in Europe* (Derby: Derby Books, 2012)

Burke, Joanna, *Working-Class Cultures in Britain, 1890–1960: Gender, Class and Ethnicity* (London: Routledge, 1994)

Byrne, Anne and Leonard, Madeleine (eds), *Women in Irish Society: A Sociological Reader* (Belfast: Beyond the Pale, 1997)

Carter, Plunkett, *A Century of Cork Soccer Memories* (Cork: Evening Echo, 1996)

Caunce, Stephen, *Oral History and the Local Historian* (Longman: Essex, 1994)

Clear, Catriona, *Women of the House: Women's Household Work in Ireland, 1922–1961* (Dublin: Irish Academic Press, 2000)

Clegg, H.A., *The System of Industrial Relations in Great Britain* (Oxford: Basil Blackwell, 1970)

Cockerill, Anthony and Silberston, Aubrey, *The Steel Industry: International Comparisons of Industrial Structure and Performance* (London: Cambridge University Press, 1974)

Cohen, Sheila, *Notoriously Militant: The Story of a Union Branch at Ford Dagenham* (London: Merlin Press, 2013)

Charlton, Thomas L., *History of Oral History: Foundations and Methodology* (Plymouth: AltaMira Press, 2007)

Clancy, Patrick, Drudy, Sheelagh, Lynch, Kathleen and O'Dowd, Liam (eds), *Ireland: A Sociological Reader* (Dublin: Institute of Public Administration, 1987)

Connerton, Paul, *How Societies Remember* (Cambridge: Cambridge University Press, 1989)

Convery, David (ed.), *Locked Out: A Century of Irish Working-Class Life* (Sallins: Irish Academic Press, 2013)

Crompton, Rosemary, *Class and Stratification: An Introduction to Current Debates* (Cambridge: Polity Press, 1998)

Cronin, Mike, *The Blueshirts in Irish Politics* (Dublin: Four Courts Press, 1997)

Cronin, Nessa, Crosson, Seán and Eastlake, John (eds), *Anáil an Bhéil Bheo: Orality and Modern Irish Culture* (Newcastle: Cambridge Scholars Publishing, 2009)

Crouch, Colin, *Class Conflict and the Industrial Relations Crisis: Compromise and Corporatism in the Policies of the British State* (London: Heinemann, 1977)

Crowley, J.S., Devoy, R.J.N., Linehan, D. and O'Flanagan, P. (eds), *Atlas of Cork City* (Cork: Cork University Press, 2005)

Curtin, Chris, Donnan Hastings and Wilson, Thomas M. (eds) *Irish Urban Cultures* (Belfast: Institute of Irish Studies, 1993)

Daly, Mary E., *Industrial Development and Irish National Identity, 1922–1939* (New York: Syracuse University Press, 1992)

Daly, Mary E., *Women and Work in Ireland* (Dublin: Dundalgan Press, 1997)

Day, Graham, *Community and Everyday Life* (Abingdon: Routledge, 2006)

DeBlasio, Donna M., Gaanzert, Charles F., Mould, David H., Paschen, Steven H. and Sacks, Howard L., *Catching Stories: A Practical Guide to Oral History* (Athens: Ohio University Press, 2009)

Delaney, Enda, *Demography, State and Society: Irish Emigration to Britain, 1921–71* (Liverpool: Liverpool University Press, 2000)

Delaney, Enda, *Irish Emigration Since 1921* (Dublin: Dundalgan Press, 2002)

Devine, Francis, Lane, Fintan and Puirséil, Niamh, *Essays in Irish Labour History: A Festschrift for Elizabeth and John W. Boyle* (Sallins: Irish Academic Press, 2008)

Dunaway, David K. and Baum, Willa K. (eds), *Oral History: An Interdisciplinary Anthology* (London: AltaMira Press, 1996)

Edwards, P.K., *Conflict at Work: A Materialist Analysis of Workplace Relations* (Oxford: Basil Blackwell, 1986)

Edwards, P.K. and Scullion, Hugh, *The Social Organisation of Conflict: Control and Resistance in the Workplace* (Oxford: Basil Blackwell, 1982)

Eldridge, J.E.T., *Industrial Disputes* (London: Routledge & Kegan Paul, 1967)

Evans, George Ewart, *Spoken History* (London: Faber & Faber, 1997)

Ferriter, Diarmaid, *The Transformation of Ireland, 1900–2000* (Dublin: Profile, 2005)

Finlay, Ian, *The Labour Court. 'Not an Ordinary Court of Law ...': A History of the Labour Court from 1946 to 1996* (Dublin: Stationery Office, 1996)

Fitzgerald, Robert, *British Labour Management and Industrial Welfare, 1846–1939* (London: Croom Helm, 1988)

Fox, Alan, *Beyond Contract: Work, Power and Trust Relations* (London: Faber & Faber, 1974)

Frankland, Mark and Bussey, Gordon, *Radio Man: The Remarkable Rise and Fall of C.O. Stanley* (London: The Institution of Electrical Engineers, 2002)

French, John D. and James, Daniel (eds), *The Gendered Worlds of Latin American Women Workers: From Household and Factory to the Union Hall and Ballot Box* (London: Duke University Press, 1997)

Friedlander, Peter, *The Emergence of a UAW Local: A Study in Class and Culture* (London: University of Pittsburgh Press, 1975)

Garvin, Tom, *News from a New Republic* (Dublin: Gill & Macmillan, 2010)
Gillespie, Raymond and Hill, Myrtle, *Doing Irish Local History: Pursuit and Practice* (Belfast: Institute of Irish Studies, 1998)
Girvin, Brian, *Between Two Worlds: Politics and Economy in Independent Ireland* (Dublin: Gill & Macmillan, 1984)
Gray, Jane, *Poverty and the Life Cycle in Twentieth Century Ireland: Changing Experiences of Childhood, Education and the Transition to Adulthood* (Dublin: Combat Poverty Agency, 2010)
Grele, Ronald J., *Envelopes of Sound: The Art of Oral History* (London: Praeger, 1991)
Guiry, Ruth, *Pigtown: A History of Limerick's Bacon Industry* (Limerick: Limerick City and County Council, 2016)
Hall, David, *Working Lives: The Forgotten Voices of Britain's Post-War Working Class* (London: Transworld, 2012)
Hannigan, Dave, *Terence MacSwiney: The Hunger Strike that Rocked an Empire* (Dublin: O'Brien Press, 2010)
Hart, Peter, *The IRA and Its Enemies: Violence and Community in Cork, 1916–1923* (Oxford: Clarendon Press, 1998)
Hastings, Tim, *Semi-States in Crisis: The Challenge for Industrial Relations in the ESB and Other Semi-State Companies* (Dublin: Oak Tree Press, 1994)
Henige, David, *Oral Historiography* (Essex: Longman, 1982)
Hill, Myrtle, *Women in Ireland: A Century of Change* (Belfast: Blackstaff, 2003)
Hillery, Brian, Kelly, Aidan and Marsh, A.I., *Trade Union Organisation in Ireland* (Dublin: Irish Productivity Centre, 1975)
Hogan, Sarsfield, *A History of Irish Steel* (Dublin: Gill & Macmillan, 1980)
Howarth, Ken, *Oral History* (Gloucestershire: Sutton Publishing, 1999)
Humphreys, Alexander, *New Dubliners: Urbanization and the Irish Family* (London: Routledge & Kegan Paul, 1966)
Hunt, Pauline, *Gender and Class Consciousness* (London: The Macmillan Press, 1980)
Hurley, Martin, *A Sign of the Times: A Commercial History of Cork* (Cork: Prufrock, 1985)
Hyman, Richard, *Industrial Relations: A Marxist Introduction* (London: Macmillan, 1975)
Hyman, Richard, *The Political Economy of Industrial Relations: Theory and Practice in a Cold Climate* (London: Macmillan, 1989)

Inglis, Tom, *Moral Monopoly: The Rise and Fall of the Catholic Church in Ireland* (Dublin: Gill & Macmillan, 1987)

Jackson, Brian, *Working-Class Community: Some General Notions Raised by a Series of Studies in Northern England* (London: Routledge & Kegan Paul, 1968)

Jacobsen, John Kurt, *Chasing Progress in the Irish Republic* (Cambridge: Cambridge University Press, 1984)

Jacoby, Sanford M., *Modern Manors: Welfare Capitalism Since the New Deal* (Princeton: Princeton University Press, 1999)

Jeffries, Henry, *A New History of Cork* (Dublin: The History Press, 2010)

Johnston, Ronald and McIvor, Arthur, *Lethal Work: A History of the Asbestos Tragedy in Scotland* (East Lothian: Tuckwell Press, 2000)

Jowlitt, J.A. and McIvor, Arthur (eds), *Employers and Labour in the English Textile Industries, 1859–1939* (London: Routledge, 1988), pp. vii–xviii

Joyce, Patrick, *The Culture of the Factory in Later Victorian England* (London: Harvester Press, 1980)

Kearns, Kevin C., *Dublin Pub Life and Lore: An Oral History* (Dublin: Gill & Macmillan, 1996)

Kearns, Kevin C., *Dublin Tenement Life: An Oral History* (Dublin: Gill & Macmillan, 1994)

Kearns, Kevin C., *Dublin Voices: An Oral Folk History* (Dublin: Gill & Macmillan, 1998)

Kearns, Kevin C., *Working-Class Heroines: The Extraordinary Women of Dublin's Tenements* (Dublin: Gill & Macmillan, 2004)

Kennedy, Liam, *The Modern Industrialisation of Ireland, 1940–1988* (Dublin: Dundalgan Press, 1989)

Kiely, Elizabeth and Leane, Máire, *Irish Women at Work, 1930–1960: An Oral History* (Sallins: Irish Academic Press, 2012)

Kirk, John, *Class, Culture and Social Change: On the Trail of the Working Class* (New York: Palgrave Macmillan, 2007)

Kornhauser, Arthur, Dubin, Robert and Ross, Arthur M., *Industrial Conflict* (London: McGraw Hill, 1954)

Leland, Mary, *Dwyers of Cork: A Family Business and a Business Family* (Cork: Ted Dwyer, 2008)

Lowenstein, Wendy and Hills, Tom, *Under the Hook: Melbourne Dockworkers Remember* (Melbourne: Melbourne Bookworkers, 1982)

Martin, Roderick and Fryer, R.H., *Redundancy and Paternalist Capitalism: A Study in the Sociology of Work* (London: George Allen & Unwin, 1973)

Maitland, Ian, *The Causes of Industrial Disorder: A Comparison of a British and a German Factory* (London: Routledge & Kegan Paul, 1983)

McCarthy, Charles, *The Decade of Upheaval: Irish Trade Unions in the Nineteen Sixties* (Dublin: Institute of Public Administration, 1973)

McCarthy, Charles, *Trade Unions in Ireland, 1894–1960* (Dublin: Institute of Public Administration, 1977)

McCarthy, Kieran, *Voices of Cork: The Knitting Map Speaks* (Dublin: Nonsuch, 2005)

McCarthy, Paddy, *Cork in the Inter-War Years, 1918–1939: An Outline* (Cork: Paddy McCarthy, 2011)

McIvor, Arthur, *Working Lives: Work in Britain Since 1945* (Basingstoke: Palgrave Macmillan, 2013)

Meenan, James, *The Irish Economy Since 1922* (Liverpool: Liverpool University Press, 1970)

Messenger, Betty, *Picking Up the Linen Threads: Life in Ulster's Mills* (Belfast: Blackstaff Press, 1989)

Meyer III, Stephen, *The Five Dollar Day: Labor Management and Social Control in the Ford Motor Company, 1908–1921* (Albany: State University of New York Press, 1981)

Montgomery, Bob, *Ford Manufacture and Assembly at Cork, 1919–1984* (Garristown: Dreóilín, 2000)

Muldowney, Mary, *The Second World War and Irish Women: An Oral History* (Dublin: Irish Academic Press, 2007)

Nevin, Donal (ed.), *Trade Union Century* (Cork: Mercier Press, 1994)

Nevin, Donal (ed.), *Trade Unions and Change in Irish Society* (Cork: Mercier 1980)

Newby, Howard, *The Deferential Worker: A Study of Farm Workers in Anglia* (London: Penguin, 1997)

Newby, Howard, Bell, Colin, Rose, David and Saunders, Peter, *Property, Paternalism and Power: Class and Control in Rural England* (London: Hutchinson, 1978)

Nye, David E., *Henry Ford: Ignorant Idealist* (London: Kinnikat Press, 1999)

Nyhan, Miriam, *Are You Still Below? The Ford Marina Plant, Cork, 1917–1984* (Cork: Collins Press, 2007)

O'Connor, Emmet, *A Labour History of Ireland, 1824–2000*, 2nd edition (Dublin: University College Dublin Press, 2011)

O'Dea, Patrick (ed.), *A Class of Our Own: Conversations about Class in Ireland* (Dublin: New Island Books, 1994)

Ó Drisceoil, Donal and Lane, Fintan (eds), *Politics and the Irish Working-Class, 1830–1945* (Basingstoke: Palgrave Macmillan, 2005)

Ó Drisceoil, Diarmuid and Ó Drisceoil, Donal, *The Murphy's Story: The History of Lady's Well Brewery, Cork* (Cork: Murphy Brewery Limited, 1997)

Ó Gráda, Cormac, *A Rocky Road: The Irish Economy Since the 1920s* (Manchester: Manchester University Press, 1997)

Ó Gráda, *Ireland: A New Economic History, 1780–1939* (Oxford: Clarendon Press, 1994)

O'Mahony, David, *The Irish Economy: An Introductory Description* (Cork: Cork University Press, 1967)

O'Malley, Eoin, *Industry and Economic Development: The Challenges for the Latecomer* (Dublin: Gill & Macmillan, 1989)

O'Sullivan, Donal, *Sport in Cork: A History* (Dublin: History Press Ireland, 2010)

Passerini, Luisa, *Autobiography of a Generation: Italy, 1968* (London: Wesleyan University Press, 1996)

Passerini, Luisa, *Fascism in Popular Memory: The Cultural Experience of the Turin Working Class* (Cambridge: Cambridge University Press, 1987)

Perks, Robert, *Oral History: An Annotated Bibliography* (London: British Library, 1990)

Portelli, Alessandro, *The Death of Luigi Trastulli and Other Stories: Form and Meaning in Oral History* (Albany: State University of New York Press, 1991)

Portelli, Alessandro, *The Order Has Been Carried Out: History, Memory and Meaning of a Nazi Massacre in Rome* (New York: Palgrave Macmillan, 2003)

Portelli, Alessandro, *They Say in Harlan County: An Oral History* (Oxford: Oxford University Press, 2010)

Quinlivan, Aodh, *Philip Monahan: A Life Apart* (Dublin: Institute of Public Administration, 2006)

Ritchie, Donald A., *Doing Oral History: A Practical Guide* (Oxford: Oxford University Press, 2003)

Ritchie, Donald A. (ed.), *The Oxford Handbook of Oral History* (Oxford: Oxford University Press, 2011)

Roberts, Elizabeth, *An Oral History of Working-Class Women, 1890–1940* (Oxford: Basil Blackwell, 1984)

Rubery, Jill and Wilson, Frank (eds), *Employer Strategy and the Labour Market* (New York: Oxford University Press, 1994)

Russo, John and Linkon, Sherry Lee, *New Working-Class Studies* (London: Cornell University Press, 2005)

Rynne, Colin, *The Archaeology of Cork City and Harbour: From the Earliest Times to Industrialisation* (Cork: Collins Press, 1993)

Sangster, Joan, *Earning Respect: The Lives of Working Women in Small-Town Ontario* (Toronto: University of Toronto Press, 1995)

Scase, Richard (ed.) *Industrial Society: Class, Cleavage and Control* (London: Allen & Unwin, 1977)

Share, Perry, Tovey, Hilary and Corcoran, Mary P., *A Sociology of Ireland*, 3rd edition (Dublin: Gill & Macmillan, 2007)

Shields, John (ed.), *All Our Labours: Oral Histories of Working Life in Twentieth Century Sydney* (Kensington: New South Wales University Press, 1992)

Silverman, Marilyn, *An Irish Working Class: Explorations in Political Economy and Hegemony, 1800–1950* (Toronto: University of Toronto Press, 2006)

Tolliday, Steven and Zeitlin, Jonathan (eds), *Between Fordism and Flexibility: The Automobile Industry and Its Workers* (Oxford: Berg Publishers, 1992)

Tolliday, Steven and Zeitlin, Jonathan (eds), *The Power to Manage? Employers and Industrial Relations in Comparative-Historical Perspective* (London: Routledge, 1991)

Toms, David, *Soccer in Munster: A Social History, 1877–1937* (Cork: Cork University Press, 2015)

Thompson, Alistair, *Anzac Memories: Living with the Legend* (Melbourne: Oxford University Press, 1994)

Thompson, E.P., *The Making of the English Working Class* (London: Penguin, 1963)

Thompson, Paul, *The Voice of the Past: Oral History*, 3rd edition (Oxford: Oxford University Press, 2000)

Tone, Andrea, *The Business of Benevolence: Industrial Paternalism in Progressive America* (New York: Cornell University Press, 1997)

Turner, H.A., Clack, Garfield and Roberts, Geoffrey, *Labour Relations in the Motor Industry* (London: George Allen & Unwin Ltd, 1967)

Upham, Martin, *Tempered – Not Quenched: The History of the ISTC, 1951–1997* (London: Lawrence & Wishart, 1997)

Verdon, Michael, *Old Cork Remembered: Shawlies, Echo Boys, the Marsh and the Lanes* (Dublin: O'Brien Press, 1993)

Vinyard, Joellen, *The Irish on the Urban Frontier: Nineteenth Century Detroit, 1850–1880* (New York: Arno Press, 1976)

Walker, Charles R. and Guest, Robert H., *The Man on the Assembly Line* (Cambridge: Harvard University Press, 1952)

Wallace, Joseph, Gunnigle, Patrick and McMahon, Gerard, *Industrial Relations in Ireland*, 3rd edition (Dublin: Gill & Macmillan, 2004)

Wallman, Sandra (ed.), *The Social Anthropology of Work* (London: Academic Press, 1979)

Whelan, Edward, *Ranks Mill: The Industrial Heart of Limerick City* (Limerick: Limerick Corporation, 2012)

Whyte, J.H., *Church and State in Modern Ireland, 1923–1979* (Dublin: Gill & Macmillan, 1980)

Wilkins, Myra and Hill, Frank Ernest, *American Business Abroad: Ford on Six Continents*, 2nd edition (Cambridge: Cambridge University Press, 2011)

Wilson, Thomas M. and Donnan, Hastings, *The Anthropology of Ireland* (Oxford: Berg, 2006)

Winn, Peter, *Weavers of Revolution: The Yarur Workers and Chile's Road to Socialism* (New York: Oxford University Press, 1986)

Yow, Valerie Raleigh, *Recording Oral History: A Practical Guide for Social Scientists* (London: Sage, 1994)

Index

Illustrations are indicated by page numbers in **bold**.

absenteeism, 87, 135
advertising, 36, 124
agriculture, 52, 72, 84, 96, 175–6, 187, 208, 235, 240
Aiken, Frank, 59
Allied Textiles Ltd, 43, 44
Amalgamated Union of Engineering Workers (AUEW), 61–2, 159–60
Anglo-Irish Free Trade Agreement (AIFTA), 30, 40
apprenticeships, 171, 179–81, 182
Ardfinnan, 41
Arklow, 53
Arks Publicity, 36
asset-stripping, 169–70

banks, 43, 44–5
bargaining power, 48, 133, 135–6, 165, 179, 181, 219, 236, 239
Barker, Trevor, 48
Barrington Commission, 146
Barry, Madge, 115, 116
basketball, 117, 232
baths, 115, 128
Belfast, 126
Belgium, 30, 41, 56
Beynon, Huw, 83, 88, 106
Birmingham, 191, 192, 208
Black Monday stock market crash, 48
blacklegging, 125, 225
Blarney Woollen Mills, 87, 127, 133, 194

blue-collar workers, 5, 209–17
bonuses, 74, 214
Bord Gáis, 170
Bord na Móna, 158
Brady, Donal, 156, 161, 162, 169, 180, 188, 208, 211
breadwinners, 104–5, 150–51, 160, 196, 198–205, 234, 237
Breen, Richard, 173
Britain
    companies purchased by Sunbeam Group, 43, 44–5, 47
    emigration to, 27–8, 96–101, 174, 175, 181–2, 186–95
    Ford plants, 22–5, 27–9, 81, 86–8, 97–101, 106, 110–11, 194–5, 221, 242
    free trade with, 30, 40, 44–5, 65
    import dumping, 41
    labour historiography, 2
    naval presence in Cobh, 53, 54
    paternalism, 113
    Second World War, 54, 96–100, 175
    social class, 185
    steel industry, 57, 65, 67, 68, 149, 152–3
    trade unions, 18, 91, 99, 101
    wages, 18, 110–11
British army, 39, 177, 181
Bruno, Robert, 109, 149, 230
Bruton, Richard, 70–71

293

Buckley, Christy, 144, 152, 171, 176–7, 201
Buckley, Lesley, 167
Buckley Motors, 28, 103
Business and Finance, 29
Byrne, Nancy, 216

canteens, 108, 115, 117, 123, 211
Carey, Dominic, 100
Carrigaline, 166
casual work, 175–7
Catholic Action movement, 128–9
Catholicism, 118, 126–30, 195, 203, 237, 241
Celtic Tiger, 9, 14, 239
childcare, 200
choirs, 117, 232
Church of the Annunciation, Blackpol, 119
City of Cork Steam Packet Company, 89–90
Civil War, 20, 162
Clarke, E.L., 22, 83, 87
cleanliness, 80, 123
Cleary, Eddie, 102
clerical workers, 131, 158, 197, 210–17, 219
Coakley, D.J., 33, 127
coal, 55, 62
Cobh
  dearth of historical research, 11
  de-industrialisation, 9, 170–72, 240
  economic history, 9, 53–4, 170–72, 239–40
  employment opportunities, 170–72, 181–2
  housing, 160–61
  impact of Irish Steel strike, 160–62
  labour pool, 52
  population size, 53–4, 160
  tourism, 172
  as treaty port, 54
  unemployment, 53–4, 59, 62, 170–72
Cobh Urban District Council, 54, 55, 59, 160
Cockerill, Anthony, 66
Cohen, Sheila, 99
Coloroll Plc, 48
commercial travellers, 125–6, 212
Commercial Travellers Federation (CTF), 125–6
Commission Dyers, 44
Committee on Industrial Organisation (CIO), 28, 29, 44, 103
company newspapers, 80–81, 90–91
company shops, 79, 116
Constitution of Ireland, 198
construction industry, 63, 64, 147–8, 177, 188, 226
contraception, 209
Convery, David, 1
Coogan, Eamonn, 59
Córas Iompar Éireann (CIÉ), 52, 102
Corcoran, Mary, 173
Corcoran, Patsy, 224, 230
Cork city
  burning of, 20, 92
  economic history, 9, 11–14, 72, 172, 235, 239
  growth in trade union membership, 236
  Henry Ford's visit to, 16–17
  housing, 77, 82, 127
  impact of Celtic Tiger, 14, 239
  industrial development, 11–14
  labour pool, 17, 18, 84–6, 98
  local philanthropy, 118–19
  population size, 11
  poverty, 16
  transport links, 17, 18

unemployment, 14, 18, 34, 48, 72, 81–2, 91, 111, 139, 175, 186–7, 235–6
  and the War of Independence, 20, 92–4
Cork Corporation, 19, 20–21, 91
Cork Economic Development Council, 130
Cork Examiner, 27, 82, 85, 89–90, 92–3
Cork Folklore Project (CFP), 4, 7–8
Cork harbour, 11, **12**, **13**, 18, 52–3, 169
Cork Industrial Development Association, 73–4
Cork prison, 93
Cork Spinning and Weaving Company, 34, 36, 127
Cork Spinning Company, 38, 41
Cork Workers' Council, 36, 124, 125
Costelloe, Michael, 106, 175–6, 181–2, 186–7, 189–92, 212–13, 219, 221
craftsmen, 6, 141, 154–5, 157–64, 167–8, 178–81, 197, 210–11, 213, 217–19, 225, 239; *see also* skilled labour
Cronin, Jim, 138–9, 162, 171–2, 181, 192–3
Cronin, Mary, 189–90, 191–2, 194, 207–8, 224
Crowley, Ethel, 206
Cumann na nGaedheal, 35
Cummins, Tony, 150, 165, 183, 184, 198–9, 218, 222–3

Dagenham, 23, 24–5, 29, 81, 86–8, 97–101, 194–5, 221, 242
Dairy Disposal Company, 52
Danus Clothing Company, 133
Davignon plan, 70
Dearborn, Michigan, 20, 25, 76–7, 86, 88
deaths, 9, 141, 142–3, 144–53, 242
Delaney, Enda, 186, 189, 194

Denmark, 68
Department of Finance, 59, 68
Department of Industry and Commerce, 32, 55–8, 65, 83, 97
Detroit, Michigan, 16
Detroit Free Press, 88
developing countries, 42, 70
Devine, Francis, 147, 148, 152
Dineen, Pat, 167–8
discrimination, 205–7
District Nursing Association, 119
dock workers, 89–90, 161–2, 177
Douglas, 33, 41
Downey, Liam, 100
Downey, Vaunie, 98, 194–5
Drogheda Manpower Survey, 174, 207, 215
Dublin, 30, 36, 43–4, 52, 77, 157–8, 159, 178
Dublin Corporation, 157–8, 159
Dublin Council of Trade Unions, 61
Dunlea, Patrick, 99, 205
Dunlop, 48, 105, 161, 166, 176, 213
Dwyer, Declan, 115, 127, 134
Dwyer, Kevin, 41–2
Dwyer, William, 34–6, 37, 39, 49, 112–13, 115, 118–20, 123–9, 134, 212, 232

Economic and Social Research Institute (ESRI), 173–4, 184–5
economic policy, 11–14, 25–6, 31–2, 35–9, 49, 60, 64–5, 235–6, 238
economies of scale, 65, 66
education, 74, 122, 173–4, 178, 179, 181–5, 217, 236, 239
Elders, Marian, 224
electricians, 155, 172, 179, 180
Electricity Supply Board (ESB), 161, 162, 170, 213

Elliott, Bob, 81, 88
emigration, 16, 27–8, 48, 62, 73, 97–100, 141, 172–6, 181–2, 186–95, 235–6
employee welfare policies, 73–81
European Economic Community (EEC), 14, 30, 32, 40–42, 46, 49, 65–7, 70, 156, 161
Evening Echo, 160

Factories Act, 152
Factory Inspectorate, 146–9, 151–2
factory study approach, 2, 3
factory tours, 80
family, 79, 104–5, 120–22, 151, 160, 177, 179–82, 190, 194–6, 198–208, 237–8; *see also* breadwinners; homemakers; kin recruitment; marriage
Federated Union of Employers (FUE), 158
Fianna Fáil, 11, 25, 35, 36, 38, 54, 58, 96, 130, 166
Fiat plant, Dublin, 30
Fine Gael, 51, 59, 119
First World War, 76
FitzGerald, Garret, 51
Fitzgerald, Michael, 93
Fitzgibbon, Kathleen, 124, 199, 224–5
Foley, Billy, 120, 121, 215–16
football *see* Gaelic football; soccer
Ford, Eleanor, 189, 191–3, 199–200, 230–31
Ford, Henry, 16–17, 19, 21, 23–4, 73–4, 76, 78, 80, 87–8, 90
Ford, Henry, II, 31, 103
Ford Dagenham plant, 23, 24–5, 29, 81, 86–7, 88, 97–101, 194–5, 221, 242
Ford Dearborn headquarters, 20, 25, 76–7
Ford Genk plant, 30

Ford Highland Park plant, 74, 84
Ford Leamington Spa plant, 97, 99, 105
Ford Liverpool Halewood plant, 106
Ford Manchester plant, 22, 91, 98
Ford Marina plant
 absenteeism, 87
 acquisition of site, 19
 age profile of workforce, 104–5
 business history, 3, 16–32
 canteen, 108, 211
 car assembly, 25–9, 96, 103, 106–9
 closure, 9, 31, 48, 111, 166
 company newspaper, 80–81, 90–91
 dispute with Cork Corporation, 20–21, 91
 employee welfare policies, 73–81
 employees transferred to British plants, 27–8, 97–100, 194–5
 establishment, 17–20, 73, 235
 experiences of work at, 3, 72–111
 fiftieth anniversay celebrations, 29
 foundry, 22, 23, 24, 86–7, 98, 242
 gender balance of workforce, 6, 104
 green labour, 84–7
 and hunger strikes protests, 92–4
 industrial relations, 3–4, 73, 87–95, 100–106, 108–11, 236, 238
 internal promotions, 208–9
 investment scheme, 79
 job security, 82–3, 91, 103, 186, 208
 labour representation committee, 91, 94
 labour turnover, 79, 81, 82–3
 medical care, 79–80
 Model T production, 22
 modernisation of plant, 30
 occupational safety, 80, 242
 pensions, 111
 pictured, **83, 104, 110**
 in popular memory, 9, 10, 241

INDEX

production quality, 22, 30
public tours, 80
recruitment practices, 97–8, 104–5
redundancy packages, 9, 31
shop, 79
social clubs, 78, 80, 228–9, 232
sports, 78, 228
strikes, 4, 95, 101–3, 108–11, 162, 212–13, 236, 238
television documentary about, 9
tractor production, 19, 20–25, 82
and trade unions, 4, 73, 87–93, 101–3, 197, 212, 221, 236, 238, 242
wages, 31, 75, 84, 85, 88, 90, 95, 103, 104, 105–6, 110
working conditions, 73, 81–7, 106–9
Ford River Rouge plant, 86, 88
Forde, Denis, 99, 104–5, 189
Fordism, 72–81
Fordson soccer team, 78
Fordson tractors, 19, 23–25, 82
Fordson Worker, 80–81, 90–91
Frame, David, 52–8
France, 133
free trade, 14, 29, 30, 32, 39–46, 49, 63, 131–4, 236, 238

Gaelic football, 117, 228
garden parties, 118
gender
    devaluation of female labour, 205–8
    and discrimination, 205–7
    and duration of working life, 6, 122, 205, 207–9, 224, 234, 237
    and emigration, 192–3
    gender balance of interviewees, 6–7
    gender balance of workforces, 6, 34, 97, 104, 112, 122–3, 207, 237
    gender roles, 104–5, 150–51, 160, 196–7, 198–205, 237

male work identities, 150, 152–3, 202–3, 237, 241
and occupation types, 205–6, 207–8, 209, 213–15, 237–8
and occupational status, 213–17
and pensions, 207
restrictions on female working hours, 133
and trade unions, 197, 206, 224–5, 237–8
and wages, 205, 237
General Agreement on Tariffs and Trade (GATT), 14
general operatives, 6, 157, 158, 160, 162–3, 181, 197, 210–11, 217–19
Germany, 42, 54, 68
Glasgow, 191, 194
Goek, Sara, 187
Gouldings fertiliser factory, 102
government subsidies, 46, 47, 49
Grace, Edward, 19–22, 77, 78, 79, 89–90, 94
Great Depression, 24, 27
green labour, 84–7
Grimes, Thomas, 17, 77, 94
Guild of Goodwill, 119
Guinness brewery, 77, 123, 158

Hall, David, 149
Hammond Lane iron foundry, 52, 56
Hammond Lane Steel Company, 57
Haulbowline naval base, 52, 53
Haulbowline Steel Syndicate, 56–7
Hayes, Max, 102, 212
Hayes, Paddy, 30, 31, 111
Health and Safety Authority, 151
health impacts, 9, 141
Hickey, June, 136–7
Hickey, Marian, 136, 199, 203–4, 206, 207, 209, 225, 226

Highland Park, Michigan, 74, 84
Hill, Frank Earnest, 17, 22, 23, 24
Hogan, Sarsfield, 51, 59, 60, 63, 154–6, 211
homemakers, 122, 196, 198–201, 203–4, 207–8, 237
housing, 75–6, 77, 82, 113, 115, 127, 160–61, 199
hunger strikes, 92–4
hurling, 100, 117, 228
Hutchinson, Bertram, 185

Iarnród Éireann, 170
immigrant labour, 84
import dumping, 41
import substitution, 11, 237, 239
Industrial Inspectorate, 146–9, 151–2
industrial paternalism *see* paternalism
industrial relations
    attitudes to, 222–8
    Ford Dagenham plant, 99–100
    Ford Marina plant, 3–4, 73, 87–95, 100–106, 108–11, 236, 238
    Irish Steel, 3–4, 67, 70, 141, 153–68, 238–9
    Sunbeam Wolsey, 3–4, 42, 112–13, 122, 123–6, 130–39, 238–9
    see also Labour Court; strikes; trade unions
inequality, 173–86
informed consent, 7–8
Ingot, 232
Inisfallen, 176, 187, 192, 194, 208
initiation rituals, 229
injuries, 9, 142–3, 144–53, 242
interview procedures, 4–10
investment schemes, 79
Irish Congress of Trade Unions, 159–60
Irish Press, 32, 140–41, 160, 178–9, 205

Irish Republican Army (IRA), 92–3
Irish Steel
    asset-stripping, 169–70
    business history, 3, 51–71
    closure, 9, 71, 141, 169–71
    craftsmen, 141, 154–5, 157–64, 167–8, 181, 218, 225, 239
    deaths, 9, 141, 142–3, 242
    demolition of plant, 140
    Department of Industry and Commerce investigation into, 55–8
    establishment, 52–3
    expansion and redevelopment, 62–3, 67–8
    experiences of work at, 3, 140–72
    exports, 63, 64, 65, 68, 70
    foreign technicians, 153–4
    gender balance of workforce, 6
    Haulbowline site, 52–4, **61**, 62, 140, 169
    health impacts, 9, 141
    industrial relations, 3–4, 67, 70, 141, 153–68, 238–9
    injuries, 9, 142–3, 242
    Ispat ownership, 9, 51, 70–71, 141, 169–70
    job security, 141, 143, 150, 186, 208
    in liquidation (1941), 55–8
    modernisation of plant, 64, 67–8
    monopoly on scrap metal, 52, 57, 60, 64–5, 66, 164
    occupational safety, 9, 141–53, 242
    pictured, **61, 145**
    in popular memory, 9, 10, 140, 241
    privatisation, 51, 70–71, 141
    in receivership (1946), 58–9
    redundancy packages, 9, 167, 170
    as semi-state company, 50, 51–2, 59–60, 154

social activities, 211, 232
sports, 232
strikes, 4, 67, 141, 150, 154–64, 211, 213, 218, 225, 238–9
and trade unions, 3–4, 67, 70, 102, 154–68, 197, 236, 238
wages, 141, 143, 150–51, 155, 156, 157, 160, 163–4
working conditions, 141–53, 238
Irish Steel Holdings (ISH), 59–61
Irish Steel Sports and Social Association, 232
Irish Sugar, 52
Irish Textiles Federation, 46
Irish Times, 29, 30, 36, 39, 48, 84, 101, 126–7
Irish Transport and General Workers Union (ITGWU), 42, 88–9, 101–3, 112, 122–4, 130–31, 154–5, 161, 167, 180, 219, 222, 225, 236
Irish Union of Distributive and Clerical Workers, 206
Irish Worsted Mills, 41
Ispat, 9, 51, 70–71, 141, 169–70

Japan, 70
job security, 82–3, 91, 103, 141, 143, 150, 175–7, 186, 208, 237
job sharing, 207
John Crowther Group, 47–8
Johnston, Ronald, 152–3

Keating, Justin, 67
Kelly, Aidan, 214
Kenny, Joseph, 93
Kermesse, 118, 119
Kerrigan, Fionnán, 149, 150, 169, 170, 184, 189, 202–3, 208, 223
Kerrigan, Gene, 178
Kerry Fashions Ltd, 48

Kiely, Elizabeth, 127, 198, 201, 203–4, 206–7
Kiley, William, 44–5, 132–3
Kilspindie Ltd, 43
kin recruitment, 120–22, 179, 180–81; *see also* family

labour categorisation, 197, 209–19
Labour Court, 101, 131, 167
labour historiography, 1–2, 242
labour turnover, 79, 81, 82–3
Lahiff, Edward, 127
Lane, Fintan, 1–2, 242
Leamington Spa, 97, 99, 105
Leane, Máire, 127, 198, 201, 203–4, 206–7
Lee Boot Company, 34, 116–17
Lee Hosiery, 34
Lemass, Seán, 29, 53, 54, 57, 58, 59, 61, 63
Lenihan, Michael, **104**, 105, 107–9, 188–9, 201–2, 225, 227–8, 230–32
Lever, Sir Ernest, 62
Liberty, 102, 112, 124, 129, 135, 209–10
libraries, 113, 128
life insurance, 79
life-story approach, 7
Limerick, 133
linen, 33–4, 35, 126
Little Island, 172
Liverpool, 106
London, 190–92
loyalty, 106, 114, 117, 120, 121, 129
Luxembourg, 68
Lynch, Jack, 162

Mac an tSíthigh, Domhnall, 100
McCabe, Conor, 2
McCarthy, Charles, 222
McCarthy, Linda, 120, 122, 137–8

McCarthy, Rena, 116–17, 204, 214–15, 216, 225
McCourt, Kevin, 67, 166
MacCurtain, Tomás, 92
MacEntee, Seán, 55–6
McIvor, Arthur, 150, 152–3, 185
McLoughlin, Gus, 81, 88, 98–100, 107, 177, 181, 193–4, 196, 210, 220–21, 233, 241–2
McMurty, Billy, 144, 150–51, 152, 182, 183, 189
MacSwiney, Terence, 92–3
Madden, Paddy, 121
Magee, John, 168
male work identities, 150, 152–3, 202–3, 237, 241
Manchester, 22, 91, 98
Maritime Industries, 162
marriage, 115, 122–3, 176–7, 193, 198–201, 203, 205, 207, 209, 237–8; *see also* family
marriage grants, 115, 122–3
Marsh Building Society, 119
masses, 92–4, 118
medical care, 74, 79–80, 115, 128, 129
memory *see* popular memory
Messenger, Betty, 126
Meyer, Stephen, 74, 76, 84
Midleton Worsted Mills, 39, 41, 47
Millfield Flax Spinning and Weaving Company, 33
mini-mills, 65–6, 67–8
Mittal, Lakshmi, 169
Model T, 22
monopolies, 13, 36–9, 52, 57, 60, 64–5, 66, 131–2, 164
Monopolies and Mergers Commission (UK), 48
Morocco, 39
Morris, Bob, 130

motor industry quota, 32
Muintir na Tíre, 129
Mulcahy-Redmond, 41, 43–4
Muldowney, Mary, 215
Mullins, Eddie, 103
Mulvihill, John, 169
Murphy, Tim, 87, 108–9, 178, 189, 194, 202, 208–9, 221, 228–9, 231, 233
Murrough Brothers, 41

National Electrical and Engineering Trade Union (NEETU), 130
National Union of Vehicle Builders, 221
Netherlands, 41
New York, 39
Newby, Howard, 119
nicknames, 229
Nissan, 30
Nítrigin Éireann Teoranta, 52, 162, 171
nostalgia, 9, 199
Nyhan, Miriam, 4, 17, 82, 105, 106, 108

O'Callaghan, Arthur, 211
O'Callaghan, Catherine, 115
occupational safety, 9, 80, 141–53, 242
occupational status, 197, 209–19
O'Connell, John, 47
O'Connor, Emmet, 2, 165, 184, 242
O'Donnell, Reverend, 128
O'Donoghue, Michael V., 81, 93
Ogilvie, James, 33–4, 36, 127
oil crisis, 66
O'Kelly, Seán T., 55
O'Mahony, Denis, 220
O'Neill, John, 22, 31, 88, 97
O'Rahilly, Alfred, 125
oral history, 2, 4–10, 240–42
O'Riordan, Michael, 143
O'Shea, John, 175, 176, 186–7, 201, 208, 222

INDEX

O'Shea, Tom, 59, 60
Owens, Arthur, 102

part-time labour, 183, 207–8
paternalism, 39, 75, 80, 112–30, 132, 139, 232
pay freezes, 157, 166
Payne, Peggy, 118, 120
Pendleton, Andrew, 160
pensions, 111, 207, 214
Perry, Percival, 17–19, 23, 24–5, 26, 75–7
petrol rationing, 27, 96
Pfizer, 14
philanthropy, 17, 18–19, 78, 119
pilgrimages, 127
popular memory, 9–10, 112, 115, 122, 140, 241
Portelli, Alessandro, 125, 164
Portlaoise, 41
professional occupations, 178, 179, 205
profit-sharing, 113
promotions, 206, 208–9, 233, 236, 237
property ownership, 173
protectionism, 11–14, 25–7, 31–2, 35–9, 49, 52, 58, 60, 64–5, 96, 124, 130, 156, 163, 235–6, 238, 239
protests, 91, 92–4, 138

Quadragesimo Anno, 127, 128
Quakers, 126
Quinn, Ruairí, 168
quotas, 32, 35, 70

radioactive scrap, 169
rationalisation, 44, 49, 67, 166–7
raw materials, 18, 38, 41, 55, 62, 96
ready-made clothing, 35
recruitment practices
    Ford Marina plant, 97–8, 104–5
    Sunbeam Wolsey, 120–23

redundancy packages
    Ford Marina plant, 9, 31, 111
    Irish Steel, 9, 167, 170
    Sunbeam Wolsey, 138–9
republicanism, 92–4
Richard Ingham and Company, 48
Ringaskiddy, 14, 172
Ríoghacht, An, 128
Rome, 127
rural areas, 174, 175–6, 187

safety committees, 152
St Vincent de Paul Society, 119
Salts Ltd, 41, 43
sampling methods, 5, 186
Sangster, Joan, 91, 120, 121
saving schemes, 230–31
Scott, Harry, 85–6
Scott, Tom, 40–41, 43–4, 45, 132
Scranton, Philip, 131
scrap metal, 52, 57, 60, 64–5, 66, 164
Seafield Fabrics, 39, 119, 124
seasonal work, 175–7
Second World War, 27, 38–9, 54–5, 58, 73, 96–100, 116, 175, 215
Sectoral Consultative Committee of the Irish Textiles and Clothing Industries, 46
semi-state companies, 50, 51–2, 59–60, 154, 205
Services, Industrial, Professional and Technical Union (SIPTU), 138, 167
Shandon butter market, 35, 36
Share, Perry, 173
Shealy, Jim, 142–6, 149, 151, 156, 171, 181, 188–90, 210–11, 221–3, 226
Sheridan, Jean, 160
short-time working, 132, 157
sickness benefits, 115, 129, 214
Silberston, Aubrey, 66

Sinn Féin, 92, 94
Sisk, Rita, 199–200, 204, 207, 225
Skibbereen, 174
skilled labour, 18, 96, 111, 153–64, 178–81, 197, 217–19; *see also* craftsmen
slackage, 82–3, 100, 193–4
Smith Haywood and Company, 44
Smyth, Jim, 130
soccer, 78, 117, 228, 232, 233
social activities, 78, 80, 115, 117–18, 211, 232
social class, 1–2, 28, 113, 173–86, 195, 197, 235–6
social clubs, 78, 80, 228–9, 232
social mobility, 173, 178, 184, 236, 239
socialisation, 203–4
solidarity, 122, 136–7, 158, 161–2, 230–32
Sorensen, Charlie 'Cast-Iron', 19, 21–2, 76–7, 79, 94
Soviet Union, 23
sports, 78, 100, 115, 117–18, 216, 228, 232–3
Squires, William, 86
Stanley, Charles Orr, 35–6, 39–40, 126
Steel Company of Wales, 62
steel production quotas, 70
Steel Times, 68
strikes
    craftsmens' strikes, 156–64, 218, 225, 239
    decline in from 80s onwards, 4, 135–8, 165, 223, 239
    dock workers' strikes, 89–90, 161–2
    Ford Dagenham plant, 99
    Ford Marina plant, 4, 95, 101–3, 108–11, 162, 212–13, 236, 238
    Irish Steel, 4, 67, 141, 150, 154–64, 211, 213, 218, 225, 238–9
    national steel strike in Britain, 68
    respect for pickets, 109, 122, 130, 157, 158, 162, 222, 225–6
    Sunbeam Wolsey, 3, 4, 112, 122, 125–6, 130–31, 133–4, 137, 157, 212, 225, 238–9
    in support of independence movement, 92–4
    textile industry strikes, 133
    trade union recognition strikes, 101, 102, 221, 236, 238
    unofficial strikes, 103, 108–10, 130, 136, 154, 161–2, 211, 222, 225, 238
    and white-collar workers, 211–13
    see also industrial relations
Summerfield, Penny, 10
Sunbeam Group, 37–9, 41–6, 47–8, 132–4, 135
Sunbeam Response Group, 48
Sunbeam Social Services Society, 122–3, 127–8
Sunbeam Wolsey
    baths, 115, 128
    British military contracts, 39
    business history, 3, 13, 33–50
    canteen, 115, 117, 123
    and Catholicism, 118, 126–30
    closure, 49, 120, 138–9
    establishment, 34–5
    expansion, 35–9, 43–5, 49
    experiences of work at, 3, 112–39
    export markets, 39, 40, 47
    garden parties, 118
    gender balance of workforce, 6, 34, 112, 122–3, 207
    grounds, 115, 118, 119
    housing provision, 115
    industrial relations, 3–4, 42, 112–13, 122, 123–6, 130–39, 238–9
    job security, 186
    library, 128

medical care, 115, 128, 129
Millfield site, 36, **38**, 38, 49, 118
monopoly status, 13, 36–9, 131–2
musicals about, 9
paternalism, 39, 75, 112–30, 132, 139, 232
  pictured, **38**, **116**
  in popular memory, 9, 10, 112, 115, 122, 241
  recruitment practices, 120–23
  redundancy packages, 138–9
  sickness benefits, 115, 129
  shop, 116
  social activities, 115, 117–18, 232
  sports, 115, 117–18, 216
  strikes, 3, 4, 112, 122, 125–6, 130–31, 133–4, 137, 159, 212, 225, 238–9
  and trade unions, 3–4, 102, 121–6, 130–31, 133–4, 137–9, 197, 206, 236, 238
  travelling salesmen, 125–6, 212
  wages, 37, 115, 117, 132, 136
  welfare officer, 121
  working conditions, 115, 116–17, 132, 134, 136, 238
Sweetman, Gerard, 61

Tara Zinc, 158, 159
tariffs, 25–7, 31–2, 35, 40, 52, 60, 65, 95, 124, 163
tennis, 115, 216, 228, 232
textile industry quota, 35
Thompson, Paul, 106, 227
Thornley, David, 30
Timmerman, E.D., 62
Toms, David, 233
Tone, Andrea, 80–81, 113
tourism, 172
Tovey, Hilary, 173
Toyota, 30

tractors, 19, 20–25, 82, 97
trade unions
  attitudes to, 197, 219–28
  bargaining power, 48, 133, 135–6, 165, 179, 181, 219, 236, 239
  in Britain, 99, 101
  and Catholicism, 129, 220
  craft unions, 123, 154–68, 179–81, 217, 239
  experiences of union membership, 197, 219–28
  and the Ford Marina plant, 4, 73, 87–93, 101–3, 197, 212, 221, 236, 238, 242
  and gender, 197, 206, 224–5, 237–8
  growth of union membership, 236
  and Irish Steel, 3–4, 67, 70, 102, 154–68, 197, 236, 238
  and occupational safety, 152, 153
  and paternalism, 123–6, 129
  strikes to achieve recognition of, 101, 102, 221, 236, 238
  and Sunbeam Wolsey, 3–4, 102, 121–6, 130–31, 133–4, 137–9, 197, 206, 236, 238
  and white-collar workers, 211–13
tradesmen *see* craftsmen
training, 85–6, 184, 209; *see also* apprenticeships; education
transport links, 17, 18
travelling salesmen, 125–6, 212
treaty ports, 54
Tullamore Yarns Ltd, 39, 41, 44, 47

unemployment, 14, 18, 34, 48, 53–4, 59, 62, 72, 81–2, 91, 111, 121, 139, 165, 170–72, 175, 186–7, 235–6
United States, 2, 16, 26–7, 39, 41, 47, 70, 72, 74–7, 84, 88, 101, 113–14, 149, 230

University College Cork, 4
unskilled labour, 18, 75, 84–7, 153–7, 197, 217–19
Upham, Martin, 149
Uruguay, 65

Verolme dockyard, 48, 105, 141, 162, 166, 171, 188

wages
    for apprenticeships, 179
    for casual and seasonal work, 175–7
    differential between craftsmen and general operatives, 155, 157, 179, 217–18
    Ford Dagenham plant, 98
    Ford Marina plant, 31, 75, 84, 85, 88, 90, 95, 103, 104, 105–6, 110
    and gender, 205, 237
    handed over to family members, 204–5
    Irish Steel, 141, 143, 150–51, 155, 156, 157, 160, 163–4
    national wage agreements, 157
    pay freezes, 157, 166
    Sunbeam Wolsey, 37, 115, 117, 132, 136
Wallace, Frank, 133–4, 187–8, 219–20, 223–4, 233

Walsh, Robert, 144, 146, 150, 156, 163–4, 213, 218, 221, 225
War of Independence, 20, 92–4
Warren, Kenneth, 65, 66
welfare capitalism, 74–6, 81, 113–14, 121
welfare officers, 121
Westport Textiles, 133
Whelan, Christopher T., 173, 218–19
white-collar workers, 184, 197, 209–17
Wilcrest Ltd, 43
Wilkins, Myra, 17, 22, 23, 24
Williams, John, 59
Winn, Peter, 2, 3, 242
Wolsey Knitwear, 36
Women's Oral History Project (WOHP), 4, 7
wool, 33, 35, 38, 39, 41, 127
Woolcombers Ireland, 38, 41
working conditions
    Ford Marina plant, 73, 81–7, 106–9
    Irish Steel, 141–53, 238
    Sunbeam Wolsey, 115, 116–17, 132, 134, 136, 238
workplace communities, 228–33
Wyse, Pearse, 166

Youghal, 119
Young Christian Workers, 220, 241